AUTOMATIC ARCHITECTURE

AUTOMATIC ARCHITECTURE

MOTIVATING FORM AFTER MODERNISM

SEAN KELLER

THE UNIVERSITY OF CHICAGO PRESS | CHICAGO AND LONDON

The University of Chicago Press, Chicago 60637
The University of Chicago Press, Ltd., London

Published 2017
Printed in the United States of America

26 25 24 23 22 21 20 19 18 17 1 2 3 4 5

ISBN-13: 978-0-226-49649-8 (cloth)
ISBN-13: 978-0-226-49652-8 (e-book)
DOI: 10.7208/chicago/9780226496528.001.0001

Publication of this book has been aided in part by a grant from the Graham Foundation for Advanced Studies in the Fine Arts.

LIBRARY OF CONGRESS CATALOGING-IN-PUBLICATION DATA

Names: Keller, Sean (Architectural historian), author.
Title: Automatic architecture : motivating form after modernism / Sean Keller.
Description: Chicago ; Illinois : The University of Chicago Press, 2017. | Includes bibliographical references and index.
Identifiers: LCCN 2017009034 | ISBN 9780226496498 (cloth : alk. paper) | ISBN 9780226496528 (e-book)
Subjects: LCSH: Architecture, Modern—20th century. | Architectural design—History—20th century. | Architectural design—Philosophy. | Eisenman, Peter, 1932– | Otto, Frei, 1925–2015.
Classification: LCC NA680 .K39 2017 | DDC 724/.6—dc23
LC record available at https://lccn.loc.gov/2017009034

∞ This paper meets the requirements of ANSI/NISO Z39.48-1992 (Permanence of Paper).

CONTENTS

ACKNOWLEDGMENTS

Generous support for this book has come from the Graham Foundation for Advanced Studies in the Fine Arts. Research and writing have been supported by Harvard University through a Frank Knox Memorial Fellowship and an Eliot Fellowship. I am grateful for the steadfast faith and wise counsel of Susan Bielstein, my editor at the University of Chicago Press, and for the dedication of everyone at the press who has helped give this material its final form, especially James Toftness and C. Steven LaRue. I also thank the anonymous readers of my manuscript. Their comments evince the best and most selfless intellectual support one could hope to find.

I have presented this research to more groups and institutions than can be listed here. I am grateful to all of my interlocutors. From the start, I benefited from the encouragement and insight of Michael Hays, Hashim Sarkis, and Peter Galison. The responses of Daniel Abramson, Lucia Allais, Zeynep Çelik Alexander, Christine Boyer, Beatriz Colomina, John Harwood, Timothy Hyde, Mark Jarzombek, and Reinhold Martin have also been especially helpful. Early portions of this material have appeared in the volumes *Atomic Dwelling* and *Architecture and Authorship* and in the journal *Grey Room*. I thank the editors of these publications—Robin Schuldenfrei, Tim Anstey, Katja Grillner, Rolf Hughes, and T'ai Smith—for their tireless attention and many beneficial suggestions.

Crucial if less formal support has come from generous colleagues and friends who have formed my intellectual communities at and beyond several universities. I am thankful to them all, especially Luke Ogrydziak, Zoë Prillinger, Tamsin Todd, Sarah Churchwell, Charissa Terranova, Scott Rothkopf, Harry Mallgrave, Frank Flury, David Goodman, John Ronan, Michelangelo Sabatino, Aden Kumler, Ralph Ubl, Maja Naef, Heinrich Jaeger, Jessica Stockholder, Patrick Chamberlain, and Bill Brown.

Finally, this work has been sustained by my family: Ralph and Mary Ann Keller, Sharon Tanner, Helma Mehring-Keller, Leo, Elza, and—beyond all others—Christine Mehring. Thank you all.

INTRODUCTION: INTO THE AUTOMATIC

WHERE DOES architecture come from? How is it authored and how is it authorized? These are the fundamental concerns of the architects and near-architects considered here. They are questions as old as the discipline that we call architecture itself, occupying treatise writers from Vitruvius onward. In this regard, the theories and practices examined here extend the long line of architects justifying themselves—to others and to themselves—by constructing arguments about where their forms come from. More than anxious hand-wringing, this continual justification of form is the constitutive feature of architecture as a discipline, as a self-aware practice. It is the engagement with the problems of motivation that distinguishes the understanding of architecture as a discipline from models of architecture as an unreflective though perhaps expert practice, whether as a traditional craft or as a modern service profession.

Though long-standing, questions of motivation reached an unprecedented depth in the nineteenth century as the strain between advancing industrialization and the hypertrophying of historical styles provoked the first formulations of architectural modernism. It is also characteristic of the modern period generally that each discipline has been forced to question its methods, its principles, its subject matter, and its legitimacy. This is the critical legacy of the Enlightenment, and within the arts such questions define modernism itself. Yet while all of the arts confronted their modernist crises of motivation, the scale, expense, technical complexity, public presence, and comparative permanence of architecture put special pressure on architects to justify their work. Often this seemed to require demonstrating that it was not they and their limited subjectivities that authored their works but some larger, more objective authority. Indeed this sense of responsibility is the chief reason that some—Kant, for one—have preferred to remove building from the sphere of the fine arts entirely.[1] This is not to say that architects' responses to questions of motivation have been better than those of other artists. In fact, more often the reverse has been true. Because they so intensely feel called on to explain themselves, the justifications of architects are often forced—with the best alibi often being simply one that works.

So while Enlightenment modernism as a general frame stood for ongoing self-critique, architectural modernism in most of its most iconic forms—from the techno-classicism of Le Corbusier in *Vers une architecture* and of Ludwig Mies van der Rohe to the industrial standardizations of the Bauhaus—was a grand but historically doomed attempt to establish collective order: to formulate a new but stable set of conventions that would rescue the world from the uncertainties of modernism itself. In this crucial respect architecture has largely never been modernist. It has rarely understood self-critique as its fundamental and unsurpassable task. Instead, with rare exceptions architects have repeatedly attempted to overturn existing frameworks (e.g., the classical orders, historical styles generally, modernism, postmodernism) only to claim the establishment of some new universal and permanent paradigm. In this we can also see architectural thought being shaped by practice's contradictory needs for both the excitement of the new and the assurance of stability.

Since the various strands of architectural modernism before 1960 were united in their belief that such questions of design motivation could be answered and the discipline thereby stabilized, the dissolution of these modernisms during the 1960s and 1970s led to the return of these questions with renewed, even existential, intensity. What the architects considered here confronted then is a second-order failure: modernism's inability to bring coherence to a discipline that had already come apart during the long nineteenth century. These two centuries of repeated failure to establish coherence reflect architecture's inability to reconcile its slowness with the ever-more-rapid churn of global capitalism.

In this book I examine one response to this uneasiness, one that held that architects no longer had a natural or conventional relationship to what they did and that it was this relationship itself—that is to say, a method of design—that needed to be established first. Also shared here is the belief that such a design method should be so complete, rigorous, well regulated, and objective that it would be, in some significant sense, *automatic*. By various paths these figures sought an architecture that escaped artistic intuition and individuated taste, an architecture that formed itself spontaneously from its context: an automatic architecture. While the problem confronted is as old as architecture itself, the solutions suggested here are part of a historical context in which the automatization of complex cultural activities was a prominent theme across the cultural range, from Stockhausen to *Desk Set*.

The theories considered here offer an explanation of architectural authorship that runs counter to much of the discipline's history, for which architectural creation has been understood as the exercise of individual intuition within a framework of strong disciplinary conventions. Condemning both artistic intuition and historical precedent as inadequate to the postwar condition, the variations of automatic architecture argued that architectural authority—the motivation of form—could only be secured through methodology, through design processes that were rational, systematic, and transparent enough to be self-justifying. By extension, these figures also shared a belief that such systematic methods would closely connect architecture to mathematics and science. Despite their differences, these approaches all advocate a displacement of architectural authorship away from personal intuition and onto externalized processes that are thought to be, in some way, objective, logical, or natural and therefore also, in some way, automatic. In this book I am concerned with three versions of this displacement during the 1960s and 1970s, each of which posits an automatic architecture emerging from a distinct source: program, form, or nature.

My first case is the "design methods" research initiated by Christopher Alexander and pursued with more intellectual rigor by Lionel March at Cambridge University's Centre for Land Use and Built Form Study. Alexander, March, and their colleagues attempted to apply mathematics and computation to the analysis of architectural problems in the hope of formulating a scientific method of design that could proceed (semi-) automatically from data—needs, costs, site conditions, material properties—to design. For March this explicitly meant reframing constructivist goals and methods within the newly available context of electronic computation. Importantly, however, over the course of a decade or so, the role of this new context shifted for March from one of direct scientistic calculation to one in which computation provided a new working space for the collective development and assessment of design.

My second case examines the early work of architect and theorist Peter Eisenman, who, though adamantly opposed to the design methods approach of figures such as Alexander, also attempted to develop a rigorous, quasi-autonomous system of architectural form generation during the same years. In contrast to the data-driven approach of the design methods movement, Eisenman posited a Neoplatonic logic of form with ties to the contemporaneous work of the linguist Noam Chomsky and to conceptual and minimal art. Eisenman is admittedly better known and more widely written about than the other figures discussed here, especially in the American architectural community. Nonetheless, the complex presence of the automatic in his work is undeniable. What I attempt here, then, is a detailed and noninstrumental accounting of his early thought within a wider context in order to more closely articulate the similarities and differences between his work and other parallel intellectual projects.

The third historical example treated here is the German Frei Otto's research into form finding and natural models for design with a particular focus on the West German Pavilion for Expo 67 in Montreal and the 1975 Multihalle in Mannheim, both projects in which Otto played a leading role. Otto's work was based on the premise that, parallel to nature, architectural forms could be shaped as optimal responses to their physical environments. Confronting the challenges of postwar Germany, Otto gave an explicitly political valence to this naturalistic methodology, describing it as both antifascist and protoenvironmental.

In the concluding section I attempt to expand our understanding of the automatic and the role it plays both in these historical cases and in contemporary architecture by reexamining it through Stanley Cavell's concept of "automatism." What Cavell suggests is that, although some form of the automatic is inherent in postwar artistic practices, these practices must also move beyond the merely automatic—which is empty of meaning—and into the conscious deployment of the automatic as a technique within the realms of cultural production. As such, his interpretation of the postwar condition sheds light on both the historical cases gathered here and their various extensions in contemporary architectural practice, for which computation has made confrontation with the automatic inescapable. A shift in tone and time frame marks this final chapter. This is by design. My aim is to pull back from the historical cases of the 1960s and 1970s to address the conceptual terrain these cases share with the influential role of computation in contemporary architecture. This is certainly not intended to naively instrumentalize the historical analysis but rather to unfold an alternative notion of the automatic by which both the historical cases and present-day computational practice can be read.

To be clear, although the architects studied here occasionally used the term *automatic*, none of them deployed the term in the self-conscious or generalized way that I do here. There was no movement devoted to automatic architecture. Instead, I am using this term to call out a tendency, a conceptual attractor, that emerged during the 1960s and runs through to the present. Other terms suggest themselves: *spontaneous*, *self-generating*, or *computational*, for instance. However, it seems to me that *automatic* does the best job of capturing the widespread desire of this period for an architecture that arises impersonally and procedurally. *Automatic* also suggests the highly influential context of early electronic computation while allowing that hopes for automatic design might be carried out without, or even in opposition to, computer programming itself. Finally, it is no small advantage that *automatic* provides a smooth passage by which I can reconsider these historical practices, as well as contemporary ones, through the thinking of Cavell, allowing the discussion to shift into related terrain in music and the visual arts.

While ambitions for automatic processes were spread widely throughout postwar architecture, in selecting these cases I have focused on figures for whom automatic design methods were the central concern. Given the importance of the intellectual, technological, and social conditions created by World War II, it has also seemed important to provide cases that emerge from different sides of the war, and on both sides of the Atlantic, so that it is possible to see how these differing postwar contexts shaped interpretations of the automatic. Admittedly the cases, and thus chapters, relate in a somewhat asymmetrical manner: there are biographical and institutional connections between Alexander, March, and Eisenman that do not extend to Otto. Again, I have allowed the significance of the automatic within the practices to determine their inclusion rather than attempting to fulfill a more formalized historiographic arrangement.

Also shared here are the somewhat unusual positions of the key figures: all were academics throughout the period considered, with three of them (Alexander, Eisenman, and Otto) holding PhD degrees. Today, when the PhD in architecture is almost exclusively associated with historical research, this convergence reminds us of the longer history of doctoral programs in architecture and their previous relationships to practice. All of these figures were also deeply involved with—often founding and directing—academic research institutes. Though far from comprehensive, this book thus also provides insight into how architecture functioned as a field of inquiry within the postwar university system. In fact one of the strongest shared characteristics of these diverse approaches is a desire to emulate in architecture the structure of physical or social science research groups. It is also telling that the academic context encouraged each to offer supposedly justifiable "solutions" to postwar problems rather than either criticism of, or speculative responses to, these problems. This can be seen as characteristic of major research universities in the age of "Big Science" and of the somewhat troubled place of architecture (and other arts) within such contexts.

What becomes apparent through the gathering of these cases is that as a supposed solution to cultural dilemmas, the meaning of automatic design processes was highly adaptable. It could be used to revive constructivist goals of functional determinism (March et al.) or to establish disciplinary autonomy (Eisenman) or to harmonize human constructions with nature (Otto). What is shared in all of these forms is the effort to naturalize design: to shift architectural design from the realm of culture and politics to the realm of objective fact. While Otto's appeal to nature makes this explicit, it is an underlying motivation of all three approaches. These figures understood the automatic as a way of giving strong, perhaps computer-assisted, coherence to the methodologies of design as a substitute for, or antidote to, the disturbing lack of coherence in postwar culture generally. They saw the automatic as a way to deploy postwar science to solve the dilemmas created by postwar science itself.[2]

All of the strategies of automatic architecture attempt to defer one key problem: that of meaning. On its own terms this work is supposed to be thoroughly syntactic: antisemantic and iconoclastic. There are supposedly no figures, objects, or meanings to be found here—only relationships and forms. This is, of course, only a fiction proposed by the projects themselves. Once released into the world, the semantic dimension cannot be eliminated from these works. Eisenman's projects, or Otto's, have turned into icons as rapidly as any architectural products of the postwar period. These buildings have become *signs* of a systematic design process. It takes great effort to actually read the syntactic arrangements of their systems and even greater effort to determine whether the systems are systematic.

What we will see is that some of these practitioners—Eisenman and Otto—acknowledge (some of the time) that representation is unavoidable, and their projects are successful as much because they *look* systemic as because they are rigorously generated. In contrast, the more devout iconoclasts—early Alexander and March, for instance—were stymied in part by architecture's inevitable representational component. Part of my project here is to consider not only quasi-automatic processes but also the *look* of the automatic and its meanings.

Echoing the past century's anxiety over the incoherence of architecture, these theorists of automatic architecture describe the postwar condition as profoundly confused and disorienting and architecture's relationship to this condition as arbitrary and unsatisfying. There is a shared assumption here that architects have in some way become external, even alien, to their work and to the world that it inhabits. By this view, architects no longer know what is asked of them or what would constitute a meaningful response. It is as if they do not understand what architecture itself is any longer. This is why design process looms so large in their thinking—it is not merely a path for solving problems but a way of delimiting architecture, of defining architecture through its process rather than its results.

The belief shared here is that the practice of architecture can and should be unified and made coherent. Each case presents its new methodology as a solution to a state of crisis. Each presents a way of working that will establish coherence within the discipline of architecture and between the discipline and the public. So if an automatic architecture were to fulfill its aim of establishing (or restoring) a holistic and integrated architectural language, it needed to be not just a sensibility, an attitude, or a catalog of procedures but a complete system that described a total design process.

Though differing in their foundational assumptions, each proposed methodology also purports to be "scientific" in the sense that it attempts to solve the dilemmas of architecture in the postwar period "externally"—that is, not by organically reconciling the architect, the public, and buildings themselves but by offering a method that supposedly supersedes the confusion via objective analysis. Within the proposed design methods, the architect and the context of design—the clients, users, sites, and cultures—essentially remain alien to each other. As an externality, this context is treated by the architects as something that is essentially unknown and can only be approached through the mediation of new and highly formalized processes.

I have been drawn to these examples because they represent important historical and conceptual transitions between the "heroic" interwar architectural modernism of the 1920s and 1930s and the conditions of architectural practice today. The nearest historical and theoretical precursors of this work were the Soviet constructivists, who pursued questions of artistic motivation and design methods to unprecedented lengths. As in so much else, the architects of revolutionary Russia anticipated many of the paths that figures of the 1960s and 1970s would follow (the Cambridge researchers particularly were aware of and expressly devoted to their Soviet predecessors). Still, as we will see, while addressing what were essentially constructivist questions, the architects discussed here were doing so in a dramatically different context, not only politically and economically but also technologically, with electronic computing available as a tool with which constructivist goals might be reached. Rather than working in the mechanical world of the constructivists (or at least the world to which they aspired), the architects of the 1960s and 1970s operated in a world of systems, environments, and cybernetics—a shift that permeates their theories and projects.

ARCHITECTURE AND SCIENCE AFTER 1945

In 1960, *Architectural Review* marked the start of the era under consideration here with a series of articles edited by Reyner Banham under the title "Stocktaking."[3] Assessing the present and advocating for certain directions forward, Banham emphasized the importance of science and technology, with features on computers, weapons systems, and mathematics (fig. 0.1). In the following years Banham's proposal for what he called a "scientific aesthetic" would be tested in a wide range of work: the sci-fi imagery of the Archigram group, the high-tech buildings of Richard Rogers and Norman Foster, the aformal cybernetic projects of Cedric Price, as well as in the various methodological explorations that are the focus of this book. These were architectural responses to the scale and importance of science and technology in the postwar period—the "Big Science" that had emerged from the massive military research projects of World War II and the Cold War: radar, electronic computing, nuclear weaponry, jet aircraft, rocketry, and satellites.[4] Given its prominence—and the size of its budgets—science became a widely emulated model for other disciplines, so that the reach of postwar science was determined not just by the scope of scientific research itself but by the influence of science as a cultural paradigm.[5]

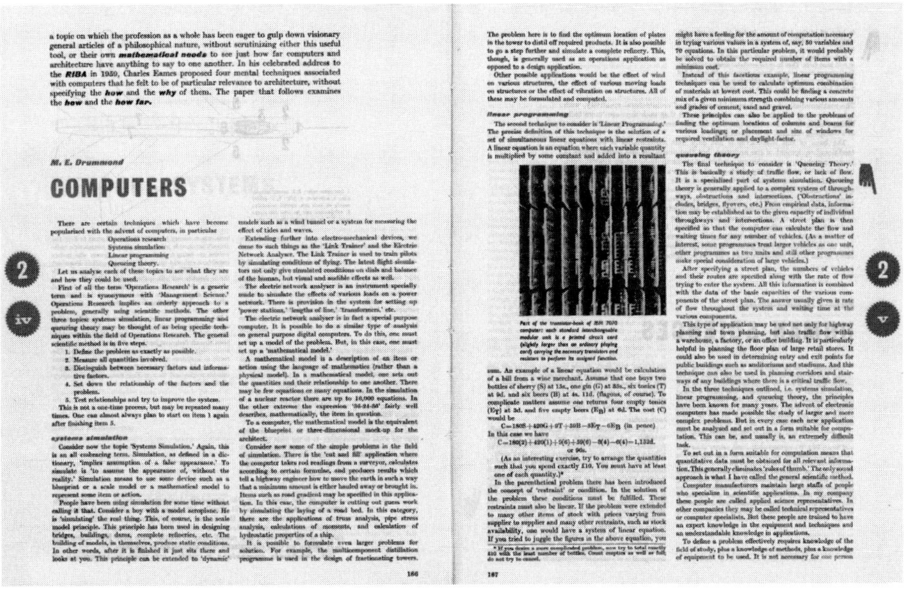
a topic on which the profession as a whole has been eager to gulp down visionary general articles of a philosophical nature, without scrutinizing either this useful tool, or their own ***mathematical needs*** to see just how far computers and architecture have anything to say to one another. In his celebrated address to the ***RIBA*** in 1959, Charles Eames proposed four mental techniques associated with computers that he felt to be of particular relevance to architecture, without specifying the ***how*** and the ***why*** of them. The paper that follows examines the ***how*** and the ***how far***.

M. E. Drummond

COMPUTERS

There are certain techniques which have become popularized with the advent of computers, in particular

Operations research
Systems simulation
Linear programming
Queueing theory.

Let us analyse each of these topics to see what they are and how they could be used.

First of all the term 'Operations Research' is a generic term and is synonymous with 'Management Science.' Operations Research implies an orderly approach to a problem, generally using scientific methods. The other three topics: systems simulation, linear programming and queueing theory may be thought of as being specific techniques within the field of Operations Research. The general scientific method is in five steps.

1. Define the problem as exactly as possible.
2. Measure all quantities involved.
3. Distinguish between necessary factors and informative factors.
4. Set down the relationship of the factors and the problem.
5. Test relationships and try to improve the system.

This is not a one-time process, but may be repeated many times. One can almost always plan to start on item 1 again after finishing item 5.

systems simulation

Consider now the topic 'Systems Simulation.' Again, this is an all embracing term. Simulation, as defined in a dictionary, 'implies assumption of a false appearance.' To simulate is 'to assume the appearance of, without the reality.' Simulation means to use some device such as a blueprint or a scale model or a mathematical model to represent some item or action.

People have been using simulation for some time without calling it that. Consider a boy with a model aeroplane. He is 'simulating' the real thing. This, of course, is the scale model principle. This principle has been used in designing bridges, buildings, dams, complete refineries, etc. The building of models, in themselves, produce static conditions. In other words, after it is finished it just sits there and looks at you. This principle can be extended to 'dynamic' models such as a wind tunnel or a system for measuring the effect of tides and waves.

Extending further into electro-mechanical devices, we come to such things as the 'Link Trainer' and the Electric Network Analyser. The Link Trainer is used to train pilots by simulating conditions of flying. The latest flight simulators not only give simulated conditions on dials and balance of the human, but visual and audible effects as well.

The electric network analyser is an instrument specially made to simulate the effects of various loads on a power network. There is provision in the system for setting up 'power stations,' 'lengths of line,' 'transformers,' etc.

The electric network analyser is in fact a special purpose computer. It is possible to do a similar type of analysis on general purpose digital computers. To do this, one must set up a model of the problem. But, in this case, one must set up a 'mathematical model.'

A mathematical model is a description of an item or action using the language of mathematics (rather than a physical model). In a mathematical model, one sets out the quantities and their relationship to one another. There may be few equations or many equations. In the simulation of a nuclear reactor there are up to 10,000 equations. In the other extreme the expression '36-24-36' fairly well describes, mathematically, the item in question.

To a computer, the mathematical model is the equivalent of the blueprint or three-dimensional mock-up for the architect.

Consider now some of the simple problems in the field of simulation. There is the 'cut and fill' application where the computer takes rod readings from a surveyor, calculates according to certain formulae, and produces results which tell a highway engineer how to move the earth in such a way that a minimum amount is either hauled away or brought in. Items such as road gradient may be specified in this application. In this case, the computer is cutting out guess work by simulating the laying of a road bed. In this category, there are the applications of truss analysis, pipe stress analysis, calculations of moments, and calculation of hydrostatic properties of a ship.

It is possible to formulate even larger problems for solution. For example, the multicomponent distillation programme is used in the design of fractionating towers.

186

The problem here is to find the optimum location of plates in the tower to distil off required products. It is also possible to go a step further and simulate a complete refinery. This, though, is generally used as an operations application as opposed to a design application.

Other possible applications would be the effect of wind on various structures, the effect of various moving loads on structures or the effect of vibration on structures. All of these may be formulated and computed.

linear programming

The second technique to consider is 'Linear Programming.' The precise definition of this technique is the solution of a set of simultaneous linear equations with linear restraints. A linear equation is an equation where each variable quantity is multiplied by some constant and added into a resultant

Part of the transistor-bank of IBM 7070 computer: each standard interchangeable modular unit is a printed circuit card (slightly larger than an ordinary playing card) carrying the necessary transistors and resistors to perform its assigned function.

sum. An example of a linear equation would be calculation of a bill from a wine merchant. Assume that one buys two bottles of sherry (S) at 15s., one gin (G) at 35s., six tonics (T) at 9d. and six beers (B) at 4s. 11d. (flagons, of course). To complicate matters assume one returns four empty tonics (E_T) at 3d. and five empty beers (E_B) at 6d. The cost (C) would be

$$C=180S+420G+9T+59B-8E_T-6E_B \text{ (in pence)}$$

In this case we have

$$C=180(2)+420(1)+9(6)+59(6)-8(4)-6(4)=1,132d.$$
or 94s.

(As an interesting exercise, try to arrange the quantities such that you spend exactly £10. You must have at least one of each quantity.)*

In the parenthetical problem there has been introduced the concept of 'restraint' or condition. In the solution of the problem these conditions must be fulfilled. These restraints must also be linear. If the problem were extended to many other items of stock with prices varying from supplier to supplier and many other restraints, such as stock availability, one would have a system of linear equation. If you tried to juggle the figures in the above equation, you might have a feeling for the amount of computation necessary in trying various values in a system of, say, 80 variables and 70 equations. In this particular problem, it would probably be solved to obtain the required number of items with a minimum cost.

Instead of this facetious example, linear programming techniques can be used to calculate optimum combination of materials at lowest cost. This could be finding a concrete mix of a given minimum strength combining various amounts and grades of cement, sand and gravel.

These principles can also be applied to the problems of finding the optimum locations of columns and beams for various loadings; or placement and size of windows for required ventilation and daylight-factor.

queueing theory

The final technique to consider is 'Queueing Theory.' This is basically a study of traffic flow, or lack of flow. It is a specialized part of systems simulation. Queueing theory is generally applied to a complex system of throughways, obstructions and intersections. ('Obstructions' includes, bridges, flyovers, etc.) From empirical data, information may be established as to the given capacity of individual throughways and intersections. A street plan is then specified so that the computer can calculate the flow and waiting times for any number of vehicles. (As a matter of interest, some programmes treat larger vehicles as one unit, other programmes as two units and still other programmes make special consideration of large vehicles.)

After specifying a street plan, the numbers of vehicles and their routes are specified along with the rate of flow trying to enter the system. All this information is combined with the data of the basic capacities of the various components of the street plan. The answer usually given is rate of flow throughout the system and waiting time at the various components.

This type of application may be used not only for highway planning and town planning, but also traffic flow within a warehouse, a factory, or an office building. It is particularly helpful in planning the floor plan of large retail stores. It could also be used in determining entry and exit points for public buildings such as auditoriums and stadiums. And this technique can also be used in planning corridors and stairways of any buildings where there is a critical traffic flow.

In the three techniques outlined, i.e. systems simulation, linear programming, and queueing theory, the principles have been known for many years. The advent of electronic computers has made possible the study of larger and more complex problems. But in every case each new application must be analysed and set out in a form suitable for computation. This can be, and usually is, an extremely difficult task.

To set out in a form suitable for computation means that quantitative data must be obtained for all relevant information. This generally eliminates 'rules of thumb.' The only sound approach is what I have called the general scientific method.

Computer manufacturers maintain large staffs of people who specialize in scientific applications. In my company these people are called applied science representatives. In other companies they may be called technical representatives or computer specialists. But these people are trained to have an expert knowledge in the equipment and techniques and an understandable knowledge in applications.

To define a problem effectively requires knowledge of the field of study, plus a knowledge of methods, plus a knowledge of equipment to be used. It is not necessary for one person

* If you desire a more complicated problem, now try to total exactly £10 with the least number of bottles. Count empties as well as full, do not try to cancel.

187

FIGURE 0.1. M. E. Drummond, "Computers." Part of the series "Stocktaking: 1960," *Architectural Review* 127 (1960), edited by Reyner Banham. Reproduced by permission of EMAP Publishing Limited.

In the case of architecture, this influence was especially intense, because the discipline has always had ties to science and technology while not being reducible to either (a condition that haunts much of the work described here). Speaking in 1967 about the state of architectural theory, Eduard Sekler singled out the influence of science:

> The high degree of attention and—one is tempted to say—reverence accorded to research in connection with architecture today, can probably be explained by the fact that architecture is more closely linked to science than any other art. When the demand for a theory of architecture is voiced, what is at work is less a desire for concepts of a kind that characterize art-theories than a wish to parallel in some way what is believed to be the *modus operandi* of scientific theory.
>
> There are few contemporaries, in any field, who would not consider it high praise to describe something as "scientific."[6]

Formed within this science-oriented postwar context, the positions examined here were also influenced by the legacy of the prewar architectural avant-garde and its attitudes toward science and technology as both continuations and refutations of that earlier work. Reviewing the wide range of approaches architects took toward science in the first half of the twentieth century, three general strategies can be distinguished: the formal, the technical, and the methodological. In the broadest terms, formal strategies sought buildings that looked appropriate to the science and technology of their era. This might be achieved, as in the case of Le Corbusier, by imitating the forms of advanced technology, which around 1920 meant steamships, automobiles, airplanes, and hydroelectric generators. Alternatively, the form of a building could be representative of an ideology that was modern and scientific, as in the buildings of the German neue Sachlichkeit movement.[7] At a technical level, the use of new construction processes and building products—such as reinforced concrete, steel frames, large plate glass, mechanical heating and cooling, and electric lighting—continued to expand and develop. These new ways of building were often, but not necessarily, paired with the formal approach to produce the exemplars of prewar modernism. Finally, formal and technical attempts to integrate architecture and science might also be accompanied by some commitment to new design methodologies, for example, in the constructivist argument that a truly modern architecture required a revolution in the means of its production. The long-held view of the architect as an artist employing his imagination within a context of traditional forms was to be replaced by the idea of the architect as a sort of scientist, engineer, or economist. Inspiration was to be replaced by calculation.

Before World War II, it was largely possible for an architect to pursue all three of these approaches—the formal, the technical, and the methodological—simultaneously. Understandably, they were seen to be complementary: scientific methods in architecture would lead to forms that utilized and were harmonious with advanced technology. And, although the methodologies of architectural practice may never have matched the claims of objectivity made for them, a new formal vocabulary and new means of construction emerged that did, in significant ways, correspond to other advanced technologies of the time. However, as Banham's "Stocktaking" series highlighted, the developments in technology and science brought about by World War II drastically challenged this arrangement. For it was—and remains—unclear what, if any, architectural lessons are to be taken from iconic postwar technologies such as computers, radar, global telecommunications, television, and the space program. As the fantastic character of Archigram's early efforts such as "Plug-In City" demonstrate, Le Corbusier's biplanes and steamships could not simply be replaced by transistors and circuit boards. The new technologies operated at scales that were outside that of buildings or, more radically, that seemed to defy architecture's very conceptions of scale. For instance, what would it mean to talk about the "scale" of the global television broadcast of the moon landing?

One reaction to the postwar dilemma—that taken by the architects considered here—was to look beyond the formal and technological strategies of modernism in order to focus on making the methods of architecture scientific. Drawing on an aesthetic language that attempted to distinguish "deep" connections of conceptual structuring from "superficial" similarities of appearance, adherents of this approach argued that it was the methodology of architectural design that needed to be scientific, not the outward appearance of any particular building (just what buildings should look like was an often deferred question).

The potential circularity of automatic architecture, its Munchhausian use of process as its foundation, was somewhat contradictorily tied to the argument that such design methods would connect architecture more deeply to science and mathematics. Indeed, these researchers seem to have always been thinking of something else. When they looked at buildings they saw mathematics, biology, geology, and linguistics. When they read mathematical and scientific theories or looked at nature, they imagined architecture. Repeatedly they turned to other disciplines (mainly the sciences) to justify their work, as if, perhaps, architecture itself had no authority to offer. As Alan Colquhoun saw it,

> The 1960s were characterized by . . . tendencies . . . which emphasized the "process" of architectural production, rather than its final achievement . . . a tendency toward seeking the laws of architecture outside of architecture itself—in mathematics, computer technology, systems analysis, or social analysis.[8]

I would only add that in the 1960s and 1970s, mathematics and systems theory often provided the dominant models and metaphors even for attempts, such as Eisenman's, that tried to discover laws of architecture *within* architecture.

Further complicating the situation of postwar architects was a conflict internal to architectural modernism itself. Evaluating the anxious architectural scene of the

1960s and early 1970s, Colin Rowe famously identified the rift between *morale* and *physique* that became apparent as modernism passed beyond its revolutionary phase and became an internationally established mode of practice.[9] In the postrevolutionary period—that is, after 1945—architects encountered a dilemma: should they cling to the *morale* of modernism, which demanded ever-new forms tied to ever-advancing technological and social conditions? Or should they simply accept that the revolution was finished and that prewar modernism had established a lasting vocabulary that only needed to be refined and elaborated by those who followed? The first position would require that the forms of modernism, which had only recently gained acceptance, be overturned by new forms appropriate to the needs and technologies of the postwar period. The second would perpetuate the forms of modernism—and so accept a secondary, derivative, historical role—but in so doing would turn away from modernism's primary explanation of itself. Rowe himself argued for the latter approach, rejecting the argument of Banham and others that "in default of the convenient anti-'art' entity of the twenties called the 'machine,' we substitute the equally useful entities designated 'the computer' and 'the people.'"[10]

But not all attempts to apply computation to architectural methodology were as naive as Rowe would have them, and work with computers and mathematics in the sixties and seventies created the ground for the wide range of formal and procedural developments that were to follow. We should then recall the more subtle and engaged critique of scientistic design methods offered by Colquhoun. Concluding his 1967 essay "Typology and Design Method," Colquhoun noted that despite his reservations, "a certain scientific detachment toward our problems is essential and with it the application of the mathematical tools proper to our culture. But these are unable to give us a ready-made solution to our problems. They only provide the framework, the context within which we operate."[11] This suggests a limitation of Rowe's thinking, one that may also prove to limit the longevity of its effect: his inability to think about operating productively *within*, rather than *against*, the postwar world. As the subject of historical consideration, in this book I make this science-oriented context, which Rowe sidelined, central: What did it mean to operate within this context? How were significant architectural practices established through postures of scientific detachment and the use of mathematical tools?

COMPUTING THE AUTOMATIC

Within this context, the computer immediately became a focal point for the profession's science envy. In the 1960s the use of these calculating machines—which, we should remember, were exotic, expensive, cumbersome, and mainly devoted to military and scientific research—bolstered architects' claims to intellectual and professional seriousness (fig. 0.2). In turn, approaching architecture through the computer demanded new mathematical descriptions of form and, at least for some, parallel

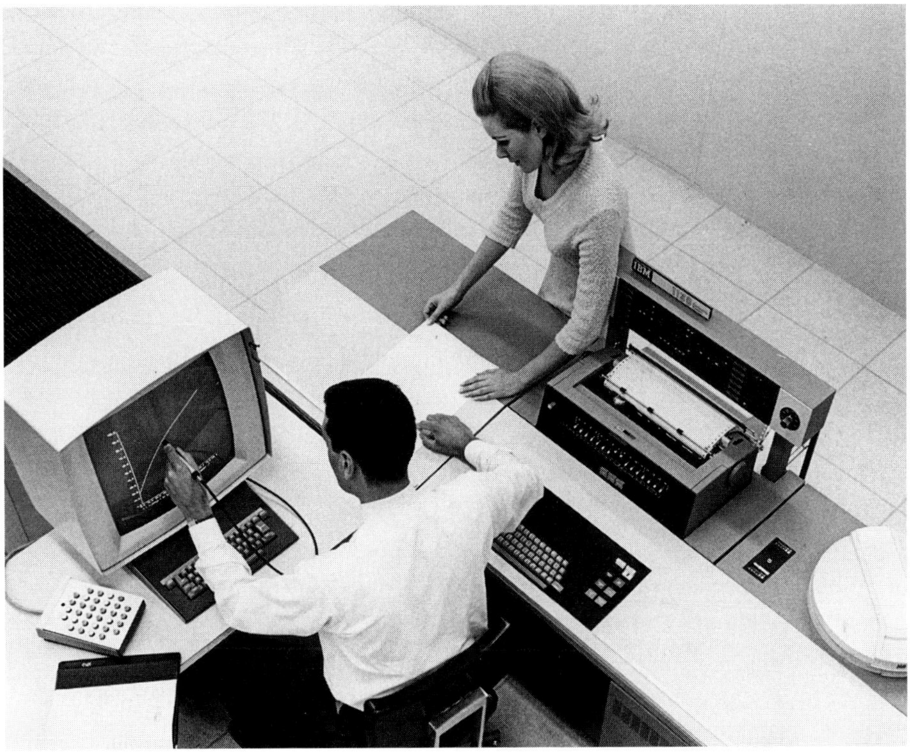

FIGURE 0.2. IBM 1130 computer system showing CRT 2250 display terminal, ca. 1970. Courtesy of IBM archives.

redefinitions of design methodologies. Summarizing what he called the "logic" of architecture in the late 1960s, Royston Landau described the "New Direction" set by the presence of computing:

> Perhaps the single most important factor . . . has been the computer, which offers its services for the solution of any question which can be characterized in a suitably quantified way. Even if the psychological optimism encouraged by the computer might be distinguished from its current mathematical possibilities, it has, nevertheless, been responsible for an increasingly "scientific" attitude (sometimes pseudo-scientific).[12]

As this passage suggests, the influence of the computer extended beyond its actual use. This makes sense in a context where the mythology of science and mathematics was strong but computers themselves were still scarce, time consuming, and costly. In its first decades then, the computer affected architecture in two ways that were not always congruent: as an actual programmable electronic device and as a model for advanced intellectual activity. This doubled aspect echoes the history of computation. The first "computers" were not machines but teams of people organized to perform rote calculations.[13] Also, while computation was an important node in the postwar context, the individuals considered here held widely divergent and evolving views of its role in architecture: March was always a tempered advocate and Otto a consistent skeptic; Alexander pivoted from an enthusiastic initial embrace to vigorous rejection, while Eisenman gradually, and almost resentfully, accepted the machines within a trajectory of work that had long appeared to have a computational dimension.

Looking back at these cases, it is important to recognize that although it now seems obvious that the principle role for the computer in architecture is as a sophisticated modeling and graphics device, limitations of memory and speed meant that exploration of the computer's potential as a graphical medium was difficult and slow to develop. Instead, before the wide availability of graphic displays, architects in the early 1960s such as Alexander and March used computers algebraically, creating mathematical models of needs analysis, space planning, and circulation problems. The most extreme advocates believed that the solution of these problems could lead to optimally functional buildings that were derived scientifically from empirical data. The practical lack of graphic opportunities was accommodated at a theoretical level by a strong iconoclasm that was both antiaesthetic and anti-intuitional and that was also linked to selected readings of prewar functionalism.

While today the computer has been completely integrated into architecture and many strands of advanced work are entirely based on the possibilities provided by computation, there has been until very recently almost no history of architectural computing. So if during the last two decades we have often heard that architectural authorship will be revolutionized by computation, we should remember Mark Wigley's warning that much of this is perhaps only "an echo of an echo" of ideas explored decades earlier.[14] I hope that this account will help interrupt the further echoing of naive myths about scientific, mathematical, and computational solutions to the inescapable complexities of architectural, or any other, authorship while also illuminating the real novelties of process-driven methods. This work contributes to the history of architectural computation by discussing developments from the early 1960s, when computer systems first began to be available for architectural research at universities, through the later 1960s, when computing became a popular theme in architectural journals and at conferences, to the mid-1970s, when computer-aided drafting systems started to enter routine use in larger private practices.

One indication of computation's ideological significance during this period, despite its practical limitations, is given by Rowe's characterization quoted above. If in the 1960s the computer replaced the (mechanical) "machine" as an icon for architects, then one need only recall the important rhetorical and formal role that the machine played in the creation of modernism to understand the centrality of the computer in the postwar period. Whatever one may think about computation's proper role in architecture, a full historical account of the period from 1945 to the present cannot follow Rowe's dismissal of this culturally significant development. Despite their many early limitations, computers entered an architectural setting already looking to take direction from science and technology, already searching for a logic to call its own, so that since the early 1960s, architects have repeatedly been both seduced and troubled by the possibility that these machines might be harnessed to create form automatically.

DEPLOYING THE AUTOMATIC

Considered broadly, the dominant disciplinary conditions that shaped these attempts at automatic architecture continue to define our present: we still confront both the absence of a consensus architectural vocabulary and the presence of electronic computation as a protean design space. While there are occasional resemblances of architectural form to be found here, the more general similarity to contemporary architecture is procedural. It lies in the ways that these architects conceive of design as a process rather than a product. By focusing on design methods and by examining evidence at a range of scales—from institutions to individual buildings—I am offering an alternative to historical narratives of this period that focus on postmodernism as a style. In this respect the approach of this book runs parallel to other recent reassessments of the 1960s and 1970s.[15] Here a temptation arises to imitate my subjects and say that this focus on methods reveals a "deeper" historical truth about the period than that given by discussions of postmodernism as a style, but I reject this hierarchy. The surfaces of any architecture—and especially of postmodernism—are an indispensable site of meaning, not something to be looked past. My approach is guided only by the belief that there were also *methods* of architectural design formulated during this period that are equally important to our historical comprehension and that have a vital bearing on contemporary practice.

By carrying forward architectural modernism's goal of cultural coherence, automatic architecture remained resistant to, and attempted to overcome, the broader modernist condition itself. These cases stand, then, as counterpoints to the contemporaneous efforts of Robert Venturi, which—though termed "postmodernist" in relationship to architectural modernism—were *modernist* in their desire for an architecture that reflected rather than superseded the disjunctive culture of the late twentieth century (as Venturi himself makes clear in the opening of *Complexity and Contradiction*).[16] By one light these figures might appear naively utopian, clinging to a notion of a cultural coherence that they should have known was not to be found. Yet both because of the techniques they deploy in pursuit of this coherence and because architects continue to pursue such coherence (it may be the most unifying trait of their disparate practices), these automatic architectures are the forerunners of today's practices in ways that Venturi is not.

Confronted over the past decades by the rapid expansion of architectural computation, by its highly technical means of production, and by its equally specialized vocabulary, it has been all too easy to see only its novelty. We have been encouraged to believe that a revolution has occurred (even if an apolitical one) and that the forms created by computational methods reside on the near side of a historical rift technologically, formally, and conceptually severed from architecture's past. Against this I want to suggest that the automatic architecture of the 1960s and 1970s offers an important precedent for contemporary practices in which process-driven computational techniques are increasingly integral. The methods and techniques identified here have been more persistent than the stylistic shifts of the last half century. In this book I provide an account of the development of such automatic design processes, a historical shift that both extended selective principles of modernism and presaged the expanding role of computational methods in contemporary architecture.

More specifically, each of these cases anticipates a major theme of contemporary architectural speculation. By relaying constructivist principles, the Cambridge research foreshadowed the data-driven, objectivist approach generally associated with Dutch firms of the last two decades, especially Rem Koolhaas's Office for Metropolitan Architecture (the neoliberal application of such methods reveals the common techno-bureaucratic ground of both constructivism and market speculation). Eisenman is clearly a significant intellectual and genealogical precursor of today's computer-driven formal speculation, with its emphasis on process and exotic mathematics, while Otto is a pioneer for architects and engineers invested in genetic design methods who continue to see nature as the model of architecture.

Of course none of these research projects resulted in a fully automatic design process, one in which architectural forms were generated spontaneously out of given conditions. One good explanation of why in principle such efforts could not succeed—if such an explanation is needed—was already offered by Colquhoun in 1967.[17] In brief, his argument is that any such effort at automation of the design process would have to eliminate the representational aspect of architecture, its role as signification as well as shelter, and that this is simply not a possibility of the human condition. Works of architecture, indeed any artificial objects, cannot be designed in a way that insulates them from the field of meanings.

The terms of Colquhoun's argument suggest a central theme running through this book: the tension between the automatic and signification. Each of the cases considered here begins with a vision, perhaps never fully dispelled, of completely automatic, fully determined design processes. In each case this drive for the automatic is linked to an essentialist claim about an ultimate, singular ground of architecture—in either program, form, or nature—and leads to its own architectural system. Yet in each case this tendency to total determination is countered by a realization that architecture is always technically underdetermined and nondeterministic and is therefore open to choices out of which meaning can arise. So, while the rhetoric of these figures often emphasizes the automatic aspects of their various methodologies, it is important to look past this to see that the compelling issue here is the artistically productive tension between what is automatic and everything that is not. That is, it is not the impossible-to-realize automatic itself that is significant here but the ways in which the notion of the automatic is deployed rhetorically, conceptually, methodologically, and technically.

My aim therefore is not to demonstrate that these attempts to create an automatic architecture were naive. Though some such criticism may be unavoidable en route, it is too reductive and too unsympathetic to the historical context in which this work was conducted. Instead, branching out from Colquhoun's observations, I want to consider the meaning of the various quasi-automatic methods these architects established and the ways in which the rhetoric of the automatic played an important role in their work. And not just rhetoric—we must also acknowledge the limited, partial, fragmentary aspects of these practices that were, in fact, automatic by any reasonable meaning of the term. The common orientation of these figures toward the quixotic goal of the automatic is itself one of the most revealing historical symptoms of the postwar period.

1. FENLAND TECH: DESIGN METHODS AT CAMBRIDGE

IN THE FALL OF 2004 the General Board of the Faculties of the University of Cambridge recommended closing the school's department of architecture. Although others suggested that financial pressures were to blame, the board stated that their recommendation was based purely on academic grounds, specifically, "concerns within the University about aspects of the Department's research profile going back over two decades."[1] The primary evidence for this concern was a weak rating—by Cambridge standards—in a national assessment, which influenced the allocation of funding. Opponents of the closure, including the acting head of the department, Marcial Echeñique, argued that the assessment was flawed because it improperly evaluated architecture as a science and failed to recognize the distinct type of research pursued by design.[2] While the guidelines used by the assessment panel did not suggest that architecture be considered as a science, and while they noted that design work would be taken into consideration, the assessment criteria greatly emphasized typical academic markers of research accomplishment such as publication in peer-reviewed venues.[3] At issue here was not only the relative importance given to research versus teaching at a leading university but the particular difficulty of fitting architecture into an academic framework defined by research. After months of criticism in the press, protests on campus, and a restructuring proposal from the department that pledged to focus full-time faculty on research, the general board relented and allowed the department to remain open.

Particular irony surrounds this round of the long-running debates over architecture's place in academia and over its relationship to science. For at least two decades, from the 1950s through the 1970s, much of the Cambridge department—including Echeñique—had been explicitly committed to establishing architecture *as* a science, as a field that would finally reject its artistic pretensions and produce a body of quantifiable knowledge through research. We should understand the reversal of the department's attitude over five decades not as inconsistency or opportunism or even mere change but as an indication of architecture's persistently troubled disciplinary boundaries over the past half century and of the particular difficulties faced by architecture within academic contexts that have become ever more dominated by the sciences.

Unlike France, where formal architectural education began as early as 1671 with the founding of the Académie Royale d'Architecture, architectural training in England continued to be based on apprenticeships well into the nineteenth century. The first university instruction began as late as 1893 at Liverpool, and it was only in 1911 that the School of Architecture there offered a full-time degree with a final examination approved by the Royal Institute of British Architects (RIBA).[4] At Cambridge, the School of Architectural Studies was established in 1912 under the direction of Edward Schroeder Prior, a practicing architect and scholar of medieval art and architecture. Prior's inaugural lecture argued that the school should include a program of "research and experiment" that would undertake both a "systematic examination of first principles" and practical investigations of materials, particularly the new medium of reinforced concrete.[5] In this way, he established architecture within the heart of the English academy and set architectural studies at Cambridge on a path of technical and theoretical research.

Significant expansion of the school would come only after the upheavals of the Second World War with the appointment of Leslie Martin as head and as the university's first professor of architecture in 1956. The son of an architect, Martin, whom Richard Rogers has characterized as "the doyen of postwar British architecture," first led an architecture school in 1934, when, at the remarkable age of twenty-six, he was made head of the School of Architecture at the University of Hull.[6] Embodying the new academic standing of the discipline, he also completed a PhD in architecture at the University of Manchester soon after. During Martin's time at Hull, Marcel Breuer, László Moholy-Nagy, and Serge Chermayeff all lectured.[7] This firsthand contact with key figures of European modernism—many of whom had immigrated to England during the mid-1930s—had a lasting influence on Martin's work and on the pedagogical views he would implement at Cambridge after the war. He thus served as an important link between European and British—as well as pre- and postwar—architectural thought, particularly, as we will see, by carrying an interpretation of constructivism into the postwar period.

The character of Martin's prewar intellectual world is conveyed by the publication *Circle: International Survey of Constructive Art* (fig. 1.1), an art and architecture compendium that he coedited with the artists Ben Nicholson and Naum Gabo. The volume included contributions from Breuer, Moholy-Nagy, Siegfried Giedion, Walter Gropius, Le Corbusier, Henry Moore, Piet Mondrian, Lewis Mumford, and Richard Neutra.[8] Though intended as a serial, *Circle* appeared only once, in 1937, and few copies were sold before stocks of the journal were destroyed in the Blitz.[9] Yet as a rare statement of modernist principles in Britain before World War II, *Circle* had an effect greater than its small circulation would suggest—an effect evidenced and reinforced by its appearance as a reprint in the 1970s.

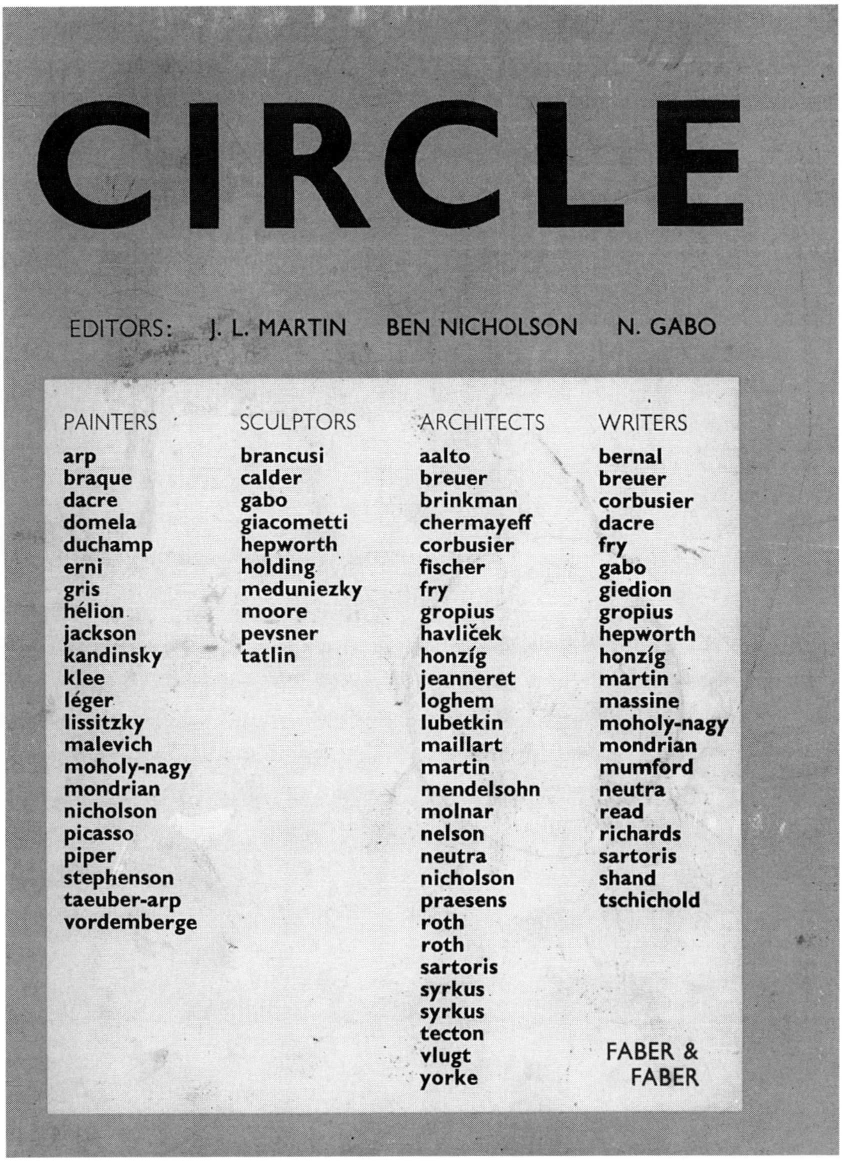

FIGURE 1.1. Leslie Martin, Ben Nicholson, and Naum Gabo, eds., *Circle: International Survey of Constructive Art* (1937; 1971 repr. pictured). Courtesy of Faber and Faber Ltd.

Tellingly, *Circle*'s two introductory editorials both speak of science before they speak of art or architecture. Echoing what was by this time established modern movement ideology, these introductions claim that the sciences had made greater and more revolutionary advances than the arts and that the arts must follow a similar revolutionary course in order to remain intellectually and socially relevant. After the radical and cleansing upheaval of cubism, described as the artistic parallel to the new physics of relativity, what they call "the Constructive idea" emerges as a synthetic strategy for the positive creation of new works. Most significantly for the architecture program Martin would shape at Cambridge after the war, this "Constructive idea" rejected art's historical dependence on "Content"—which Gabo describes as "the external images of Nature"—to focus exclusively on "Form." Further, the introductions posit that the elements of "Form" in art—line, shape, color—have intrinsic qualities and effects, making possible a sort of science of artistic production.[10]

Martin's own contribution to *Circle* is in part a similar summary of modernist rhetoric. In his view, architecture in the nineteenth century was severed from scientific advances and became mired in the groundless reworking of historical styles. Martin saw the division continuing into his present: "the general public does not as yet observe the incongruity between its motor cars and its tudor villas."[11] Modernism's goal is to synchronize the spheres of human activity, which in the 1930s meant the proliferation of an architectural aesthetic appropriate to the machine age. This much was already established polemic. More unusual is the iconoclastic turn taken in Martin's description of the epistemology that accompanies this new aesthetic.

> It is a matter of common knowledge that in science, the world of "appearances" . . . has been abandoned. The world of appearances has given place to a world in which things unrelated to each other in appearance are united in the completeness of a single system. In science as in art, "appearance" has been jettisoned in favour of a world discovered only through the penetration of appearances.[12]

Extending this view to architecture, Martin argues that our understanding of buildings must unite internal and external conditions, static form and environmental performance, the individual building and its surrounding context. Here are two notions that would be fundamental to the postwar work under Martin's direction at Cambridge: first, that there could be an ordering system for architecture that operated at a level deeper than aesthetics, and second, that this system would determine architectural production across all scales, or as the postwar vocabulary would have it, throughout the "built environment."

Such theoretical tenets were extended in practice during the Second World War as Martin served as principle assistant architect to the London, Midland and Scottish Railway, where, anticipating his later interests at Cambridge, he established a research group to study the prefabrication of railway stations. In 1953 he was appointed Chief Architect of the London County Council, an influential post in which he was able to foster a wave of modernist building.[13] It was also in the years just after the war that he designed his best known work, the Royal Festival Hall in London, completed in 1951.

Two years into his tenure at Cambridge, Martin chaired the 1958 RIBA Oxford Conference on Architectural Education. His statement for the conference can be taken as a manifesto for his leadership at Cambridge:

> If architecture is to take its proper place in the university and if the knowledge which it entails is to be taught at the highest standard, it will be necessary to establish a bridge between faculties; between the arts and the sciences, the engineering sciences, sociology and economics. Furthermore, the universities will require something more than a study of techniques and parcels of this or that form of knowledge. They will expect and have a right to expect that knowledge will be guided and developed by principles: that is by theory. . . . Research is the tool by which theory is advanced. Without it, teaching can have no direction and thought no cutting edge.[14]

Faced with a continuing need to justify architecture's presence in universities, Martin offered a threefold argument: first, architectural education would rely on other established fields for much of its content; second, it would establish a coherent body of theory as a means of self-definition; third, architects would conduct research that would advance not just technical aspects of the field but also its theoretical foundations. In the 1960s, this need for intellectual justification, Martin's constructivist beliefs, and his planning experience during reconstruction were forcefully combined with the new technology of computing to encourage the rapid expansion of architectural research at Cambridge. It was also during Martin's tenure that a group of figures who would become internationally influential came to the school of architecture, including new faculty members such as Colin St. John Wilson, Colin Rowe, and Peter Eisenman, as well as students drawn to the program such as Anthony Vidler, Christopher Alexander, and Lionel March.

These developments within the study and teaching of architecture were part of a greater shift in attitude at the university. In postwar Cambridge architects were not alone in adopting a scientific attitude. As a visiting scholar noted in 1961, "The university itself . . . should get a different name. Not the University of Cambridge, it really should be called Fenland Tech; and we should all go out and get T-shirts to advertise this message."[15] Recalling the influential work coming out of other Cambridge departments and directly echoing the tone of *Circle*, March remembered that "Models, quantitative techniques, structuralism seemed to be in the Fenland air. . . . [T]here opened up the prospect of disciplines merging together through the form of approach, despite the ever-increasing specialization of content."[16]

In fact these developments of the 1960s and 1970s would soon outrun Martin's own position, for while he pushed architecture at Cambridge toward the sciences, architecture did not, in his view, simply collapse into science. One of his colleagues, Dean Hawkes, has emphasized both sides of this attitude as well as the influence of the postwar context, recalling that Martin had

> [a] determination to guarantee the status of architecture as a valid academic discipline. . . . [W]hen the principles of scientific rationalism were influential in many fields of critical study, it was, perhaps, inevitable that the model of theory and,

hence, of research in architecture would look to the paradigms of science. . . . But, while this early research observed, and undoubtedly benefited from the discipline of the scientific model, Martin's constant concern was to make connections between these studies and the broad themes of architecture, *not* to make architecture itself "scientific."[17]

Somewhat contradictorily, then, the validity and autonomy of architecture as an intellectual discipline is in this view supported by and modeled on the sciences. As we consider the theories that emerged from Martin's school, we will see that each is built on this assumption: that architecture is a domain that can be investigated in the way that science investigates nature and that analogous laws for architecture can be discovered.

Though understandable as a reaction both to architecture's comparatively new place within the academy and to the generally scientistic context of the postwar years, the internal tensions, even instability, of Martin's vision would be constantly evident over the subsequent decades of architectural research at Cambridge, reaching a critical point with the 2004 recommendation to close the department. By suggesting that architecture be closely connected to science, Martin provoked a cluster of nagging questions: If architecture was not in fact a science, then what, exactly, did it learn from the sciences? If there was only a parallelism between architecture and science, what did that mean? If the methods were the same, then architecture *was* a science, but if, presumably, the methods were not the same, then what was it that the two fields had in common? And what was it that belonged particularly to architecture?

These and similar questions would continue to haunt the Cambridge research. What is under debate here is a question of objectivity: whether within a university context architecture can deliver knowledge that is objective according to the terms of the sciences (here I bracket the many questions about those terms themselves). This can be restated as a question of motivation: Can architecture become "unmotivated" in the manner of science? For, although the processes of discovery in science and mathematics are certainly not unmotivated, the discoveries themselves—facts, laws—are by conception meant to be unaffected by the interests of any individual. The motivation of the researcher cannot play a role in the outcome of an experiment, the validity of a theory, or the proof of a conjecture (that would be patently unscientific bias). They are in this sense automatic. What Martin established at Cambridge was a program of architectural research that explored the possibilities and limits of an automatic architecture modeled on the sciences, a program that projected a scientific attitude onto what was, by his own argument, not science. This attitude also explains, as we will see, the inexorable drift of the Cambridge work away from buildings as material, social, and symbolic constructions and toward the abstractions of geometry and mathematics.

In this chapter I will show how, over a period of about a decade, the original goal of an automatic, value-free, ex nihilo scientific methodology was undercut by a range of criticisms. In its place came a carefully constructed new methodology based on typology, evolution, and value judgments explicitly distinguished from science itself. This shift mirrored the historical and typological interests that overtook architecture generally in the form of postmodernism. Like other architects and architectural theorists, the Cambridge methodologists, too, passed from modernism to postmodernism during the 1960s.

PROFESSIONAL REDEFINITIONS

The growth of architectural research after World War II, like that established at Cambridge, represented a significant shift away from the traditional conception of the architect as an artist-craftsman working with a personalized combination of talent, practical experience, and historical knowledge. In England the turn to collective research was motivated in part by professional anxiety. During the war English architects had been frustrated in their attempts to demonstrate the value of their training, and they emerged fearing that they might be displaced entirely by planners and engineers. The extremities of war had forced to the surface many doubts about architecture as a modern profession: Did architects possess particular expertise? Was their expertise objective in some sense, or based merely on taste? In times of real need, such as war, were architects even necessary? In short, was architecture serious business?

The context for this crisis of confidence is illustrated by the fluctuation of British architects' official status during the war. At the start of World War II, architecture was considered an essential occupation, and architects twenty-five and older were reserved from military service and restricted to employment within their profession. Presumably they were meant to aid the construction of military and industrial facilities and to coordinate the planning of evacuations and the use of air-raid shelters. However, most of this work was actually given directly to large contracting firms with few architects involved. In the fall of 1940, private building was restricted by law, and architects were left without work. Awkwardly, RIBA was then forced to push for its members' status to be reevaluated as nonessential so that they could join the military. Architects were first removed completely from the category of reserved occupations, enabling them to enlist in the armed services, and later fractionally reserved. When enlisted, architects struggled to be treated as favorably as engineers.[18]

At the same time, the entire British construction sector was put under the control of the Department of Works and Buildings. Statistics were gathered regarding available materials, sites, and personal so that resources could be allocated by the department: "under the administration of career civil servants and recruited technical experts, the vast building industry was brought under government direction through controls that were mainly still in use at the end of the war when they were available for planned reconstruction."[19] In such a context, which considered building to be a problem of logistics, architects struggled to be viewed as anything other than superfluous aesthetes.

After the war, the reconfiguration of the profession was intensified by the massive scale of postwar building, for both reconstruction and expansion, with public construction exerting a dominant influence. At a peak in 1955, 45 percent of architects practicing in Britain worked in public departments, and by 1964 that fraction was still as high as 39 percent.[20] One result of this centralization of planning and construction was the growth of architectural research as an organized and fundable activity. The scope of architectural research also shifted from limited prewar concerns with the performance of materials to immediate postwar work on an expanded range of technical issues such as heating, lighting, and estimating to a focus in the 1960s on the general relationship of structures to user needs—what became known as "environmental design." Somewhat paradoxically, in this context, research modeled on the sciences became an important way for architects to assert the legitimacy and relevance of their own discipline.

Looking back from 1968, Royston Landau noted the lasting effects of the war on the architectural profession:

> That the job of the architect can now be seen to be concerned, among other things, with strategic planning, economic planning, and rationalization of communications and transport is not simply a matter of commitment or even wishful thinking. Central planning of physical amenities has been a committed government concern ever since Lord Reith took office as Minister of Works in Churchill's wartime government.[21]

Landau goes on to describe the "theories of knowledge" that troubled the thinking of postwar architects: Karl Popper's notion that an increase in knowledge entails an increase in knowledge of ignorance, Bertrand Russell's failure to establish an unquestionable foundation for mathematics, F. A. Hayek's observation that the natural sciences often do not provide a good model for the social sciences, Buckminster Fuller's warning against overspecialization, and Norbert Wiener's distinction between the general propositions of human thinking and the limited operations of the computer. Such references illustrate not only the turmoil felt by British architects in the latter 1960s but also the extent of their preoccupation with science and the philosophy of science—a preoccupation that, while causing anxiety, could also easily take on positivist tones:

> The idea that the successes of science might be emulated in areas such as architecture and planning swiftly gained ground; not only was there the notion that design might be pursued scientifically, systematically, but the idea that all the

components of cities, from rooms in buildings to entire urban regions, might be understandable and predictable from the new science also generated wide appeal.[22]

It was in this atmosphere that the Cambridge researchers struggled with what might be called "architectural epistemology," making painstaking attempts to establish the principles and methodologies of architectural knowledge.

It was also in the context of this broadly defined research program that architects, especially at Cambridge, began to use computers in the hope of formulating a "scientific" design methodology. As the scope of building research expanded after 1945, computer research at universities was also growing. Begun during the war by the famous British code breaking program, computing research was continued by universities, where it became a tool for scientists in many fields. By the early 1960s architects at universities, following the lead of social scientists, also began to make alliances with computer researchers—though access to machines themselves was not easy.

In a revealing anecdote John Paterson, then deputy county architect of West Sussex, describes how in 1965 he saw a promotional film of the IBM CRT 2250, a graphics-capable display with a light-pen input (fig. 0.2). Attempting to acquire one, he discovered that the film was based on a demonstration at MIT and that IBM had "no back up" in place for the device and that any software would have to be developed "from very first principles." Nonetheless, he received approval to buy the "very expensive" machine in 1966 and began working with a small group on graphics-based architecture programs. While waiting for delivery, the group tested their programs at IBM Hursley on what Paterson claims was one of only six graphics terminals in the entire United Kingdom. When a machine was finally delivered in December of 1967, it did not include the display he had expected but only an IBM 360 computer. The CRT 2250, he learned, was sold only to "high status organizations" such as "Rolls Royce, Atomic Weapons Research, etc. which later became an exclusive club."[23]

CHRISTOPHER ALEXANDER: THE ANALYSIS AND SYNTHESIS OF FORM

The first internationally significant graduate of Cambridge's new model of architectural education was Christopher Alexander, although by his own account his time there was somewhat schizophrenic, and although he would go on to spend most of his career in the United States. Alexander had been raised to become a scientist but at seventeen decided that he wanted to be an architect instead. His recollection of his father's reaction to this news reflects in miniature the troubled standing of architects throughout postwar Britain: "[my father] was horrified. He thought architects were disreputable and idiotic. Here was his son that he was taking so much care of in the direction of science and it was as if I had announced to him that I was going to be a clerk."[24] As a compromise, Alexander agreed to complete a bachelor's degree in mathematics, including the famous Cambridge "tripos" honors examination, before going on to study architecture. During his first years at Cambridge he also devoted time to the study of aesthetics, employing an outside philosophy tutor to assist his readings of Kant, Schopenhauer, and early British philosophers. As agreed, he finished the mathematics tripos and, remaining at Cambridge, entered the architecture program.

Yet having pressed to study architecture, Alexander quickly became dismayed by what he saw as the lack of clarity in studio instruction. He "admired Mies and Corbu but could not understand what they were doing."[25] At some point in this first year, he had a revelatory meeting with Martin:

> [My] experience in the Director's office . . . led me to believe that there was something strange going on. . . . By accident I had got a glimpse of the sheer absurdity of it all. And this was very fortunate. Since I was supposed to be at one of the tap roots of contemporary modern architecture at that time, recognizing that absurdity was much more fundamental than if I had been in some architectural backwater.[26]

Apparently uninterested in spending too much time learning what might be going on, Alexander insisted on hurrying through the program by taking the second and third years concurrently. He received a BA but declined to pursue the two additional years required for a professional degree.

His reaction to the Cambridge program and his mathematical training came to be reflected in his early publications. The first, written in the summer of 1958, just after he finished his degree, reviews the Golden Section ratio. Alexander argues in favor of a more general mathematical principle, which he relates to modular construction.[27] The following year the *Architect's Yearbook* published his polemical rejection of the modernist tenets he had (or believed he had) discovered at Cambridge.[28] "The Revolution Finished Twenty Years Ago" argued that architects, and especially students of architecture, must not be fooled into taking the heroes of the prewar modern movement as role models; that the architectural revolution of the early twentieth century could not be repeated; and that what was needed instead was the gradual and collective refinement of the already established modernist vocabulary. (Although differing in tone, this denial of the possibility of continual revolution was at root similar to that made twelve years later by Colin Rowe in his well-known introduction to *Five Architects*.[29])

Alexander went on to explore the possibility of using mathematics to overcome perceived flaws in modernist design thinking in a much fuller manner and to much greater effect as a student in the new PhD program in architecture at Harvard, which he entered after finishing at Cambridge. While at Harvard he became involved with a number of academic communities and research projects beyond the PhD program, including Harvard's Society of Fellows, the Center for Cognitive Research at Harvard, the Joint Center for Urban Studies of MIT and Harvard, and the Civil Engineering Systems Laboratory at MIT. A number of publications came out of these associations, most notably *Community and Privacy*, written with Serge Chermayeff, and two studies of highway design methodology, written with Marvin Manheim of the Civil Engineering Department at MIT.[30] Pursuing the desire for a collective, cumulative architectural process that he had expressed in "The Revolution Finished Twenty Years Ago," in these collaborative works Alexander turned his mathematical interest away from the more obvious topic of proportional systems and toward design methodology. Using the mathematics of graph theory and the electronic computers provided by the MIT Civil Engineering Department, he began to develop a method for analyzing the contexts of design problems by which, he believed, architectural forms could be determined.

Alexander articulated this design methodology in his dissertation, completed in 1962, and published in 1964 as *Notes on the Synthesis of Form*.[31] Echoing the concerns of his Cambridge years, the book attempts to demonstrate that mathematics and computer programming can dispel the fog of individual intuition and enable better design for the masses. Though later rejected in part by Alexander himself, *Notes on the Synthesis of Form* proved surprisingly popular for a technical tract on design methodology: the book has had at least fourteen English printings and was translated into Italian in 1967 and French in 1970. The book also brought together nearly all of the themes that would occupy architectural methodologists throughout the 1960s and 1970s: mathematics (particularly graph theory), computer analysis, the quantification of programmatic and environmental requirements, and an overriding reliance on scientific analogies. Although many subsequent researchers took pains to distance themselves from the specifics of Alexander's proposals, his book was clearly the founding work of the computational approach in architectural methodology and remained its principal reference into the early 1970s. An amalgam of broad epistemological, historical, and sociological claims; suggestive diagrams; and mathematical demonstration, the book reveals much about the motivations and difficulties of early attempts to marry the computer and architecture.

In brief, Alexander argues that design is essentially a problem-solving activity. Contemporary designers, however, face problems that are both too new and too complex to be adequately solved either by modification of received forms or by the mysterious work of artistic intuition. Given this, he argues, the only sure route to successful design is through the creation of a "formal picture" that retains only the "abstract structural features" of the design problem. Mathematics, particularly set theory, provides a language and group of tools that, when coupled with computer analysis, can generate this formal picture. Finally, it is proposed that the formal picture of the problem can be straightforwardly converted into a solution—a design—

the success of which is assured because it responds only to a rational analysis of the design problem.

In order to begin this process, Alexander posits that any design problem can be represented by a list of requirements and by the linkages between these requirements. In contemporary design—whether of products, buildings, or cities—difficulties arise because these requirements are so complexly interdependent that the designer, unable to sort and weigh their many entanglements, is overwhelmed and therefore cannot proceed rationally. Alexander's proposed solution is to use the computer to mathematically disentangle the web of requirements into nested subsets (fig. 1.2) that are relatively independent. At the lowest level of the resulting hierarchy are comparatively autonomous groups containing only a small number of requirements that can then supposedly be more easily solved by a "constructive diagram," that is, a design proposal of some sort. These small diagrams are then to be recombined (fig. 1.3) through a process that steps back up the analytical tree via the eponymous "synthesis of form."[32]

Importantly, Alexander claims that this formalization of the design process and the introduction of computational analysis is intended to return to contemporary design the same virtues that he finds exemplified in what he calls the "unselfconscious" design of premodern cultures. Alexander's method is an artificial means of achieving a new automatism for contemporary design: the description of the design problem is supposedly objective, the analysis into subproblems is carried out automatically by a computer program, each subproblem is simple enough that its solution is transparent, and the synthesis of these partial solutions is also assumed to be obvious and without conflict. This supposedly complete articulation of the design problem and its solution is intended to displace the role of individual authorship and judgment, returning design to a collective—though now scientific rather than ritualistic—basis and thereby escaping the dilemmas of modernist subjectivity.

Alexander's argument rests on the general premise that, at a fundamental level, hidden from intuition, both physical forms and social contexts are organized by logical structures that can be discovered by mathematical analysis. He uses a range of terms for these structures: *form*, *conceptual order*, *organization*, *pattern*, *abstract structure*, *logical structure*, *logical picture*, *diagram of forces*, *field description*, *formal picture*, *constructive diagram*, and finally, in his mathematical treatment, "the graph G(M,L)"—where M is the set requirements and L the set of connections between these requirements for a particular design problem. However, the connection between these logical structures, which are understood purely as sets of relationships, and the material organization of the objects they are supposed to describe remains entirely ambiguous.

On the one hand, the entire book seems intended to show that the logical analysis of requirements into a diagram will directly inform the physical pattern of the

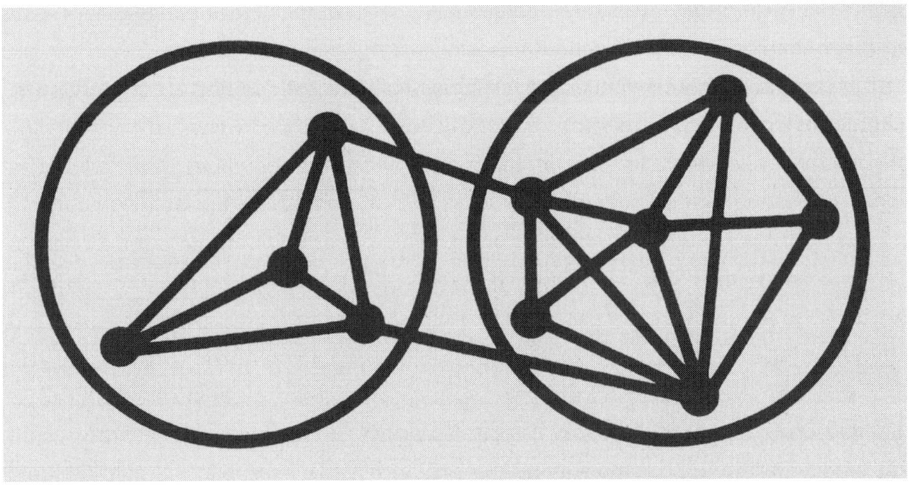

FIGURE 1.2. Disentangling sets of programmatic requirements. From Christopher Alexander, *Notes on the Synthesis of Form* (1964). Cambridge, MA: Harvard University Press. Copyright © 1964 by the President and Fellows of Harvard College. Copyright © renewed 1992 by Christopher Alexander.

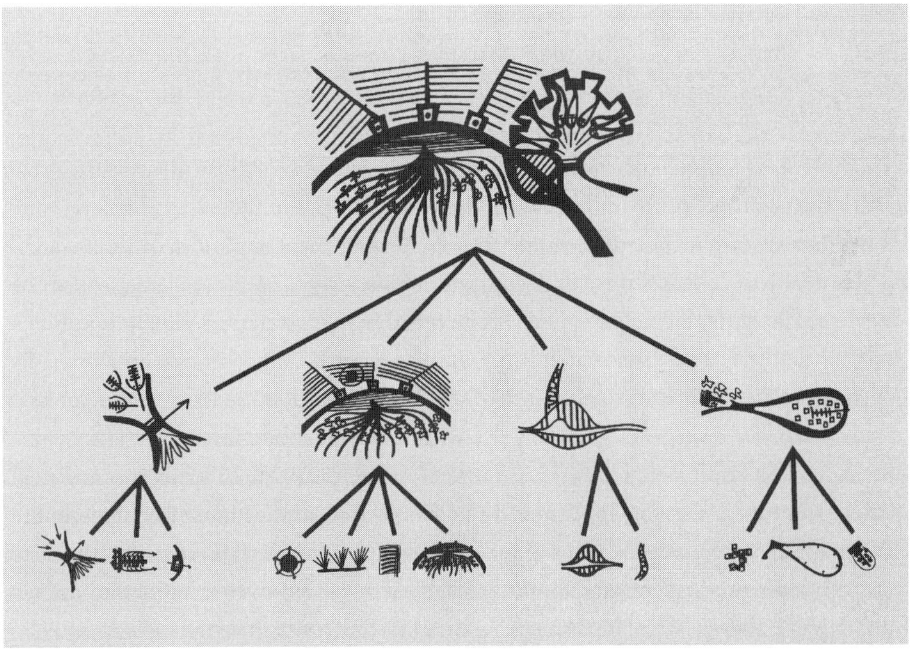

FIGURE 1.3. Tree of diagrams illustrating the "synthesis of form" for the design of a village in India. From Christopher Alexander, *Notes on the Synthesis of Form* (1964). Cambridge, MA: Harvard University Press. Copyright © 1964 by the President and Fellows of Harvard College. Copyright © renewed 1992 by Christopher Alexander.

object being designed. Alexander uses the analogy of iron filings in a magnetic field to argue that a properly designed object is entirely determined by its requirements and makes those requirements perfectly visible. This point is also made in the final chapter of the main argument:

> The hierarchical composition of these diagrams will then lead to a physical object whose structural hierarchy is the exact counterpart of the functional hierarchy established during the analysis of the problem; as the program clarifies the component *sources* of the form's structure, so its realization, in parallel, will actually begin to define the form's *physical* components and their hierarchical organization.[33]

Yet near the beginning of the text Alexander appears to argue in exactly the opposite direction. Describing the modern mathematics of "order and relation" that he plans to use, he notes that

> though even this kind of mathematics may be a poor tool if used to prescribe the physical nature of forms, it can become a very powerful tool indeed if it is used to explore the conceptual order and pattern which a problem presents to its designer. Logic, like mathematics is regarded by many designers with suspicion. . . . But no one shape can any more be a consequence of the use of logic than any other, and it is nonsense to blame rigid physical form on the rigidity of logic. . . . There is no legitimate sense in which deductive logic can prescribe physical form for us.[34]

What then is meant to be the outcome of Alexander's method? He is clearly concerned with architects and designers and with their role in producing material objects; and, as the first excerpt indicates, he appears to believe that his method will lead directly to physical forms. Yet the second passage denies the possibility of this, especially because Alexander never again mentions building a "particular plastic emphasis" into his method. The dilemma is ultimately condensed into, though hardly solved by, a scattering of almost ideographic diagrams collected at the back of the book.

Notes on the Synthesis of Form ends with a "worked example" that offers one of the earliest examples of computer use in architecture outside of structural engineering calculations.[35] Having emphasized that his mathematically based design method is demanded by the unprecedented novelty and complexity of modern architectural projects, strangely, Alexander's test case is a six-hundred-person village in India—not, it would seem, a novel or modern program (although perhaps the premise of designing such a village, ex nihilo, is a modern problem). The contradiction here suggests that a newly formalized design process was demanded not so much, or not only, by design problems themselves but by Alexander's desire for methodological rigor as epitomized by mathematical techniques and computation.

This computer envy also helps to explain the level of complexity displayed in the worked example. There, Alexander lists 141 requirements that will define his hypothetical Indian village, such as

> 20. People of different factions prefer to have no contact. . . .
> 67. Drinking water to be good, sweet. . . .
> 92. House has to be cleaned, washed, drained.[36]

Left unexplained is how Alexander hit on these 141 requirements and not others and why there are roughly one hundred requirements and not just ten or perhaps one thousand. What we can suspect is that 141 requirements and their linkages gave Alexander a number that was too large to be sorted by hand yet small enough to be handled within a reasonable amount of time by the IBM 7090 to which he had access. If so, the computer not only analyzed the design problem but shaped its very definition.

After the IBM 7090 sorted the requirements of his Indian village example, Alexander was left with subsets of seven to twenty-three requirements that could not be further disentangled. At this critical point of transition from analysis of the problem to the proposition of a solution, where a physical form must finally, somehow, be suggested, mathematics and the computer drops out, and it is a long-established type of architectural sketch, the *parti pris*, rendered with a broad pen, that is brought in to "solve" the conflict among these requirements. Alexander never explains how he arrives at these diagrams or whether these are the only possible solutions. Instead, these sketches apparently emerge from exactly the sort of private, intuitive, formal language he had promised to overcome. Deep within this mathematical and iconoclastic method it is a version of the architect's cocktail napkin sketch that is left to perform the crucial tricks of design. In a work ostensively devoted to mathematical clarity, it is just their ambiguity that makes these diagrams indispensable.

In order to function as they do, the diagrams hover between representing abstract relations and representing concrete plans. Their wide strokes and irregular forms appear to record very general relationships, what Alexander would call the logical structure of the problem, and yet also very tentatively suggest ground plans for the problem's physical solution. The implication of the diagrams is that the detailed, concrete, design of the village is yet to come. However, his brief explanations reveal that Alexander is, in fact, proposing very specific configurations of buildings, wells, roads, fields, and trees but without venturing to show how these would actually be laid out, at what scale, with what geometry, and in what materials. The diagrams give the impression that Alexander's method has produced a design for an entire village, but without daring to show what that village would look like.

This troubled transition from the logical analysis of program to the synthesis of architectural form became the focal point for Alexander's work immediately after

Notes on the Synthesis of Form. He returned to England from May 1965 to June 1966 to serve with the Directorate General of Research and Development in the Ministry of Public Buildings and Works. His work there with Barry Poyner was later published as *Atoms of Environmental Structure*, which attempts to elucidate the process of using form to resolve programmatic conflicts that had remained so obscure in *Notes*:

> We believe that it is possible to define design in such a way that the rightness or wrongness of a building is clearly a question of fact, not a question of value. We also believe that if design is defined in this way, a statement of what a building ought to do, can yield physical conclusions about the geometry of the building, *directly*. We believe, in other words, that it is possible to write a programme which is both objectively correct, and which yields the actual physical geometry of a building.[37]

Without mention of the mathematical analysis that had taken up so much of *Notes on the Synthesis of Form*, Alexander and Poyner immediately address the challenge of logically translating programmatic statements into architectural forms. The bulk of their book is devoted to examples of such translations and is intended to show that a direct and objective translation is possible. The general method they describe follows these steps: first, create hypotheses about the tendencies of the people using the environment under consideration; second, catalog architectural arrangements that cause conflicts between these tendencies; third, define "an abstract geometric property" that avoids these conflicts; and finally, design a specific manifestation of this abstract geometric property.

Though hardly unquestionable, this method does seem to give greater detail about the process of moving from analysis to synthesis than *Notes* had provided. But like much of Alexander's work during this period, it remains conflicted about its central thesis. In describing the general approach, Alexander and Poyner claim that the "relations" they are interested in are abstract geometric properties and that the class of concrete arrangements that have these abstract properties, and that therefore prevent conflicts, are theoretically infinite. Thus, their introductory example of designing an urban corner demonstrates that, practically, there are numerous distinct physical manifestations that satisfy the "relationship" they define. According to their argument, if the goal is to create an urban building corner that prevents pedestrians from colliding, then the corner may be beveled or rounded, it can be made transparent, or a low obstruction can be placed just beyond the corner to force people to walk around it.[38]

Yet in the more elaborate case studies presented later in the book and in the book's more polemical moments—"it is possible to write a programme which is both objectively correct, and which yields the actual physical geometry of a building"—Alexander and Poyner seem to forget that their abstract properties are not *sufficient* to generate architecture. Certain forms may be ruled out, but no form is positively determined. Again the logical determination of form seems to have slipped away.

Finally, while *Atoms of Environmental Structure* does not include any computational analysis, Alexander and Poyner still insist on the "scientific" nature of their approach. However, where the mathematical method of *Notes on the Synthesis of Form* was developed explicitly as a synchronic replacement for the loss of the traditional "unselfconscious" development of forms over time, *Atoms of Environmental Structure* recommends a new sort of formal development modeled on scientific progress:

> The point of view we have presented is impartial. This is its beauty. Because it is impartial, it makes possible a sane, constructive, and evolutionary attitude to design. It creates the opportunity for the cumulative improvement of design ideas. . . . The body of known relations must, therefore, grow and improve. Design, if understood as the invention and development of relations, is no longer merely a collection of isolated and disconnected efforts. It becomes a cumulative scientific effort.[39]

This suggests a tempering of the cataclysmic tone projected by *Notes on the Synthesis of Form*, which argued that the contemporary condition was so radically new, complex, and fast changing that gradual responses were impossible. In some respects the shift to an evolutionary model anticipates the methodological system soon to be developed at Cambridge. It also begins the trajectory of Alexander's subsequent work at the University of California, Berkeley, on what he would call "pattern languages," which, at least initially, were to be compiled in an ever-expanding, collective catalog taken from all architecture and urban languages.

The problems with Alexander's method were numerous and would be sharply noted by later critics, especially those at Cambridge discussed below. The questionable role of his diagrams attracted immediate attention, and Alexander's introduction to the 1971 paperback edition of his book focuses explicitly on them. There, in a surprising inversion, Alexander argues that "once the book was written, I discovered that it is quite unnecessary to use such a complicated and formal way of getting at the independent diagrams."[40] Instead, "you can create, and develop, these diagrams piecemeal, one at a time, in the most natural way, out of your experience of buildings and design."[41] This, of course, is nothing less than a complete rejection of the book's foundational premise that the formalized mathematical analysis and the computer were needed precisely because the intuition of the individual designer could no longer be relied on. (The reversal foreshadows his later dogmatic espousal of a "timeless way of building.") In its difficulties and reversals Alexander's troubled attempt to marry mathematics and design, logical analysis and graphical production, computation and architectural design, revealed the fault lines that would run through all of the methodological work to come.

POSTWAR FORM

Throughout Alexander's early writings, the word *form* plays an important role, and its ambiguity does invaluable work. On the one hand, *form* seems to mean the shape and qualities of physical objects: in one example the dimensions, shape, and materials of a tea kettle. On the other, it suggests an underlying logical organization that is not related to physical appearance: the "form" of Alexander's mathematical analysis of programmatic requirements. The ambiguity of physical and logical form leads to passages such as this:

> The shapes of mathematics are abstract, of course, and the shapes of architecture concrete and human. But that difference is inessential. The crucial quality of shape, no matter of what kind, lies in its organization, and when we think of it this way we call it form.[42]

This suggestively vague notion of form is taken directly from several prewar sources that Alexander encountered at Cambridge.

The most obvious influence on Alexander's dissertation, echoed even by its title, is *On Growth and Form* by the biologist D'Arcy Thompson. First published in 1917 and expanded for a second edition in 1942, Thompson's book is a wide-ranging "introduction to the study of organic Form, by methods which are the common-places of physical science"—this is to say, by mathematical methods.[43] Thompson argues that organic morphology is the result not only of evolution but also of physics, that the form of an organism can be explained, in part, by the physical forces that affect the organism at any instant. This shift in emphasis from diachronic to synchronic explanation is mirrored by Alexander's attempt in *Notes on the Synthesis of Form* to replace a slowly evolving "unselfconscious" craft tradition with a mathematical analysis of the immediate present. Alexander also borrows his fundamental metaphor, that form is a "diagram of forces," directly from Thompson.[44] This metaphor is crucial for Alexander both in his initial assertion of a parallel between design problems and scientific problems and in his final attempt to move from an analytic to a synthetic procedure. But Alexander also significantly alters what he takes from Thompson. When using the term *force*, Thompson, as a scientist, refers only to literal physical forces, such as gravity, magnetism, and friction. In contrast, Alexander applies Thompson's term to an entirely different category of entities. Moving without hesitation between natural and social phenomena, Alexander begins speaking of human preferences and desires as "forces." What is literal in Thompson becomes metaphoric in Alexander: programmatic requirements should shape a building *like* the wind shapes sand dunes. This transference naturalizes the context of design so that user preferences appear to be as predictable and as quantifiable as the forces occurring around a magnet. Objectified in this manner, these preferences are able to become the stable, unquestioned objects of Alexander's mathematical analysis.

Alexander himself understood this application of the form-forces model as a legitimate, even emulative extension of Thompson's work. Just as Thompson set out to carry mathematical techniques beyond mechanics and into biology, Alexander attempted to move beyond the animal organism and into the realm of social relations and the aesthetic activities of men. In 1917 Thompson claimed that

> It is but the slightest adumbration of a dynamical morphology that we can hope to have until the physicist and the mathematician shall have made these problems of ours their own, or till a new Boscovich shall have written for the naturalist the new *Theoria Philosophiae Naturalis*.[45]

Forty-five years later, Alexander's epilogue to *Notes on the Synthesis of Form*, in which he compares his own efforts to those of the mathematician Bernhard Riemann, echoes and extends Thompson's call:

> Man's feeling for mathematical form was able to develop only from his feeling for the processes of proof. I believe that our feeling for architectural form can never reach a comparable order of development, until we too have first learned a comparable feeling for the process of design.[46]

Thompson's influence on Alexander was no quirk—*On Growth and Form* was a popular reference in postwar England, especially among artists and architects.[47] The book even inspired an exhibition titled *Growth and Form* (fig. 1.4), at London's Institute of Contemporary Arts (ICA), which was opened in July 1951 by Le Corbusier (in London for the tenth meeting of the Congrès International d'Architecture Moderne). Like several ICA shows that would follow, the exhibit was designed as a complete environment, containing photographs, slide projections, films, and three-dimensional structures. The subject matter was a mixture of scientific images of natural forms—X-rays, microphotographs, and time-lapse films of skeletons, crystals, and sea urchins—and artworks based on or resembling these images. The ICA show projected the possibility that the laws of "form" would prove so general that they could unite not only all scales of natural entities but also the entire sphere of the natural with the artificial and the sciences with the arts.

The ideas of *Growth and Form* were further advanced in a book, *Aspects of Form*, originally intended as the catalog of the exhibition (and cited by Alexander).[48] An anthology of articles devoted to "different aspects of spatial form," *Aspects of Form* includes contributions from a crystallographer, an astronomer, a geneticist, five biologists, three psychologists, and the art historian, E. H. Gombrich, represented by his classic essay, "Meditations on a Hobby Horse; or, the Roots of Artistic Form." The organization of the book and Lancelot Law Whyte's introduction make clear that we are meant to understand form as a characteristic that can be studied in similar fashion over a vast range of scales and phenomena. Although acknowledging many gaps, the book tries to present a continuum that begins with subatomic structures;

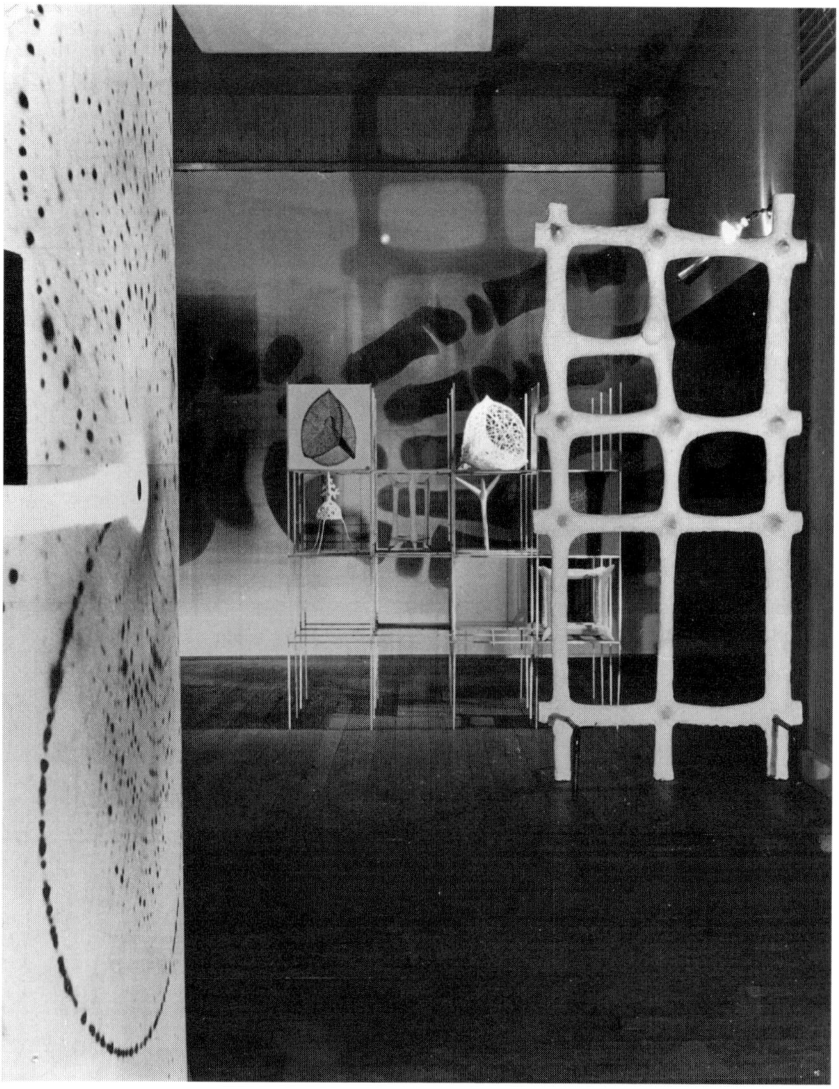

FIGURE 1.4. *Growth and Form* exhibition, Institute of Contemporary Arts, London, 1951. Copyright © Tate, London 2016. Copyright © Nigel Henderson Estate.

works up through the qualities of matter, the organization of plants and animals, and the psychology of advanced animals; and arrives at the socially conditioned activity of artistic production. Ideally, for Whyte—as for Alexander—"form" would relate these diverse phenomena and allow a unified understanding extending from muon to Manet.

Whyte's choice of *form* as the unifying term gave distinct advantages to the artists, art historians, and architects who organized the *Growth and Form* effort. For if form presented a promise of uniting the increasingly complex and remote fields of postwar science with art and social life generally, it did so in a way that would put the artist at a distinct advantage:

> There is, I think, special reason why busy scientists have responded to the initiative of the I.C.A. Form is very important and yet tantalisingly subtle. Exact science seems to know much, and yet it has so far only got to grips with the simplest forms such as crystals and bubbles. Complex forms still baffle it. All the powers of science do not let us see into the growing point of a plant, or the dominant centres of an embryo, or the grey matter of the brain, and understand exactly what is going on there when new forms develop. . . . [S]cience has not yet discovered its own method of making complex forms appear simple. . . .
>
> The artist knows well the pervasiveness and subtlety of form; his interest in external forms and his pre-occupation with the formative processes of his imagination make him what he is.[49]

Or as the ICA's Herbert Read put it,

> The increasing significance given to *form* or *pattern* in various branches of science has suggested the possibility of a certain parallelism, if not identity, in the structures of natural phenomena and of authentic works of art . . . and the gradual realisation that all of these patterns are effective and ontologically significant by virtue of an organisation of their parts which can only be characterized as *aesthetic*—all this development has brought works of art and natural phenomena on to an identical plane of enquiry. Aesthetics is no longer an isolated science of beauty; science can no longer neglect aesthetic factors. . . . It is an exciting moment in the history of human thought, and the paths that lead forward are bright with intellectual promise.[50]

Boldly, these artists, architects, and art historians attempt to take the upper hand in this postwar exchange with science. Faced with a widening gap between the scales of advanced science and the scales of architecture and art, they attempt a reconciliation through one of the most traditional concerns of their own fields. Generalizing from what are actually a wide variety of interests in the sciences and recalling Thompson as an authority, Whyte and the ICA organizers espouse a Kantian view that claims that the principles determined by science can be stated only because, first, there are principles of aesthetic judgment. Of course, the question of whether the relationship between natural phenomena and works of art is only "a certain parallelism" or an actual "identity" would seem crucial for the prospects of an aesthetically guided science. Neither *Growth and Form* nor *Aspects of Form* gave clear support to the later claim, but this is just the identity that, a decade later, Alexander would presume in order to assert that social forces and forms could be treated just as natural ones are.

Finally, although as a student at Cambridge Alexander may have been confused by the modernist orientation of the architecture program and shocked by his meeting with its director, his ideas about form nevertheless owe much to Martin's influence. Specifically, we can see the influence of the "Constructive idea" that Martin had put forward in *Circle*, which is referenced several times in *Notes on the Synthesis of Form*. Yet while important as a precedent, the idea of form espoused by *Circle* was not simply identical to conceptions of form developed by postwar theorists such as Alexander (or later Peter Eisenman). Although sharing the view that the "laws" of form are not based in mere appearances and are thus independent of traditional aesthetic preferences, *Circle* had still argued that the elements of form are "organically bound up with human emotions." Alexander pressed further, arguing that form describes logical relationships in the abstract without necessarily referring to any particular physical configuration or emotional state. He attempts to reject the aesthetics of architectural form, in favor of the abstract "form" of his mathematical analysis. The difficulty of maintaining such a rejection within architecture is evidenced by Alexander's deeply ambiguous, perhaps even desperate, diagrams. (By comparison, Eisenman's brand of formalism would, in this sense, remain on safer disciplinary ground, as the next chapter will show.)

LIONEL MARCH AND THE CENTRE FOR LAND USE AND BUILT FORM STUDIES

Alexander was not the only Cambridge student of the mid-1950s to migrate from mathematics to architecture. Lionel March, who entered Magdalene College in 1955 with a recommendation from computer science pioneer Alan Turing, thought of architecture only after arriving at Cambridge, where the "new status of the school of architecture under Prof. Martin" attracted him.[51] As discussed earlier, this new status depended in great part on an effort to make architecture more intellectually rigorous. In contrast, according to March, before Martin's arrival "architecture was considered to be a soft option, along with estate management and geography. If you were good at sports, were active in the theatre or journalism, or enjoyed the full social life, then these were the subjects to go for."[52]

March began studying architecture with Alexander in the first class under Martin's tenure; he would graduate with a first class BA in mathematics and architecture. He remembers Alexander suggesting in 1957 that "games theory and linear programming might be useful techniques in architectural design."[53] Although he has said that Alexander's references were beyond him at the time, March would soon be the one scolding Alexander for sloppy mathematical reasoning while Alexander had abandoned computers and mathematics for the intuitive knowledge of his "pattern language."[54] (Yet in another reversal, today it is Alexander's pattern language that is popular among computer programmers.) The movement of these two math prodigies to architecture was not coincidental: the "new status" of architecture at Cambridge, fostered by Martin, was largely achieved by pushing architecture toward the sciences and mathematics. His prewar involvement with modernism, particularly his "constructivist" faith in an underlying continuity between science and art, left him receptive to the postwar infatuation with science, especially the new technology of electronic computing. The result was a great expansion of architectural research during his tenure.

A distinct institutional framework for this research was established in 1967 with the creation of the Centre for Land Use and Built Form Studies (LUBFS) within the Department of Architecture, first under Martin's direction and then, from 1969 to 1973, under March's.[55] The creation of LUBFS was a direct result of the parallel early careers of March and Alexander. March had "followed" Alexander to the Joint Center for Urban Studies at Harvard and MIT, and as March recalls, "When Alexander moved [from the Joint Center] to Berkeley, I was the only architect at the Center with the exception of Kevin Lynch. The place seemed to be dominated by lawyers, economists and political scientists. Much of the research employed computer methods and models."[56] Returning to England, March reported to Martin on his "experiences at the Harvard/MIT Joint Center, and soon the idea of the Centre for Land Use and Built Form Studies (LUBFS) emerged. . . . Land use was a planner's term, built form an architect's. The new Centre would attempt to occupy the, then, no-man's land between planning and architecture."[57]

Around 1966, March and Martin received funding from the Centre for Environmental Studies in London, "a quasi-independent public-sector think-tank established with Ford Foundation and British government monies," after speaking with the young assistant director, a mathematician named Alan Wilson, and were able to launch LUBFS.[58] Naturally, the research center did not remain entirely separate from the school and soon "students in the architectural programme became interested in the research activities. Ed Hoskins was the first student to present a computer program as his architectural thesis at Cambridge as a result of Leslie Martin waiving the usual design requirements."[59] Like the scientific labs that were its models, LUBFS was financed by research contracts and grants, primarily from British public agencies including the Centre for Environmental Studies, the Department of Education and Science, the Department of Health and Social Security, the Housing Research Foundation, the Department of the Environment, and the Social Science Research Council. By 1973 the center had received nearly £250,000 and housed eighteen full-time researchers and about an equal number of postgraduate doctoral candidates and visiting associates—in total twice the number of teaching staff in the Department of Architecture proper.[60]

Further pursuing the model of the sciences, March and Hoskins also set up a commercial consulting firm, Applied Research of Cambridge, that made commercial use of the center's research (the company went on to develop early CAD and GIS systems and was acquired by McDonnell Douglas in 1985). Concerned with preserving the "academic" character of work in the center, March saw Applied Research as an outlet for practical development that would remain "completely independent" from the center's theoretical work. Where fifty years earlier Edward Prior and others had argued that professional training for architects needed to be located within universities, March repeatedly stressed that architectural research and teaching needed to remain "intellectual" and "theoretical": "I believe that it is not the function of a university to train students to be professionals *in* a subject, but to educate students *through* a subject. If some students wish to become members of a profession after their university education that should be their affair and the profession's, not the university's."[61] As is the case throughout his career, something of March's mathematical inclination shows here in his desire to construe architecture as a field with theories and methods to be examined apart from the act of proposing specific designs for specific situations. While this might seem at odds with his call for an interdisciplinary program in environmental studies, March understood mathematics as the common language of all of these disciplines as academic research fields.

Looking back on his time at Cambridge, March reveals how the central role he gave to mathematics was the result of both his belief in the rhetoric of modernism and his disappointment in its realization.

> It had been an assumption of my student education in the fifties that the *Zeitgeist* demanded of the Modern Movement a close parallel between contemporary mathematical and scientific discovery and architectural activity. Indeed, the Movement's apologists such as Giedion and Kepes claimed such a special relationship, and eductionalists like Bill and Maldonado at Ulm were translating the relationship into a practical programme for design in the guise of "scientific operationalism."
>
> My case is that the Modern Movement *qua* movement has disintegrated in part because it failed to make any but the most superficial bridges between itself and developments in mathematics, sciences, and other technologies.[62]

After criticizing Le Corbusier and Gropius for their mystification of mathematics and geometry, March suggests that only Moholy-Nagy had a "deeper understanding of the problem. At least he had read Rudolf Carnap's *Der Raum* (1922), and his lectures on space at the Bauhaus share the language of the transformational approach to geometry advocated by Klein's *Erlangen Programme* (1872)."[63] March argued that a central problem for postwar architecture arose from the fact that "the Modern Movement did not itself establish a tradition of geometrical investigation."[64] His work, and that of LUBFS, was explicitly intended to remedy the situation.

Encouraged by the mathematical forays of their colleagues in the social sciences, by the perceived failures of modernism, and by the promise of increasingly accessible computers, the LUBFS researchers began an organized effort to produce a mathematically based methodology for architecture. The center espoused an explicitly mathematical approach.

> The common method of the Centre's work is to formulate mathematical and logical models which make it possible to characterize and to explore the ranges of spatial patterns which accommodate various activities. . . . The research is mainly in the field of quantitative methods, mathematical and logical models, and computer aides for building and environmental design, planning, development and management.[65]

March hoped that these associations with mathematics and computer science would give architecture not just a sound epistemological base but also greater practical standing in a postwar society dominated by science. Architecture would be reconstructed as a serious business with a legitimate and fundable role for advanced research. Research would no longer be conducted by "lone scholars" but by "systems laboratories":

> the old Vitruvian view of architecture which related it to the study of classics, divinity, fine arts and music . . . has long since been outgrown. . . . Today most of our research workers would connect most easily to engineering, geography and geology, mathematics, and even physics and chemistry: indeed many of them come to us from these disciplines and not from architecture.[66]

For the first time since the eighteenth century, March argued, architectural studies had "touched the frontiers of knowledge," and he held out hope that architects might regain membership to the Royal Society.[67]

Yet while the mathematical turn of architecture was widespread in the 1960s, at Cambridge this turn was also explicitly framed as the revival of efforts that had been suspended thirty years earlier, lending March's program a historicist dimension as well. He opened an important anthology of Cambridge research with a long passage from Soviet constructivists Lidiia Komarova and Nikolai Krassil'nikov calling for the expansion of mathematical techniques in design beyond strict engineering problems to the "scientific-objective assessment of all the possible variants available to the projector."[68] March seconded Catherine Cooke's assessment that "perhaps more than any other single piece of work in *Sovremennaya arkhitektura* this warms the Cambridge architect's heart to a sense of intellectual community with the members of the OSA [the Association of Contemporary Architects—the constructivists]."[69] Here, Martin's influence is again evident in preparing a generation of Cambridge hearts for this sympathetic response. Cooke, who began studying architecture at Cambridge in 1961 and who completed a dissertation on Soviet town planning in 1974, was also a crucial voice in the community, providing groundbreaking research on the Soviet constructivists that was directly echoed in March's writing (he seems to have suggested her dissertation topic).[70] Indeed, while March wrote nothing explicitly political during this period, his program for the LUBFS research is nearly identical to that of the OSA as described by Cooke.[71] However, there were two important distinctions between March's program and that of his Soviet precursors. First, March almost completely neglected the expressive aspect of architectural form: he never discussed what a building would look like. Second, March and his group had access to electronic computers that made quantitative analysis of "all the possible variants"—as the OSA phrased it—seem to be a newly realizable goal.

STRUCTURAL REVOLUTION

The mathematical approach to architecture reached a high point in May 1971 with the publication of a special issue of *Architectural Design* titled "Models of Environment"—edited by March, Marcial Echeñique, and Peter Dickens—devoted to the work of Cambridge researchers and graduates (fig. 1.5).[72] (At this time March was director of LUBFS and Echeñique was the assistant director.) The introduction to the issue, subtitled "Polemic for a Structural Revolution," gives a concise summary of the beliefs underlying their work. Martin and Echeñique argue that "architecture and physical planning lack adequate theoretical foundations" and that only the certain-

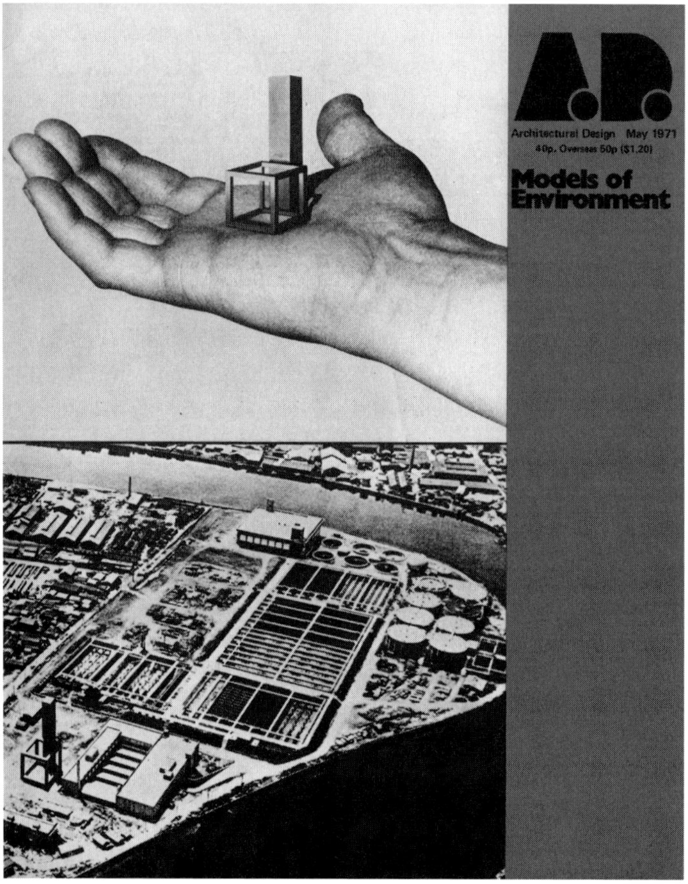

FIGURE 1.5. Lionel March, Marcial Echeñique, and Peter Dickens, eds., "Models of Environment," special issue, *Architectural Design* 41 (1971). Cover by Derek Boshier. Courtesy of Derek Boshier.

ties of mathematics can provide such a conceptual base. They describe their investigation of architecture and planning through mathematical methods as part of a more general "structural revolution" taking place in the social and behavioral sciences. Based on a new awareness of "systems and structures," this revolution intends to root out the "intuitive skill . . . confusion . . . sophistical sciences . . . individual hunches . . . court jesters and acrobats . . . private pranks . . . pricey prima-donnas . . . hallucinations . . . extravagant and empty images . . . individual expression . . . [and] personal prejudice" that plague architecture and planning. The structural revolution will also bring architecture and planning into closer relationships with other disciplines, using mathematics as a common language. This will mean abandoning professional distinctions established in the nineteenth century in favor of a holistic, interdisciplinary approach. Finally, all of these tenets are intended to encourage objective, collective, and socially responsible answers to what is described as the "environmental dilemma" of the 1960s and early 1970s.

As an architectural methodology, the Cambridge polemic is most radical in its rejection of artistic intuition and in its deep iconoclasm. Intuition is condemned on two counts: first, it is unequal to the complexity of postwar politics, economics, and technology (as Alexander had asserted), and second, it is private and opaque and thus unaccountable. Instead, the LUBFS researchers seek an explicit, quantified design process that is open to criticism and collective refinement. Regarding architectural images, the damnation is concise: "Draughtsmanship is a drug."[73] For March and his colleagues, texts, formulas, diagrams, and computer code should replace drawings, models, and photographs as the proper tools of architectural research. The common understanding of the building as an object of sensory engagement is to be supplanted, at least in the minds of designers, by an understanding of the building as a system of functional relationships—although we will see that for March, this too might be "aesthetic" in some sense. Yet an architectural theory that rejected images was rejecting the profession's dominant medium of communication, both internally and with the general public, as well as the profession's established methodologies, which were also image based. That the long history of drawing could be replaced by mathematics was not obvious and could not be easy. *Revolution* was an accurate term.

The more radical strains of prewar constructivism had attempted a similar revolution against intuition and images but within the context of the scientific sixties, and with the growing availability of digital computing, a mathematically based iconoclasm took on new force. In this regard, the Cambridge position represented both an extension of and break with architectural modernism. It condensed and exaggerated attitudes that had been developing since the end of the nineteenth century, particularly the call for the reconciliation of architecture and contemporary science. However, following Reyner Banham, the Cambridge researchers argued that prewar modernism's relationship to science had been largely metaphorical and that modernism had subsequently evolved into a number of purely subjective, unscientific styles. Also, as Banham had pointed out, where Le Corbusier's biplanes and ocean liners offered their forms directly to architects through vision, postwar technologies—such as telecommunications, radar, cybernetics, operations research, and computer science—provided few obvious formal tropes and tended to operate on scales much larger or much smaller than that of architecture. Aiming then for a "deep" connection to postwar science, the Cambridge group dismissed appearances entirely and concentrated instead on the use of mathematics and computation in the design process. Postwar architecture, they argued, should be practiced like a science but need not look "scientific."

While LUBFS contributed to research on concrete engineering problems—problems of structure, lighting, acoustics, and heating—this was not the most ambitious goal of their work. In *The Architecture of Form*, March emphasizes a distinction between "architectural engineering" and "architectural science."[74] The latter is meant to apply to the analysis and design of the built environment as a whole: it describes a mathematically based theory of architecture from which, ultimately, entire buildings and cities could be generated. "Architectural science" attracted the most ambitious research at Cambridge and became possible only "with the coming of large, fast, and reliable computers during the latter half of the 1960s."[75] March and his colleagues hoped to solve building programming with computer programming. Rigorous functionalism, they believed, could finally succeed through the merger of the two: programming programming. However, as we will see, this rigidly scientific approach would soon find itself demonstrating its own limitations, so that a major, if ironic, contribution of the Cambridge research was, in fact, its ultimate rejection of functional determinism as an intellectually viable position. Thus, what began as an apparent triumph of functionalism quickly became one of its ends.

Continuing along the trajectory set by Alexander, March's "architectural science" mainly focused on problems of spatial arrangement, particularly problems of architectural plans: the arrangement of rooms within a given perimeter, of spaces according to a given architectural program, and of activities within a given plan. Typically the goal was simply to minimize walking distances for users. Working on these sorts of problems, the Cambridge researchers, with their mathematical backgrounds, were able to draw on an existing body of knowledge in topology and graph theory. Helpfully, these arrangement problems could also be separated from the computational modeling of architectural geometry itself because the focus was on the relationships between spaces, not on the particular forms of the spaces themselves—that is to say, the concern was topological, not geometrical. This work therefore required little or no graphic output; and results, like a table of room locations or a diagrammatic floor plan, could be produced by a simple alphanumeric printer. So, in addition to the theoretical commitment to an approach based on function, there was also a practical advantage to such research at a time when graphics-capable displays remained rare and costly.

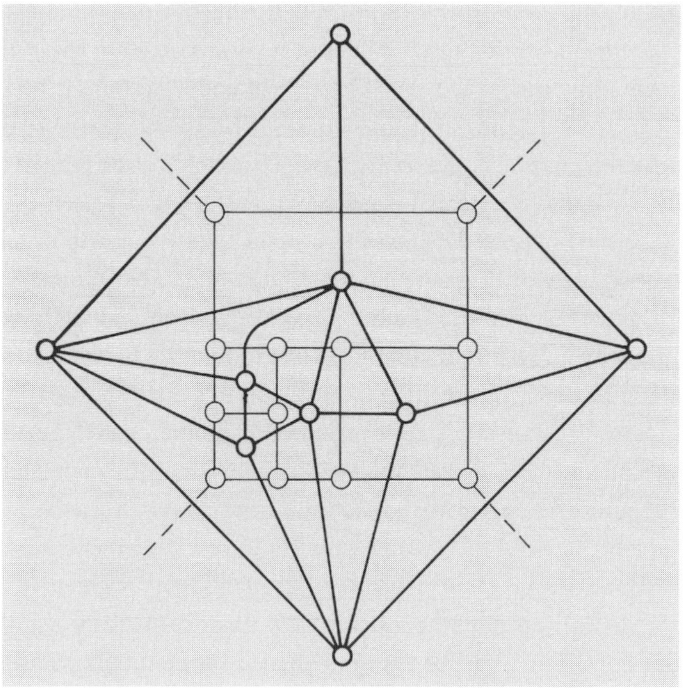

FIGURE 1.6. Philip Steadman, relationship of a plan graph and an adjacency graph. From "Graph-Theoretic Representation of Architectural Arrangement," in *The Architecture of Form* (1976). Copyright © 1976 Cambridge University Press. Reprinted with the permission of Cambridge University Press.

The Cambridge exploration of arrangement problems followed two strategies: enumeration and optimization. Enumeration sought a complete listing of all spatial configurations satisfying a set of conditions. Optimization analysis tried to calculate the best possible configuration for a particular architectural program given a controlling variable, such as the distance between related activities. To address problems of realistic complexity by either approach, the computer was essential in order to test the many thousands of possibilities that arose.

A good example of enumeration is provided by Philip Steadman's 1973 paper "Graph-Theoretic Representation of Architectural Arrangement."[76] Citing applications of graph theory in architecture, operations research, electronics, and aesthetics, Steadman explains that any architectural plan consisting of bounded subdivisions (i.e., rooms) can be associated with a mathematical graph describing the adjacencies of these subdivisions (fig. 1.6). Similarly, if a building's adjacency requirements can be defined—that is if some rooms should be located next to others—these requirements can also be represented by a graph, which simplifies the initial phase of plan making by describing only the relationships between spaces, not their size or shape. In some cases it can be shown that it is topologically impossible to construct a plan corresponding to a particular adjacency graph, and the requirements can then be reconsidered. In other cases, it will be possible to construct one or more plan graphs describing the topologies that meet the adjacency requirements. These plan graphs can then be adjusted through all manner of scalings and distortions to become actual building plans. The computer becomes valuable in this process because the number of possible plan graphs that might satisfy a given adjacency graph grows very rapidly as the number of rooms considered is increased.

However, at the time Steadman was writing in 1973, even with a computer the search for satisfactory plan graphs could be quite long. For an eight-room situation a typical program, which contained about twelve thousand instructions in the IPL-V language, took two hundred minutes just to find the first viable plan graph. Exhaustive results could be given only for five or fewer rooms—a trivial number from the architect's perspective. To overcome this limitation, Steadman proposed an alternative method. For a given number of subdivisions (rooms), there is a clear process for stepping through every possible adjacency graph. At each step the graph can be tested for "planarity," which determines whether the graph can be associated with any plan(s). If the graph is planar, then its plan(s) can be given. In this way it is possible to enumerate all of the topologically distinct plans for a given number of subdivisions (rooms). Steadman suggests that these prototype plans could then be compiled as reference books or stored as data files for rapid computer searches. His paper lists the possible topologically distinct plans for up to six rectangular rooms within a rectangular perimeter (fig. 1.7), and a note indicates that later work

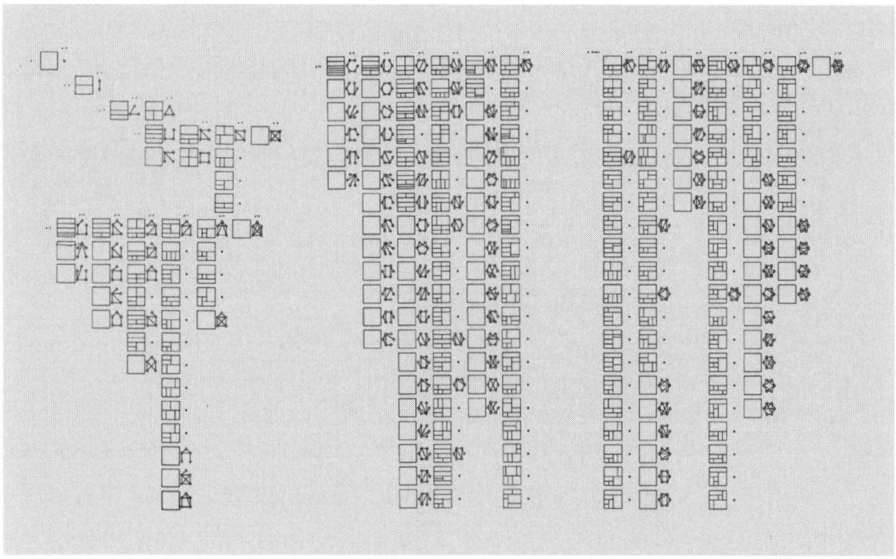

FIGURE 1.7. Philip Steadman, exhaustive enumeration of rectangular dissections and corresponding adjacency graphs for zero to six subdivisions of a plan. From "Graph-Theoretic Representation of Architectural Arrangement," in Lionel March, *The Architecture of Form* (1976). Copyright © 1976 Cambridge University Press. Reprinted with the permission of Cambridge University Press.

reached eight rooms. For five rooms there are twenty-three possibilities; six rooms give 116; seven rooms yield 694; and for eight rooms there are 5,124 topologically distinct plans.

While such enumeration of possible architectures was of theoretical interest, optimization was an obvious further goal. Surely, it seemed, a proper science of architecture should not only be able to say that certain designs were possible but would also be able to arrive at optimal designs. Like Alexander, researchers in optimization hoped that the application of the correct algorithms to sets of building requirements could produce architectural forms that were objectively "best"—thereby fulfilling the dream they had taken up from the Soviet constructivists of a fully rational design process.[77] However, as their investigations proceeded and as the results of their research began to circulate, the possibility of creating such a process became more and more remote. The "polemic for a structural revolution" began to face serious internal challenges.

THE MOST EXTRAVAGANT OF FANCIES

Optimization research at LUBFS was brought to a critical point around 1972 in the work of Philip Tabor and his student Tom Willoughby.[78] Their work is valuable because it includes both a thorough review of previous research and rigorous original efforts. Tabor and Willoughby focused on the most typical problem studied by quantitative methodologists: the "circulation" or "activity-location" problem. In this version of the classic "traveling salesman" problem, the goal is to minimize total pedestrian traffic within a building. In theory, travel can be minimized by using the amount of traffic between activities to locate spaces and, therefore, the activities they "contain": in general, the greater the amount of traffic between two spaces, the closer they should be. Typically, a large institution such as an office building, hospital, or college campus was selected as a test case.

Since Alexander's initial efforts, this sort of operations research approach to architecture had faced strong external criticism (an example of which is discussed below). Tabor and Willoughby present the unusual case of internal critique, in which precise, quantitative arguments were used to reject what Tabor called "that most extravagant of fancies, completely automatic design."[79] Their research led them to conclude that quantifiably optimized architectural solutions were largely impossible. They suggest that at best, quantitative approaches have a limited use for certain very complex problems and must always rely on many assumptions that cannot be quantified. This was a far more limited view than that held by Alexander in 1963 or even that expressed just a short time earlier in the "Structural Revolution" publication of 1971. As we will see, its implications would be central to March's mature design theory.

Tabor gives a careful account of the difficulties and misconceptions haunting the circulation problem, which can be summarized as follows (Willoughby's dissertation offers a very similar assessment):[80]

1. The dissection of programs and spaces in an architectural problem is often difficult, and is always artificial.
2. It is unrealistic to assume permanent associations of activities and locations.
3. Traffic between locations may not always be the determining criterion.
4. It is difficult to quantify both the traffic between locations and the weighting of different sorts of traffic.
5. Because the circulation problem is a permutational problem with no efficient solution, the number of possible solutions that must be considered is very large: for 12 locations there are 400 million permutations, which, in 1973, would have required two to three years of computing time to evaluate.
6. Since use patterns change much more rapidly than physical structures, any overly specific design is soon destined to be obsolete.

Tabor ends up arguing against any attempt to automatically produce designs that are too carefully tailored to specific descriptions of use, which is to say that he rejects dogmatic functionalism. Instead, he suggests, "buildings can be designed only for general ease of communication" (a view that suggests a role for typology).[81] He then takes two approaches to the problem of organization at this more general level. First, he studies methods for grouping activities into fewer, larger clusters. This is similar to the work done by Alexander ten years earlier, although Tabor is critical of Alexander's use of exclusively hierarchical classifications. Tabor suggests several alternative methods that he feels are less distorting, proposing that "non-hierarchic dendrograms, overlaid hierarchies, or scaling are all potent tools for suggesting solutions."[82] Importantly, where Alexander had initially emphasized the automatic translation of such diagrams to formal solutions, Tabor is more cautious, carefully noting the distortions and elisions that these diagrams always contain and the many partially subjective decisions needed to turn them into buildings.

Tabor's second response follows from his view that any overly specific effort to match program and building is doomed. As an alternative he attempts the evaluation of a number of generic building types—slab block, Corbusian cross tower, courtyard—to determine which, if any, provide the most efficient circulation. His results are inconclusive, and it seems that again no clearly optimal structure can be determined. Within the quantitative tradition, this recourse to existing types is unusual, for much of the rhetoric surrounding architectural computing focused on the uselessness of inherited types and on the need to create new forms directly out of the analysis of contemporary situations. Typology was typically a foil wielded by critics of computational methods, who argued for the indispensability of established building types as the initiating models of architecture. Tabor's willingness to explore the role of types within a computational design method can be seen as part of a nuanced position that began to emerge at Cambridge in the early 1970s, one for which typology came to play a surprisingly central role.

DESIGN METHODS AND TYPOLOGY

If by the early 1970s the most ambitious goals of "architectural science" were being challenged from within, they faced serious external criticism as well. In June 1967 the journal *Arena* published the essay "Typology and Design Method" by the architect and critic Alan Colquhoun.[83] In this essay Colquhoun rejected the possibility of a purely inductive architectural design method and argued instead that the use of received types was unavoidable. While Colquhoun's dismissal of hard-line methodologists, such as the early Alexander or Tomás Maldonado, is forceful and clear, his own attitude toward the appropriate role of science in architecture requires careful explication.

Colquhoun holds that while there is some distinction to be made between works of art, which are based primarily on mimesis and tradition, and those of technology, which are shaped mainly by functional requirements and physical limitations, both sorts of artifact always possess "message" values in addition to any use values they may have. This inescapable representational aspect distinguishes man-made artifacts from natural entities. Modernist functionalism attempted to collapse use value and message value so that the artifact would both be determined by and be representative of its function. However, citing the wide-ranging symbolism of cars, airplanes, steamships, and locomotives, he argues that the products of modern technology themselves demonstrate that the meaning of an object can never be restricted to its function. Moreover, almost no artifacts can be determined by function alone, especially not artifacts as socially complex as buildings, because there are rarely sufficient constraints, and value judgments must always be made in defining the design problem (as Tabor and Willoughby discovered).

Yet, he continues, by clearing away received standards of tradition and taste, modernism left no public vocabulary within which these judgments could be made and discussed. This vacuum was supposed to be filled by free intuition, but, Colquhoun claims, artistic intuition can never be pure; it is always based on knowledge of past solutions of similar problems. Similarly, as Gombrich had argued, the meaning given to forms by a viewer is never immediate, as expressionism would have it, but is always based to some degree on received conventions. So, Colquhoun concludes, to ignore the field of existing types is to ignore the context out of which both forms and interpretations arise.

The discussion progresses straightforwardly up to this point and would seem to be leading to a clear rejection of scientific methodologies in architecture or any art. Colquhoun's position, however, is more complex. He concludes his essay by arguing that despite the impossibility of complete scientific determination in design, the postwar age is nonetheless a scientific one, and science needs to be incorporated into architecture. While mathematical tools cannot give solutions directly or independently, they do provide the context within which Colquhoun believes architecture in the late 1960s must operate.

By arguing for the relevance both of historically evolved typologies and of the present context, Colquhoun describes architecture as shaped by both diachronic and synchronic dimensions (in an essay of 1981 he ascribes a similar view to Gombrich): technology determines the contemporary context within which inherited typological models are modified. It is only to counterbalance the prevailing scientistic mood of the 1960s that he minimizes the role of the contemporary technological context in order to advocate a return to typology. Granted, Colquhoun does not describe how received solutions are adapted to new problems, and figures such as Banham and Alexander were arguing that the problems faced in the postwar context were so new that comparison to past problems was impossible or irrelevant. On the other hand, by giving some importance to the contemporary context, Colquhoun avoids the purely formalist recycling of historically given typologies recommended by Colin Rowe. While his refutation of strict functional determinism in design appears indisputable, his argument for the necessity of a historically determined typology seems more open to debate. Could it not be that beginning at some point in the later twentieth century, it was no longer past architectural forms that provided the dominant shaping of architectural awareness but instead contemporary forms from other fields—perhaps cybernetics or aerospace engineering or electronic media, all of which did contribute to avant-garde architecture in the 1960s?

One answer is suggested by the fact that in addition to Gombrich, Colquhoun's model of typological development also relies significantly on Karl Popper, particularly on his *Conjectures and Refutations*, which appears in the bibliography of Colquhoun's first volume of collected essays. There is general sympathy between the thinking of Colquhoun and Popper, but an especially clear point of comparison on the roles of tradition and reason is given near the end of a 1956 speech by Popper:

> The critical rationalist can appreciate traditions, for although he believes in truth, he does not believe that he himself is in certain possession of it. He can appreciate every step, every approach towards it, as valuable, indeed as invaluable; and he can see that our traditions often help to encourage such steps, and also that without an intellectual tradition the individual could hardly take a single step towards the truth. It is thus the critical approach to rationalism . . . which for a long time has been the basis of the British middle way: the respect for traditions, and at the same time the recognition of the need to reform them.[84]

The similarity to Colquhoun's model, in which established typologies are modified by a contemporary context, is clear. Also shared are strong objections to scientistic efforts such as those of the architectural methodologists—see particularly Popper's *Poverty of Historicism*.[85] Popper's views provide support for Colquhoun's advocacy of what might be called "critical typology" over revolutionary scientism. For, viewed from Popper's middle way, it would be foolhardy to replace architecture's established disciplinary models and methods by models and methods shipped in from other fields. The critical rationalist argues that there can be no synchronic substitute for the lessons learned through the diachronic process of criticizing and refining a tradition *within* a discipline.

ARTIFICIAL EVOLUTION

As a result of this internal and external criticism, by the early 1970s it had become clear even to those most committed to "architectural science" that their neofunctionalist approach was not going to lead directly to architectural results. Even with the new analytical power of computers, there was no convincingly objective path from functions to forms. In response, March, as head of the Cambridge research center, began to acknowledge these critiques and to describe a more limited, though still central, role for mathematics and the computer in design methodology. His theory begins to share surprisingly much with the thinking of critics like Colquhoun, and the differences that remain are limited largely to issues of efficacy rather than ideology.

The fullest version of March's mature methodological theory appeared in 1976 as the introduction to *The Architecture of Form*, an anthology of papers by his LUBFS colleagues. March begins with an extended critique of Alexander, who stands as the source of naive scientism in architecture. March first attacks Alexander's positivism, noting that Alexander wrongly assumes that he has direct access to objective facts about design requirements, that these facts can be stated as a set of conflicts, and that the analysis of these conflicts can lead directly to a design that will remove all conflicts and therefore be objectively best. He goes on to argue that such talk about "scientific facts" in design programs is purely rhetorical and that because these "facts" are untestable, they remain "mere clichés."[86] Then, in a manner similar to Tabor and Willoughby, March presents a careful analysis of two of Alexander's examples, demonstrating the wide variation in conclusions that would follow from the uncertainty of his initial assumptions. The second main criticism of Alexander regards his confused use of the hypothetical-deductive model of the sciences. In *Notes on the Synthesis of Form*, Alexander describes his constructive diagram as a hypothesis. March, here following Popper, sees this as a fundamental mistake, because the design diagram, as a proposal, cannot be tested and potentially falsified, as is required by Popper's definition of a scientific hypothesis.

Reacting to Alexander's mistakes, March begins to introduce his own theory of architectural methodology, which, while under the heading "scientific approach," sounds strikingly like that of Colquhoun:

> Any scientific approach to design must confront the issues raised by the pluralism of individual values and the autonomy of social choice; and must accept the conditionality of degrees of conviction about truth, rightness and goodness.[87]

Later, he concludes that

> What Alexander says is: "If you accept my hypotheses then you have no further choice in the matter, you must accept my proposal." What is argued here is: "If you give any weight to our hypotheses, then the best that we can suggest, for what it is worth, is this proposal."[88]

March's model of architectural methodology then springs directly from his carefully shaped reaction to Popper's thought:

> Popper's philosophy of science cannot be applied directly to architecture.
>
> . . . Just as Popper draws a distinction between logic and empirical science, so too must a distinction be made between these and *design*. To base design theory on inappropriate paradigms of logic and science is to make a bad mistake. Logic has interests in abstract forms. Science investigates extant forms. Design initiates novel forms. A scientific hypothesis is not the same thing as a design hypothesis. A logical proposal is not to be mistaken for a design proposal.[89]

If, under the thrall of science envy, architects (including perhaps a younger March himself) have missed this distinction, that is largely because they have mistakenly followed Popper's rejection of synthetic logic, which, March believes, design demands because it aims to produce unique compositions rather than universal statements: "Thus in design, in contradistinction to scientific discovery as Popper would have it, the Popperian criteria must be stood on their heads *in order to* sustain an approach which is rational."[90]

What March then attempts to formulate is a rational theory of design that takes synthetic reasoning into account. He does this in two ways, first through the work of the American philosopher Charles Sanders Peirce and then through Bayesian probability theory. The model that March develops out of these two systems of thought describes design as a "cyclic, iterative procedure" (not unlike a computer program) that passes repeatedly through three phases: production, deduction, and induction, what March calls the "PDI-model" (fig. 1.8):

> We conceive of rational designing as having three tasks—(1) the creation of a novel composition, which is accomplished by productive reasoning; (2) the prediction of performance characteristics, which is accomplished by deduction; (3) the accumulation of habitual notions and established values, an evolving typology, which is accomplished by induction.[91]

These phases are borrowed from Peirce's three modes of inference: abductive (which March renames "productive"), deductive, and inductive. March believes that this

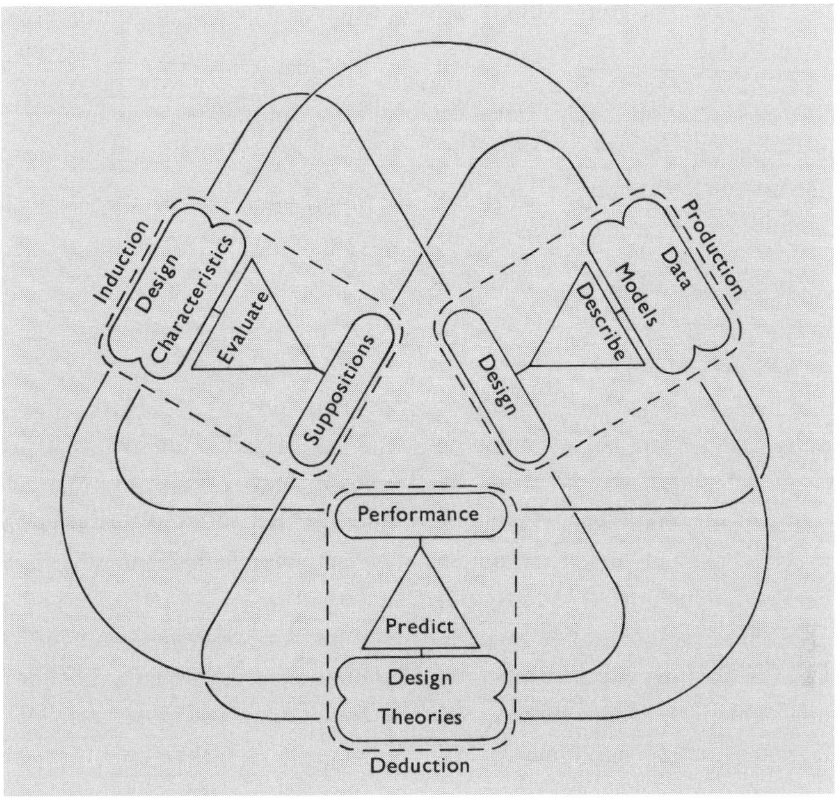

FIGURE 1.8. Lionel March, model of the design process. From *The Architecture of Form* (1976). Copyright © 1976 Cambridge University Press. Reprinted with the permission of Cambridge University Press.

has always been the way designs have been implicitly developed, whether by individuals, offices, or entire building traditions. However, he argues that in the postwar world there is a new need, and a new capability, to make the process explicit:

> If internalized personal judgement, experience and intuition alone are relied upon, the three modes of the PDI-model become inextricably entangled and no powerfully sustained use of collective, scientific knowledge is possible. Design will remain more or less personalistic and a matter of opinion, albeit professional. If the design process is externalized and made public . . . then the three stages of the PDI-model are worth making explicit so that as much scientific knowledge can be brought to bear on the problem as seems appropriate. In this externalized process it is feasible to experiment with artificial evolution within the design laboratory using simulated designs and environments. New, synthetically derived stereotypes may emerge, and old ones may be given new potential without having to wait for practical exemplification. Design comes to depend less on a single occasion of inspiration, more on an evolutionary history, greatly accelerated as

> this iterative procedure can now be—a prospect opened up by recent advances in computer representation.[92]

For March, the success of this "artificial evolution" required the creation of sophisticated computer models that simulate the demands of the real world and that, following the mandate set out by Leslie Martin in 1959, unite the disparate concerns of the architect in one design space.

> [I]t is now possible to represent a proposed design in mathematical terms in great detail—filled out, as it were (unlike the skeleton drawing) with all the flesh of its relevant physical attributes. In this form . . . a direct coupling between the art and the science becomes possible, and the two unifying paradigms—the computer program and the mathematical model—themselves unite. The mathematical model of the design may be made alive on a computer, complete with its structural integrity, with its environmental climate, with patterns of user activities; it may be disassembled into its component elements and costed; it may be speedily modified, transformed, and manipulated. . . .
>
> Architectural education around the concept of modelling—even penetrating into the teaching and methods of architectural history—becomes, I believe, an intellectually tough discipline around the theme of man and his environment. . . . It removes architecture from the invention of images which reflect the externalities of our technological culture (the machine aesthetic), and penetrates beyond appearances to the elements, relationships, and processes of its very existence: we might coin the phrase, "the systems aesthetic." It turns its back on architecture warped by the competitive individualism of the 19th century and the aggrandisement of personal genius, and faces forward to an architecture balanced in its collective design and its commitment to the promotion of cultural evolution: architecture no longer residing in the souls of individuals, but in the body of a profession.[93]

With this as a culminating vision, we can ask, what happened to architectural science? We see here the notion of an automatic scientific architecture replaced by a model of design based on typology, evolution, and value judgments—a methodology which March took pains to distinguish from scientific practice itself. In doing so, he also mirrored the typological interests that were sweeping architecture generally in the form of postmodernism. Architectural science in Cambridge underwent its own computer-aided evolution.

Still, a few tenants remained constant from Alexander to March. The most important of these was the rejection of purely subjective artistic intuition and the accompanying desire to make the design process as explicit, as open, as possible. For both men this view derives from a sense of social responsibility and a suspicion of aesthetic formalism. For March, the mathematical model assured that the architectural proposal responded to all criteria, not just the formal whims of the designer. In this way mathematics was put in the service of his socialist politics. March also continued to assert, as Alexander had, that, at least in some cases, architectural projects had become so complex that they could not be handled adequately by traditional design methods. Finally, March remained enthusiastic about the computer as a revolutionary tool that enabled new, more explicit methods of architectural design, though he now understood the computer not as an answer-giving machine but as a design environment, as a new field for human action.

THE SYSTEMS AESTHETIC

Finally, we should return to one apparent contradiction touched on above and recalled by March's phrase "systems aesthetic." For despite his iconoclastic rhetoric, all of the mathematical work March supported at Cambridge was driven by an interest that he nonetheless characterized as aesthetic: "My impelling motivation at this time was aesthetic. It still is. There are other motivations, but deep down what makes me tick is an aesthetic sense of order, of essential simplicity behind apparent complexity."[94] For March, Leslie Martin's constructivism was alloyed with serial art and computation to generate a vision of a new architectural language.

> [M]ost strongly I recollect Sandy [Colin St. John] Wilson stopping me in a corridor and saying something about the future possibility of architecture being notated as a mathematical code. This rang bells. It reinforced a thought . . . that the elements of architecture might be set out like Lavoisier's chemical table, and by a further analogy, that with such a limited means architectural works of the imaginary power of a Beethoven symphony might be constructed.[95]

What type of "aesthetic" concern is this? Not an interest in the immediate appearance of the object but a focus on its underlying relationships—what Martin and Alexander would call its "form" and Eisenman would come to call its "deep structure"—a structure of relationships that could be captured by mathematics. Following Martin, March believed that this sort of aesthetic interest could unite the two cultures of art and science.

There are few instances in March's early career in which he approached the traditional role of an architect or artist—that is, creating a specific object. However, around the time of the establishment of LUBFS, one example did appear prominently as the February 1966 cover of *Architectural Design*, which showed a study from March's *Rotations around a Square* (fig. 1.9).[96] The graphic composition is dominated by a large black square (shades of Malevich) surrounded by a seemingly arbitrary pattern of overlapping rectangular elements in translucent red, yellow, and blue. While the cover image was a study for one of sixteen prints within *Rotations around a Square*, that work, intended to be a book, was itself only one of a

FIGURE 1.9. Cover of *Architectural Design* 36 (February 1966) showing a design study for Lionel March's *Trio No. 5 "Rotations around a Square,"* 1965. Courtesy of Lionel March.

group of serial design exercises that March undertook from 1960 on, some of which were exhibited in the library of London's Institute of Contemporary Arts in the fall of 1962.

Inside the *Architectural Design* issue, a dense text titled "Serial Art: Notes on the Cover Design 'Rotations around a Square,'" explains that the design is a result—but not the end point—of an elaborate process based on serial techniques. March claims that "In a work in which serial techniques are employed, there are five stages to the process of design: intention, selection, automatism, expression and interpretation."[97] Using the passive, formalist language of serialism, March writes that the intention of

Rotations around a Square is to show "A square impinged upon by events occurring around it." In this case the "events" are the "rotating color plates" of the four-color printing process used to produce the image. March relates his graphic process to serial music and its use of "symmetry operations" such as reflection, rotation, translation, permutation, and complementarity, which may be combined by union and intersection operations (fig. 1.10). Recalling his work on the project March wrote,

> At this time, I was fascinated by the mechanisms of serial music: the inversions and reflections of the tone row, and certain rhythmic and dynamic structures then being introduced by Boulez and Stockhausen. . . . If music could be encoded in numbers, why not paintings, and ultimately architecture? The translation into painting was not difficult, especially since I was well versed in Constructivist theory and Paul Klee's pedagogical notebooks. . . . I was impressed by Stravinsky's remarks in *Poetics of Music*: "My freedom thus consists in my moving about within the narrow frame that I have assigned myself for each one of my undertakings. I shall go even further: my freedom will be so much the greater and more meaningful the more narrowly I limit my field of action and the more I surround myself with obstacles."[98]

One suspects, though, that for March the freedom to be gained through the use of serial techniques was very much a freedom *from* expression, *from* authorial intent, and *from* a finalized work. Under the heading "Automatism" he makes it clear that he should not be held entirely responsible for the design:

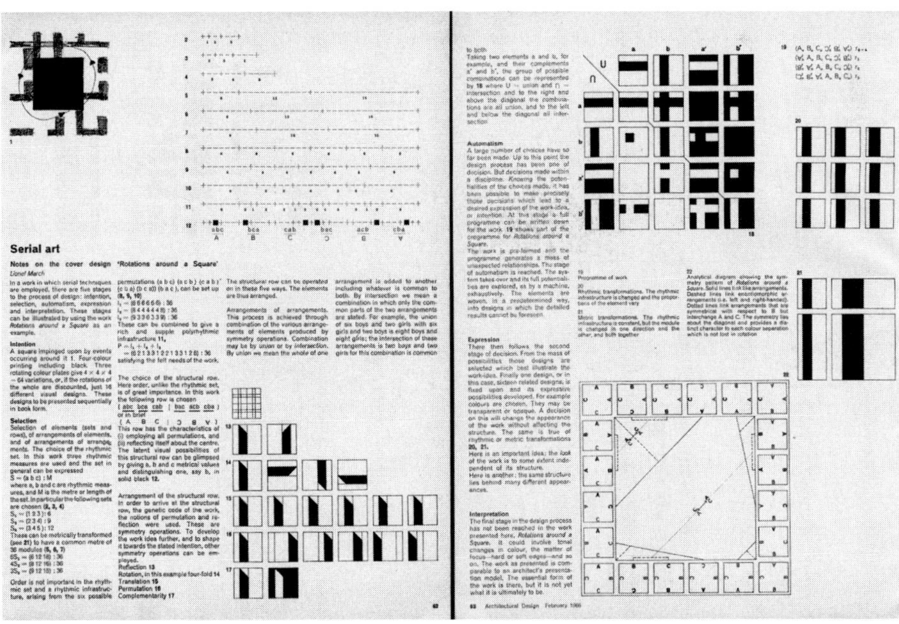

FIGURE 1.10. Lionel March, operations and serial program for *Trio No. 5 "Rotations around a Square."* From "Serial Art," *Architectural Design* 36 (February 1966): 62–63. Courtesy of Lionel March.

> The work is pre-formed and the programme generates a mass of unexpected relationships. The stage of automatism is reached. The system takes over and its full potentialities are explored, as by a machine, exhaustively. The elements are woven, in a predetermined way, into designs in which the detailed results cannot be foreseen.[99]

We also see here how March's aesthetic intentions and later interest in computing are related: before there were computer programs there were artistic ones. Yet even the partial automation of the design process did not provide enough authorial distance for March. In the last step, "Interpretation," he attempts to withdraw even the presence of the image we have in front of us:

> The final stage in the design process has not been reached in the work presented here, *Rotations around a Square*. It could involve tonal changes in colour, the matter of focus—hard or soft edges—and so on. The work as presented is comparable to an architect's presentation model. The essential form of the work is there, but it is not yet what is ultimately to be.[100]

All of this strongly echoes the attitude of Eisenman's early work (the focus of my next chapter), including his Cambridge dissertation, and suggests the extent to which the intellectual worlds of Martin, March, and Eisenman overlapped during this time. In fact the essence of Eisenman's 1972 argument for "Cardboard Architecture" is already neatly summarized here by March: "Here is an important idea: the look of the work is to some extent independent of its structure."[101] If Eisenman has attempted to pull his early houses forward as premonitions of poststructuralism, this shows that they were also tied to a context that reached backward to the constructivism of Martin and the *Circle* group. Nonetheless, a crucial distinction does exist between March and Eisenman, one with roots that stretch back to the Soviet constructivists themselves. For March, because the underlying "structure" of a work is primary, its appearance, including its physical "form," becomes at best irrelevant and at worst dangerously misleading. In contrast, Eisenman, while writing often in this period about the logical structure of his works, is also acutely concerned with their architectural form and with the tension generated by their dematerialized material presence. So, while both March and Eisenman were influenced by the constructivist revival in postwar Cambridge, March carried forward only the mathematical and methodological aspects of that tradition, setting aside concerns for the appearance of a building or for the cultural reception of that appearance (a tendency continued in his later work as founding editor of the journal *Environment and Planning B*). Again, March seems to have thought of his particular focus through an analogy to science: he and the Cambridge research center would produce "pure" architectural research that would provide the foundation for the "applied" work of others who might design particular buildings and cities.

In the other important instance of March creating projective rather than simply analytic images, they appear as the rather marginal by-product of one of his mathematical inquiries but are nonetheless potent signs of a nascent revolution. In 1973, while investigating techniques for the mathematical representation of architectural form, March generated a code for the Seagram Building. Removed from its famous Park Avenue site, stripped of its materiality, and pinned to a cubic grid, Ludwig Mies van der Rohe's iconic work was distilled into a single hexadecimal number "about the same length as some telephone dialing codes": $10_2$83EFE0F0$_2$ (fig. 1.11). Similarly, Le Corbusier's Maison Minimum—apparently not compact enough—became

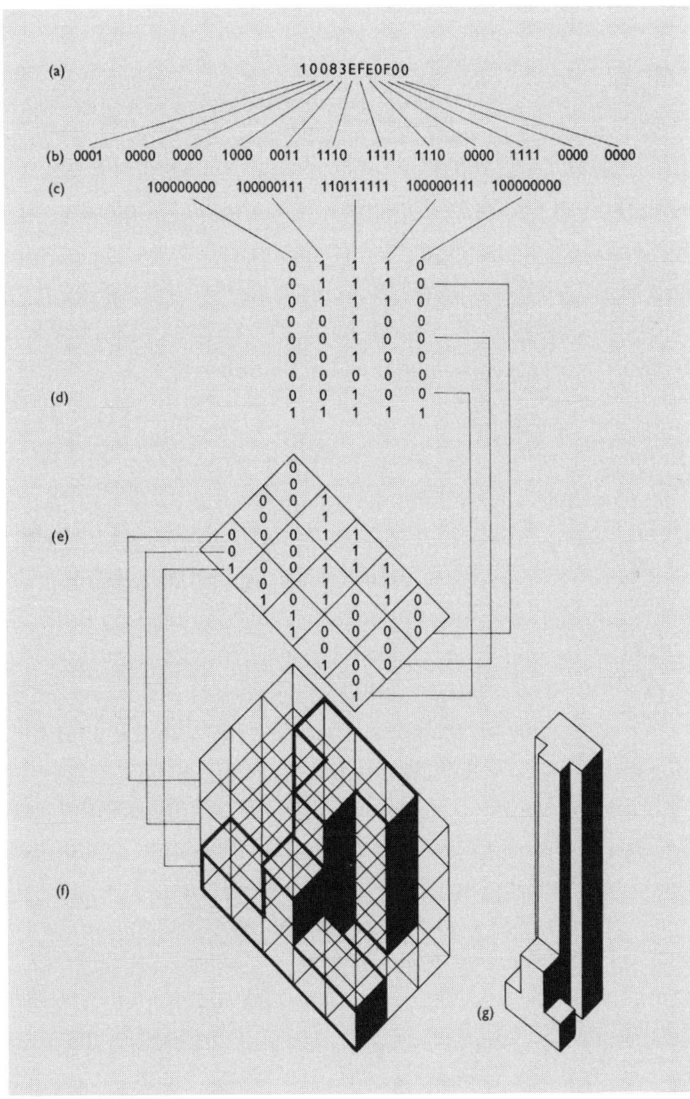

FIGURE 1.11. Lionel March, hexadecimal encoding of the Seagram Building. From "A Boolean Description of a Class of Built Forms," in *The Architecture of Form* (1976). Copyright © 1976 Cambridge University Press. Reprinted with the permission of Cambridge University Press.

F$_2$803F71$_2$80EFE03$_2$F. Such “Boolean descriptions” were intended to be part of the mathematical foundation for the computer models at the center of March’s “systems aesthetic.”[102]

For March, Boolean algebra—an algebraic treatment of logic initiated in the nineteenth century by George Boole and expanded in the twentieth by Bertrand Russell and Alfred North Whitehead—represented the mathematization of “the very processes of rational argument.”[103] He hoped that being able to describe buildings through this algebra would make architecture more rational and less intuitive, more scientific and less artistic. This representation would directly relate architecture to circuit design, topology, and information theory:

> The introduction of computer technology into architectural design made the conjunction between Boole’s mathematical structure and architectural structure, broadly understood, inevitable but not necessarily explicit. . . . By itself, the computer in architectural design is as much, and as little, a tool as a tee-square, a drafting machine, or a slide rule. The real difference lies in the fact that the computer leads us to think much more rigorously about what we are up to than those other aids ever demanded. The architectural tasks of bringing building components together, of laying out planning and structural grids, of organising space all have their counterpart in mathematical structure.[104]

As described above, March believed that computer modeling offered powerful new possibilities for analysis and simulation. Any consideration of their effect on the creation of architectural form qua form was supposed to be of no interest to him (it would be just the sort of “extravagant and empty” indulgence he was committed to rejecting). Still, even he could not resist demonstrating the novel formal potentials of his mathematics: by tweaking a few numbers one could easily produce a beveled version of the Seagram Building, suddenly transforming Mies’s classicism into expressionism (fig. 1.12). His colleague Robin Forrest used the same technique to create alternatives that were rotated, scaled, and sheared.[105] With the widening availability of graphics-capable computers, architects—even iconoclastic ones like March—were able to produce computer-generated images of buildings with increasing ease. For the first time in architectural history, transformational operations became a natural mode of production. Once the mathematical structures were in place, representing a cockeyed cube was as easy as representing an orthogonal one. We see here then, slipping out of March’s strongly iconoclastic program, signs of the new formal vocabulary of transformations, processes, and dematerialization that would come to define the architectural avant-garde of the 1980s and that has expanded since to alter wide swaths of architectural production.

Twenty years after its completion, it was no longer the Seagram Building itself but its digital encoding that signaled a new period of architectural production—a period, which we continue to occupy, marked not only by the shift from parallel rule to parallel processing and the formal consequences that followed, but by the end of the modernist social aspirations that motivated March's research. For the growth of computing led not to the rational resolutions of architectural programs envisioned by March's theory but, ironically, to a vast and expanding new vocabulary of architectural forms presaged by his images. Encoded and manipulated, Mies's monument of high modernism became, unintentionally, the first evidence of an approach to form making that has affected architecture far more deeply than the postmodern facades that dominate our view of the 1970s. March believed that the computer would become a laboratory for design in which reality was simulated with ever-greater accuracy. However, in hindsight what his paper on Boolean description shows are the first hints of the formal experimentation that could occur in such digital environments freed from the constraints of actual buildings, from gravity, from materiality, from structure, from inhabitation, and from economics.

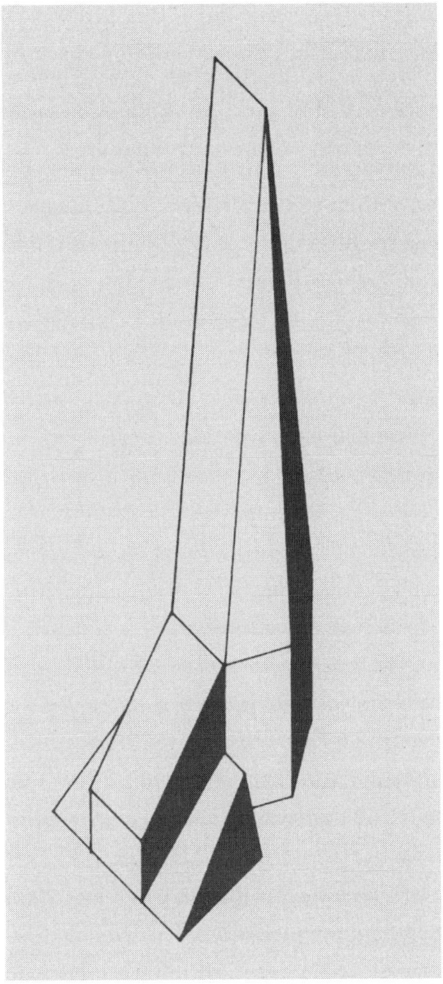

FIGURE 1.12. Lionel March, beveled version of the Seagram Building. From "A Boolean Description of a Class of Built Forms," in *The Architecture of Form* (1976). Copyright © 1976 Cambridge University Press. Reprinted with the permission of Cambridge University Press.

Subsequent events suggest that March underestimated the strength of the disciplinary self-discipline that stood against his efforts to reground architecture in mathematical rather than visual form. "Systems aesthetics" for March meant that aesthetics, traditionally understood, would give way to a totalizing science of other systems: economic, environmental, structural, and political. Yet his own early serial work and his brief experimentation with the Seagram Building reveal that "systems aesthetics" might also mean the aestheticization of systems, an involution that allows architecture to return to its established role as a representational art. Easily detached from external reference, the "artificial evolution" made possible by the computer could perfectly serve the discipline's continual appetite for novel forms (and thus perpetuating the condition Manfredo Tafuri diagnosed in the neo-avant-garde of the same period).[106]

In hindsight, March's paper can be seen to foreshadow developments in architectural form and methods over the next thirty years, most obviously Eisenman's work with transformation operations and the vocabulary of Zaha Hadid's "eighty-nine degree" architecture and of the entire "free space" wave of the 1980s and 1990s. Extended to more recent "parametric" architectures, this lineage might accurately be called an aesthetic of systems, but this is decidedly not the "systems aesthetic" March and his Cambridge colleagues hoped to establish. For despite their best efforts, architects, remaining well disciplined, continued to be concerned with appearances. What computation brought was not a solution to the modernist dilemmas of architecture but new representational systems within which those dilemmas could be further compounded.

2. THE LOGIC OF FORM: PETER EISENMAN'S EARLY WORK

DESCRIBING PETER EISENMAN'S influence on contemporary architecture, Stan Allen has singled out his "effort to produce an architecture of greater rigor and conceptual density by codifying and rethinking the process of design" so that "since the 1970s an attention to process has been the explicit sign of a conceptually ambitious, theoretically-driven work."[1] While Eisenman was certainly not alone in thinking about design methods in the 1960s, he was unusual in combining an interest in formalized design methods with a high modernist, formalist interpretation of architecture. It is also important to emphasize the extent to which terms such as *rigor* and *codifying* point to Eisenman's career-long effort to define his practice through methods that are, in some uneasy sense, automatic.

As Allen suggests, the emphasis in his early practice on quasi-automatic processes for the generation of architectural form helped prepare the aesthetic and intellectual ground for today's computational methods. However, as we will see, the relationship of Eisenman's early work to later computational architecture is mixed. In as much as this work tended toward the purely formal, the decontextualized, the procedural, and the automatic, it stands as a precursor to computational design methods. In that its formalism was based on a reading of "deep" historical structures, its isolation was self-consciously alienating, and its processes were ever only pseudoautomatic—not literally scripted—it departs from later computational architectures. If for a certain strain of contemporary architecture, Eisenman "got us there first," we should look back carefully at his early work and its context to understand how he first got there himself.

Eisenman's public intellectual career began in the same place and at nearly the same time as that of Christopher Alexander, although they would eventually come to hold antagonistic views.[2] An American with architecture degrees from Cornell and Columbia universities, Eisenman arrived to study and teach at the University of Cambridge in 1960, just a year after Alexander had graduated and moved on to Cambridge, Massachusetts. Though it would then be more than two decades until the two met, a Cambridge colleague, Colin St. John Wilson, gave Eisenman an early draft of Alexander's *Notes on the Synthesis of Form.* According to Eisenman the effect was decisive: "The text so infuriated me, that I was moved to do a Ph.D. thesis myself. It was called 'The Formal Basis of Modern Architecture' and was an attempt to dialectically refute the arguments made in his [Alexander's] book."[3]

Completed in August 1963 and supervised by Leslie Martin—the head of the Cambridge architecture department who had earlier shocked Alexander into fleeing the school—Eisenman's dissertation was the first expression of his career-long interest in the possible autonomy of architecture. Anticipating his many subsequent publishing experiments, Eisenman submitted his thesis in an unusual square format with notes running in the right margin and dozens of precise, though emphatically freehand, illustrations running on the verso pages. (The future architectural historian Anthony Vidler—then a Cambridge undergraduate—assisted with the book.) Though the full dissertation would not be published until 2006, a dense summary of its argument appeared in *Architectural Design* a few months after its completion.[4]

As in many contemporaneous polemics, "The Formal Basis of Modern Architecture" opens with the dissatisfied observation that postwar architecture lacks a proper theoretical basis. In words that echo those Alexander was writing in the same year in the other Cambridge, Eisenman describes the deeply disorienting condition of a modern world that lacks stable conventions of design. However, he quickly "refutes" Alexander, though not by name, by arguing that it is the very attempt to satisfy functional requirements, which Alexander had placed at the center of his method, that prevents postwar architecture from attaining a firm foundation. For the modern worldview generally, Eisenman argues, empirical explanations have replaced the idealism of reason, logic, and theory. Architectural modernism is a manifestation of this condition, putting the ever-changing demands of function and of a supposed zeitgeist over those of reason and logic. The modern climate, he says, is "factual rather than rational: the atmosphere being so saturated with the actual, that the theoretical is easily passed over."[5] To Eisenman, this exaggerated emphasis on the "actual" results in either a naive empiricism that wrongly imagines architecture as an applied social science surveying, analyzing, and solving quantifiable design problems or leads to a contrary escapism that takes "refuge in mannerism and the cult of self expression."[6]

Eisenman's response is essentially that of a rationalist. "The Formal Basis of Modern Architecture" attempts to escape the ceaseless churning of modernity by establishing a rational and systematic basis for architecture that, like logic and mathematics, would be transhistorical and transcultural. To avoid succumbing to the "actual," Eisenman sets out to develop an architectural theory that is thoroughly "conceptual," one that will "consider buildings as a structure of logical discourse . . . in the sense that form is considered as a problem of logical consistency. . . . The argument will try to establish that considerations of a logical and objective nature can provide a conceptual, formal basis for any architecture."[7]

Nonetheless, Eisenman's characterization of his response to Alexander as "dialectical" is especially, though perhaps unwittingly, appropriate because both began from an underlying belief in the possibility of a logical, objective, and systematic architectural vocabulary. While his methodology may differ from Alexander's—neither architectural programming nor computer programming have a place in Eisenman's approach—his motivation is nonetheless similar: he wants to obtain a nonsubjective basis for architecture. Like fellow Cantabrigians Alexander and Lionel March, Eisenman rejects intuitive composition in favor of logic and systems.

In contrast to these postwar extensions of functionalism, however, Eisenman is concerned primarily with architecture as a communicative rather than practical act, the success of which depends on the clarification of its medium, on establishing architecture as a system. Paralleling March's manifesto for "Serial Art," Eisenman explains that

> systems provide a discipline rather than a limit. . . . They are not rigid but allow for growth; they accommodate the *scherzo*; they can be elaborated to encompass infinite variations and complexities. Systems deny only the arbitrary, the picturesque and the romantic: the subjective and personal interpretations of order.[8]

Eisenman argues that architecture can only become a coherent system for communication if "temporal ends," such as "intent, function, structure and technics," are made subservient to the "absolute end" of form itself. What he means here and elsewhere by communication, and the nearly self-obliterating limits he places on what can or should be communicated in architecture, is a dilemma that will run the length of his career. Only form, because it can be detached from empirical concerns, can become truly autonomous and systematic. Yet to be available for systematic use, even form itself must be subdivided and a distinction made between "specific" and "generic" form: "The term generic form is here understood to mean form thought of in a Platonic sense, as a definable entity with its own inherent laws." Generic form has a "transcendent or universal nature" with properties that "stand above any aesthetic preferences" as well as "certain inherent dynamics" that "must be understood and respected if any grammatical usage or interpretation . . . is to be attempted."[9]

At this point, and still in the preliminary arguments of the dissertation, Eisenman makes a further observation that will have great consequences for his later work. He suggests that because the experience of a work of architecture is made up of many perceptions gathered over time by movement through and around the work, this experience builds into a conceptual, not perceptual, whole. While at this early stage Eisenman is concerned with establishing the greatest possible clarity in this conceptual entity and therefore in the "unmistakable reference to some well-understood archetypal solid," he will later take advantage of the same gap between perception and conception to create architectural works that are intentionally irresolvable. As we will see, however, the traces of this initial desire for clarity of reading are never entirely erased.[10]

Having laid out the theoretical requirements that a system of form would have to meet in order to serve as the basis for coherent architectural communication, Eisenman then extrapolates from Le Corbusier's "Four Compositions" to describe the properties and "inherent dynamics" of certain generic forms, particularly the cube and the rectangular prism, qualities that he believes to be inherent and objective (fig. 2.1).[11] What emerges is a set of procedures for the manipulation and elaboration of volumes in which "pressures" caused by a site or by programmatic requirements produce supposedly logical reactions and deformations of generic original forms. By this account, in order to be legible, specific architectural forms must be the result of systematic distortions of generic forms in response to local conditions. Here, given the completely neutral and static character of his generic forms, even Eisenman cannot avoid turning to program, or circulation, or site, as motivators, resulting in a pseudophysics of form not so dissimilar from Alexander's metaphor of good design as the unimpeded response of a neutral medium to contextual forces (e.g., sand dunes shaped by wind or iron filings organized by a magnetic field).

Having established the theoretical underpinning of his approach, the majority of Eisenman's text is then devoted to providing evidence for this theory through detailed formal analyses of works by Le Corbusier (fig. 2.2), Frank Lloyd Wright, Alvar Aalto, and Giuseppe Terragni. Here, as a rationalist, Eisenman must confront the difficulty of reconciling the world as it is with the world as it must be, and the text is largely built out of the challenges that this raises (one is reminded of the strains of Spinoza's *Ethics*). This leaves him struggling repeatedly to demonstrate not merely that there are identifiable formal considerations in each of his historical examples but that these must come together into logically coherent systems. While the elisions forced by this reconciliation may weaken the self-professed logic of the argument, they are also the most prominent signs of its place in a postwar context shaped by mathematical and pseudomathematical approaches of many sorts. Though later overshadowed by his role as architectural interpreter of deconstruction and poststructuralism, Eisenman's career begins with an argument that architecture should be understood as a logic of form, a set of operations rigorously derived from primary geometric elements. Historically, "The Formal Basis of Modern Architecture" should be seen as an especially idealist and formalist attempt to unite architecture and logic in a context that was thick with such efforts.

The questionable claims made for this architectural logic can be seen to represent a limit of Eisenman's understanding in this early period of his career. But a more complete and more sympathetic reading is that there are, in fact, two positions overlaid in the dissertation and, as will be shown, throughout the early years of Eisenman's practice: one a more dogmatic view, in which the logic of his formal system

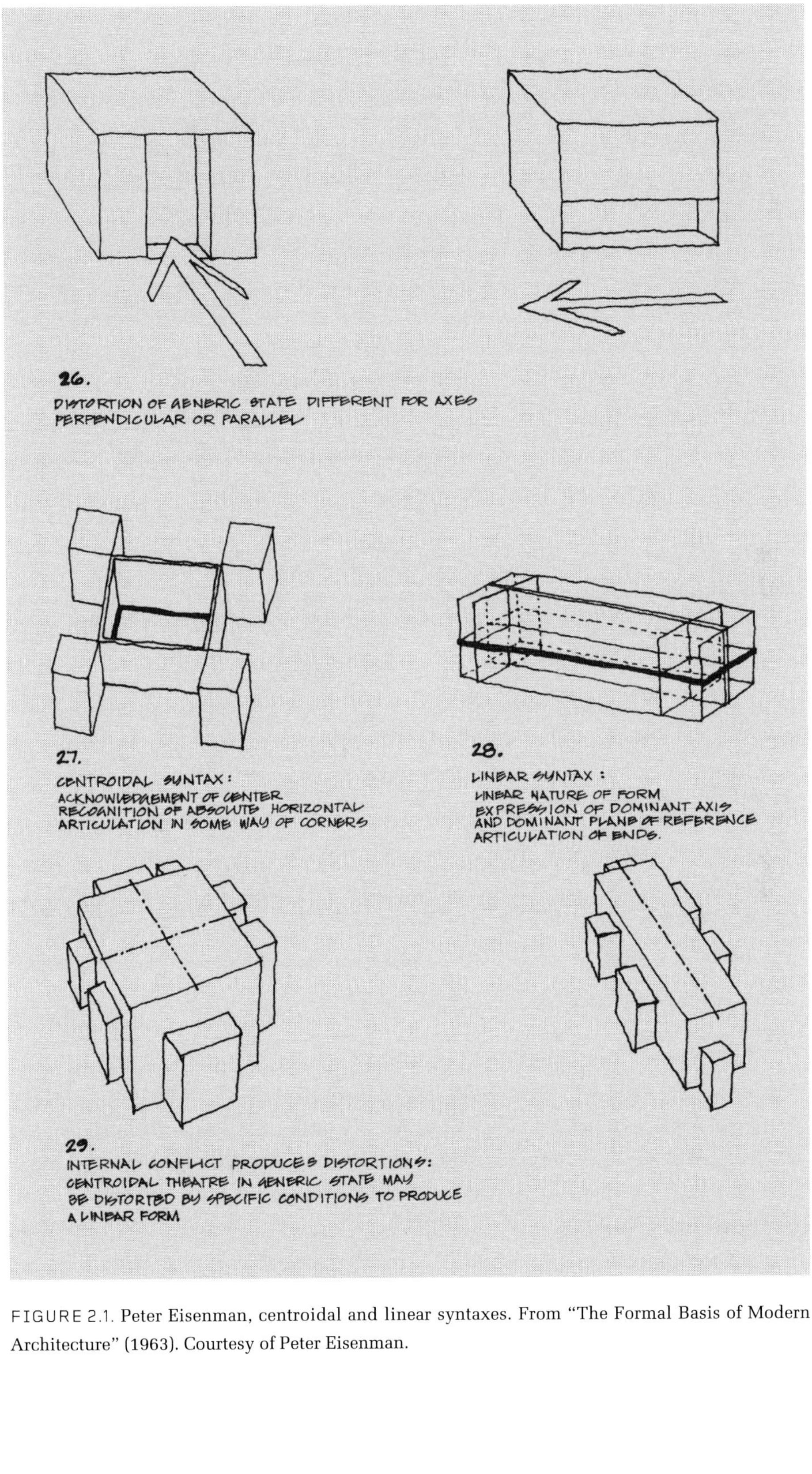

FIGURE 2.1. Peter Eisenman, centroidal and linear syntaxes. From "The Formal Basis of Modern Architecture" (1963). Courtesy of Peter Eisenman.

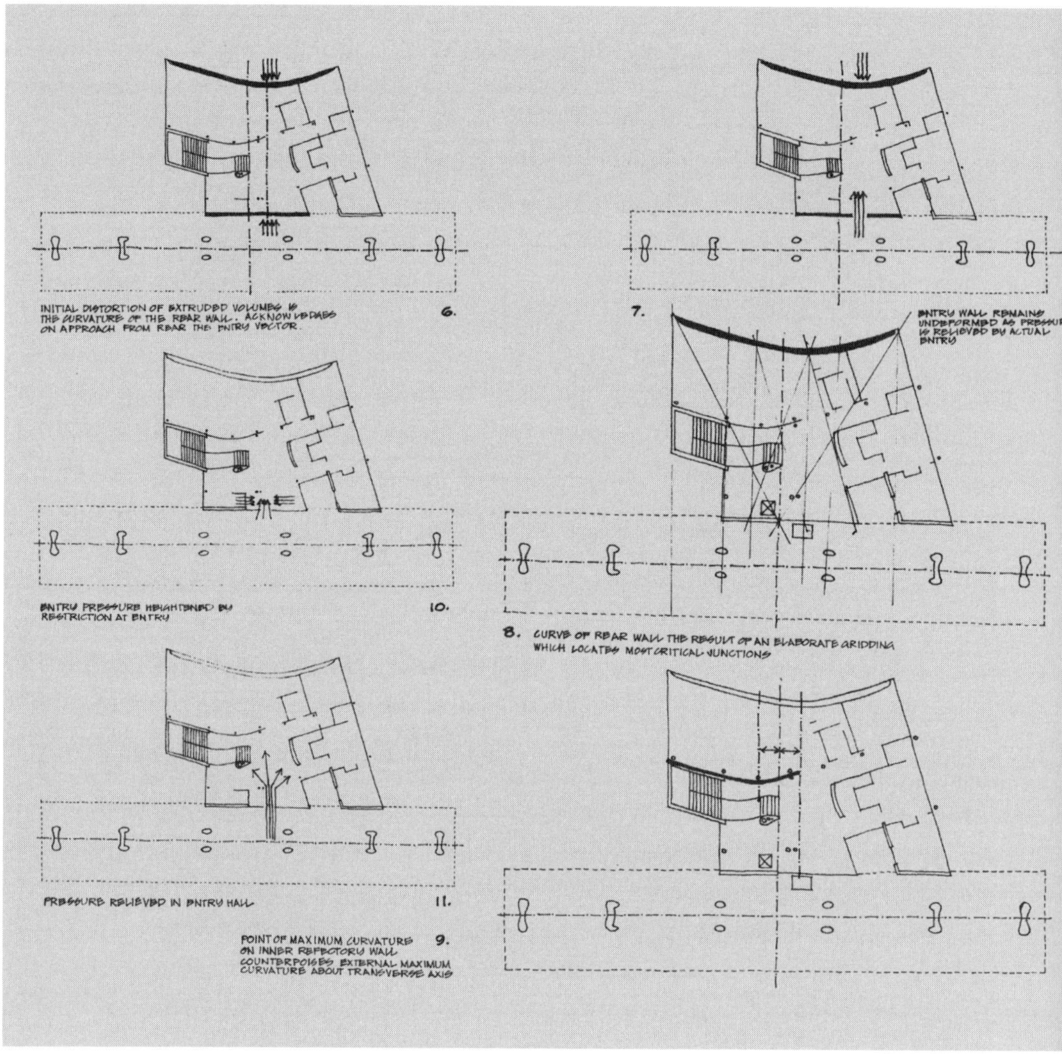

FIGURE 2.2. Peter Eisenman, analysis of Le Corbusier's Pavillon Suisse. From "The Formal Basis of Modern Architecture" (1963). Courtesy of Peter Eisenman.

is held to be (nearly) self-determining, and a second, more nuanced view, in which the formal system is understood as a historically derived grammar that can be used as a framework for the interpretation or creation of architecture. If the later view is more widely sympathetic, it also lacks the intellectual extremity to which Eisenman has always been drawn.

Nor was this intensely argued belief in an architectural logic short lived. Inflected later by ideas gathered from Noam Chomsky and conceptual art, it would continue to provide the ground of Eisenman's practice through the early 1970s. Throughout this period, he saw the logic of form as a way to give architecture autonomy from the ever-shifting field of postwar demands, thereby offering an escape from his anxiety of the "actual." *Anxiety* is the correct term here because Eisenman was concerned with what he understood to be the very existence of architecture itself—its autonomy as an intellectual endeavor—which design methods, such as those pursued by Alexander or March, threatened to subjugate to the rule of other, ostensibly more scientific, fields. This was an existential anxiety for architecture in the wake of the Second World War. Just a few years before Eisenman's dissertation, Reyner Banham's epochal conclusion to *Theory and Design in the First Machine Age* (1960) had raised the same concern while suggesting an opposing conclusion.[12] While in this early period he presented an autonomy achieved through logic as an antidote to the anxieties of the postwar condition, he would come to discover both that autonomy contained its own internal anxieties and that it offered not relief but a provocation to further anxiety.

CARDBOARD ARCHITECTURE: HOUSES I AND II

After completing his dissertation at Cambridge, Eisenman returned to the United States, began teaching at Princeton University, founded and ran both the Institute for Architecture and Urban Studies in New York and its influential journal *Oppositions*, and established his architectural practice. The first results of the practice were designs for a series of houses, some built, some not: House I (in fact, the extension of an existing house, 1967–68), House II (1969–70), House III (1969–71)—and so on, through the punningly named House El even Odd (1980). The numbering of these projects, in place of the traditional use of clients' names, reflected both Eisenman's ongoing interest in a quasi-logical exploration of architectural design and his new engagement with the New York art scene of the 1960s, especially conceptual art and minimalism, which carried their own quasi-logical explanations.

The house series began as an extension of the formal system described in "The Formal Basis of Modern Architecture" but now deployed as a syntax for the generation of architecture. Directly recalling the analytic drawings of the dissertation, the houses were presented through increasingly extensive sets of axonometric diagrams that suggest a quasi-automatic process of formal generation: step-by-step an initial rectangular volume (one of the "generic forms" of the dissertation) appears to be multiply subdivided, shifted, sheared, rotated, and intersected to arrive at a densely complex, though apparently arbitrary, end state that depicts the geometry of the built house.

When Houses I and II were presented as part of the influential book *Five Architects*, Eisenman's description of his aims directly reiterated those of his dissertation (though first published in 1972, a note indicates that the text was drafted in 1969):

> The making of form can . . . be considered as a problem of logical consistency, as a consequence of the logical structure inherent in any formal relationship. . . .

> House I was an attempt to conceive of and understand the physical environment in a logically consistent manner, potentially independent of its function and its meaning. . . .
>
> [Interpreting this underlying logic] does not depend entirely on the observer's particular cultural background, his subjective perceptions, or his particular mood at a given time, all of which condition his usual experience of an actual environment, but rather it depends on his innate capacity to understand formal structures.[13]

Yet simultaneously and in counterpoint to his earlier concern for clarity of communication, Eisenman began deploying techniques that would challenge the idea of logical consistency and began to open up possibilities for indeterminacy in his projects. Primary among these was the multiplication of "formal structures" underlying each project. For example, House I (fig. 2.3) is organized by two formal structures: one frontal and planar, the other diagonal and volumetric. Because the house itself records the fragmented result of the interaction of these two structures, the material architecture cannot be read as identical with the formal structures themselves. Instead, Eisenman believes, one is compelled to interpret these underlying structures conceptually.

However, a further step reflects the extent to which, although deploying ambiguity at one level, Eisenman is at this point still concerned with an ultimate stability of interpretation. For not only are the two formal structures themselves quite unambiguous, their interaction is intended to point to a further, and ultimate, *deep structure*, a term Eisenman had recently picked up from Chomsky. This is a single diagonal shift of the original volume as recorded in one of the diagrams.[14] Here, the idealism of the dissertation remains evident, as the incomplete state of the material architecture is put in service of a stable underlying mental construct, although the content of this construct is so vanishingly meager that it undermines Eisenman's proclaimed interest in communication or in "a new level of information."

The need to discover architectural means, such as these, that could compel "conceptual" interpretations can be seen as a consequence of Eisenman's shift from the analytical work of his dissertation to the generative task of design. While in the dissertation Eisenman, as the interpreter, brought a formalist lens to a variety of cases in order to reveal their conceptual underpinnings, he could not be assured that his own work would receive similar readings unless such readings were in some way built into the work by Eisenman himself. This need to assure a formalist reading of the houses explains not only the integral role of the diagrams to each project but also, more significantly, the disturbing sense that each house is not, in fact, a work of architecture but the demonstration of an architectural grammar. In this sense, the houses are more comparable to works of linguistics than to works of literature.

The desire to compel conceptual interpretations also lies behind another devel-

FIGURE 2.3. Peter Eisenman, House I, Princeton, New Jersey, 1972. Courtesy of Peter Eisenman.

opment. Where the dissertation had argued that form should sit atop a hierarchy of architectural concerns—including function, structure, and materiality—each of the houses was designed not just to subordinate but to negate such material considerations. Reappropriating Wright's old slur against Le Corbusier, Eisenman began to argue that the only viable materialization of a truly conceptual architecture was an antimaterial "Cardboard Architecture," one that intentionally frustrated traditional notions of structure, tectonics, performance, and scale.

> Cardboard is used to question the nature of our perception of reality and thus the meanings ascribed to reality. . . . [T]he term raises the question of the form in relation to the process of design: is this a building or is it a model? . . .

> All of the apparent structural apparatus—the exposed beams, the freestanding columns—are in fact non-structural. . . . Once one has understood that they are not structural one must ask what are they? Why are they where they are? Take them away, or change their shape, and what have you got?[15]

With this embrace of "Cardboard Architecture" Eisenman's interest in establishing architectural autonomy via form becomes polemical and oppositional rather than theoretical and coordinative. We begin to see an emerging desire to use the quasi-automatic system he has established to create works that, precisely through their "logic," challenge rather than ease interpretation.

With House II (figs. 2.4, 2.5), Eisenman extended his use of ambiguity to the elements of the composition themselves. The rather classical distinction between column and plane that House I sought to maintain by the use of round columns was

FIGURE 2.4. Peter Eisenman, House II, Hardwick, Vermont, 1970. By permission of Norman McGrath.

FIGURE 2.5. (*facing page*) Peter Eisenman, diagrams of House II, 1972. Courtesy of Peter Eisenman.

collapsed in House II so that a thin rectangular vertical element could be understood equally well as a positively determined "column" or as the remainder of an imaginary intersection between a planar solid and a prismatic void. Eisenman described this as a shift toward a generalized use of "bi-valency."[16] This interest in a simultaneity of interpretations—which had been taken up from Colin Rowe and Robert Slutzky's concept of "phenomenal transparency" and which in the dissertation had existed uncomfortably alongside the ambition for clear communication—became the central technique of what he now began to explicitly call "conceptual architecture."[17] Though initiated by an ideal of logical consistency, Eisenman's architecture paradoxically seemed to require ever-greater levels of ambiguity in the material building and in its representation to advance.

The dominant use of axonometric projection in both working sketches and formal representations of the houses, strongly evoking the prewar avant-garde movements of De Stijl and constructivism, generates ambiguities that reinforce those of the realized buildings. As representations, the axonometric drawings themselves are inherently unstable, always holding the potential to perceptually "flip" from convex to concave (a favorite Gestalt experiment) or from bird's-eye to worm's-eye viewpoint. The location of elements within a composition is often irresolvable—a condition greatly intensified by Eisenman's use of diagonal shifts within the forms themselves. Moreover, as Kenneth Frampton has pointed out, the thoroughly axonometric conception of the projects affected even the immediate experience of the houses themselves and "always allowed one to distance oneself from the immediate presence of the space" so that even when actually walking through one of houses one would be encouraged to substitute its conceptual diagram for its immediate material presence.[18]

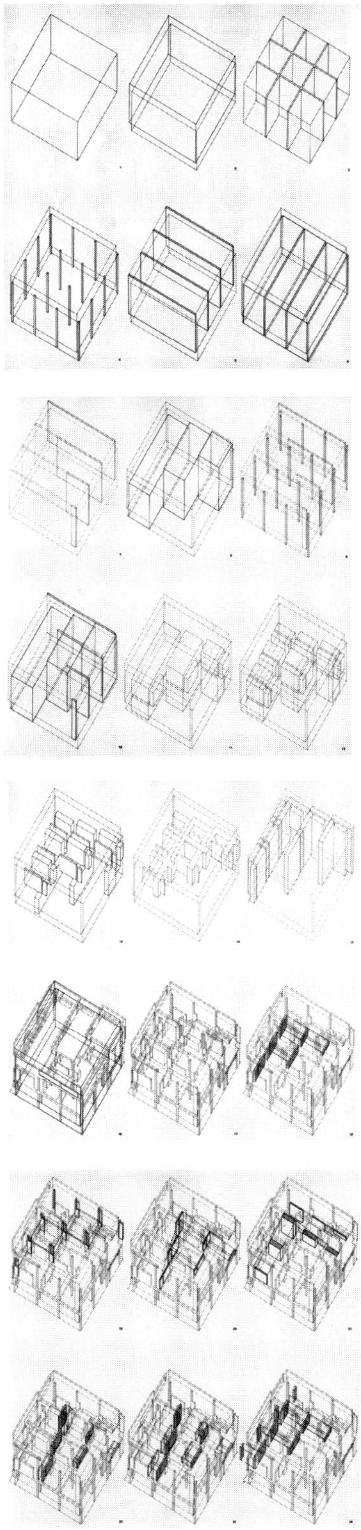

Extending and clarifying the approach introduced in House I, the diagrams accompanying House II demonstrate a new degree of sophistication in the design process as well as new means for the creation of bivalency. Directly carrying out the rhetoric of his dissertation, Eisenman begins with a set of "abstract formal propositions" and pursues their "transformation into a specific environment."[19] The formal propositions, as represented by the first six diagrams, are (1) an initial half-cube volume, recalling the proportions of Terragni's Casa del Fascio; (2) the doubling and shifting of this volume along a diagonal in all three axes; (3) the division of the initial volume into a nine-square grid by vertical planes; (4) the division of the shifted volume by vertical lines (columns); (5) the division of the initial volume into three equal parts by four parallel vertical planes; and (6) the division, in the opposite direction, of the shifted volume into three equal rectangular volumes.

Eisenman's description of these initiating forms gives a good sense of the hybrid and admittedly opaque conceptual framework within which he was working: "Any given coordinates of space can be described as either linear, planar, or volumetric. The coordinates of a cubic space are described by its edges or its center; the edge composed of lines or planes, the center by a line or a volume."[20] While a phrase such as "coordinates of space" suggests that we are in touch with mathematics, the rest of the excerpt reveals that we are, instead, in a more idiosyncratic realm, such as that of Wassily Kandinsky's *Point and Line to Plane.* As I have been arguing, however, the quasi-mathematical tone is certainly important to the character of this private language.

What follows the initial "formal propositions" are various *possible* but, as Eisenman clearly states, not *necessary* transformations of these initial propositions through their mutual interaction (in the language of the dissertation, this is the transformation from generic to specific form). Having postulated an arbitrary set of initial forms, Eisenman explores various ways in which these could overlay and interrupt one another, especially in order to articulate the motivating proposition of a diagonal shift (which had been a central example already in the theoretical section of the dissertation). By recording the accretion of these alternative interactions and wherever possible constructing an ambiguous formal condition out of them, the design process generates an ever-more complex, ever-more fragmentary formal palimpsest that at some arbitrary point is fixed to become the form of the house itself.

Characteristic of this period are Eisenman's somewhat apologetic notes in the House II text that many decisions are "at this stage of work" arbitrary, with the implication that future research will remove, or at least explain away, these arbitrary aspects. The issue of motivation looms with particular force over the early houses because in these projects Eisenman avoids even the use of the site "pressures" that got the formal mechanisms rolling in his dissertation. These moments show Eisenman continuing to aspire toward a fully systematic, nonarbitrary, formal logic of form. Such complete systems, as far as they exist, are arguably empty of meaning, but a case such as Eisenman's suggests the extent to which the unfulfilled *desire* for such complete systems may still be an important motivation within certain artistic practices.

POSTWAR PALLADIANISM

While Eisenman's idealism and formalism were explicitly set against the empiricism and functionalism of design methodologists such as Alexander and March, his work at Cambridge, and for at least a decade after, reveals that even in the formalist camp, the desire of the time was for systems and logics that could redefine architectural authorship. In one sense, Eisenman's formalism was conservative: he did not attempt to replace or ignore the primacy of formal considerations in architecture. Recognizing architecture's inherently representational aspect, he avoided the iconoclastic engagement with computers and mathematics taken up by Alexander and March. Instead, Eisenman pursued a quasi-logic of architectural form that stood in a metaphorical relationship to its historical context. This relationship is nicely captured by the contemporaneous observation that his work "is an essential part of an as yet undiscovered theory of architectural cybernetics."[21] Eisenman's early analyses and designs unfold *like* logical proofs, or *like* computer algorithms, without actually being anything other than architecture.

In an early review, Mario Gandelsonas signaled the importance of the debates surrounding computers and methodology as a context for Eisenman's thinking at this time.

> His first works, however, were not published until the 1970's, a time which no doubt denotes the decline of avant-garde attitudes, which is the result of perpetuation in the semantic dimension of architecture of the classic vicious circle of intuition versus reason or art versus technique. Art and intuition are represented by the utopian formalism of Archigram or the "reformist" formalism of Venturi's attempt to incorporate and absorb the mass culture into architecture. Technique and reason are represented in the direct rejection of forms per se expressed by the adoption of computer methods and the primacy of the "design process."
>
> Eisenman's work stands in opposition to the impasse described above and within a line of thinking first proposed by Colin Rowe, which considers the Modern Movement and the Renaissance for the analysis of some essential characteristics of architecture which are no longer seen in terms of two poles of comparison.[22]

What Gandelsonas suggests but does not spell out is that Rowe's mode of formal analysis is itself structured by (limited) mathematics and ordering systems as in his "Mathematics of the Ideal Villa." In this sense, Eisenman's intellectual position has, in part, a kinship with the "computer methods" and "design process" side of the impasse described by Gandelsonas. Thus, what Gandelsonas compresses into a linear opposition between "two poles of comparison" might be better left as a double opposition in which the axis of "art" versus "technique" is differentiated from that of "intuition" versus "reason" (fig. 2.6). This interpretation allows Eisenman to be

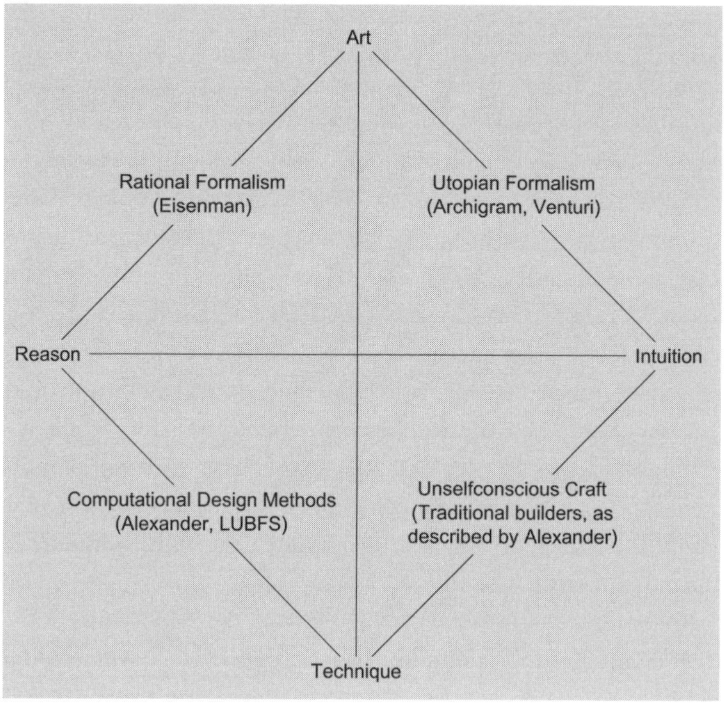

FIGURE 2.6. Eisenman's rational formalism in relation to alternative positions.

placed more accurately as an advocate of reason *and* art. It also suggests that such formalism had its own connections to more overtly scientistic methodologies of the 1960s and 1970s, connections that others, such as Sol LeWitt, consciously exploited, as discussed below.

Also introduced here is the extent to which Eisenman's early formalism, which simultaneously reasserted and strained the boundaries of the discipline, was not only shaped by the context of contemporaneous influences but also grew out of the intellectual relationship with Rowe that began in Cambridge in 1960. As Robert Somol has put it, all of Eisenman's "productive misreadings of modernist European predecessors can be understood as a swerve within and against the production of Rowe's formalism."[23] Eisenman's pursuit of a transhistorical logic of form had, naturally, its own personal and disciplinary history.

While the intellectual exchange between Eisenman and Rowe would be ongoing, Eisenman's thinking was most deeply shaped by the work Rowe had already completed when the two met at Cambridge, particularly Rowe's influential first essay, "The Mathematics of the Ideal Villa," published shortly after the end of World War II. Rowe's focus there is a comparison of Andrea Palladio's Villa Foscari (or La Malcontenta) near Venice (ca. 1550–60) and Le Corbusier's Villa Stein near Paris (1927). Using comparative formal analysis (fig. 2.7) he argues that despite great differences

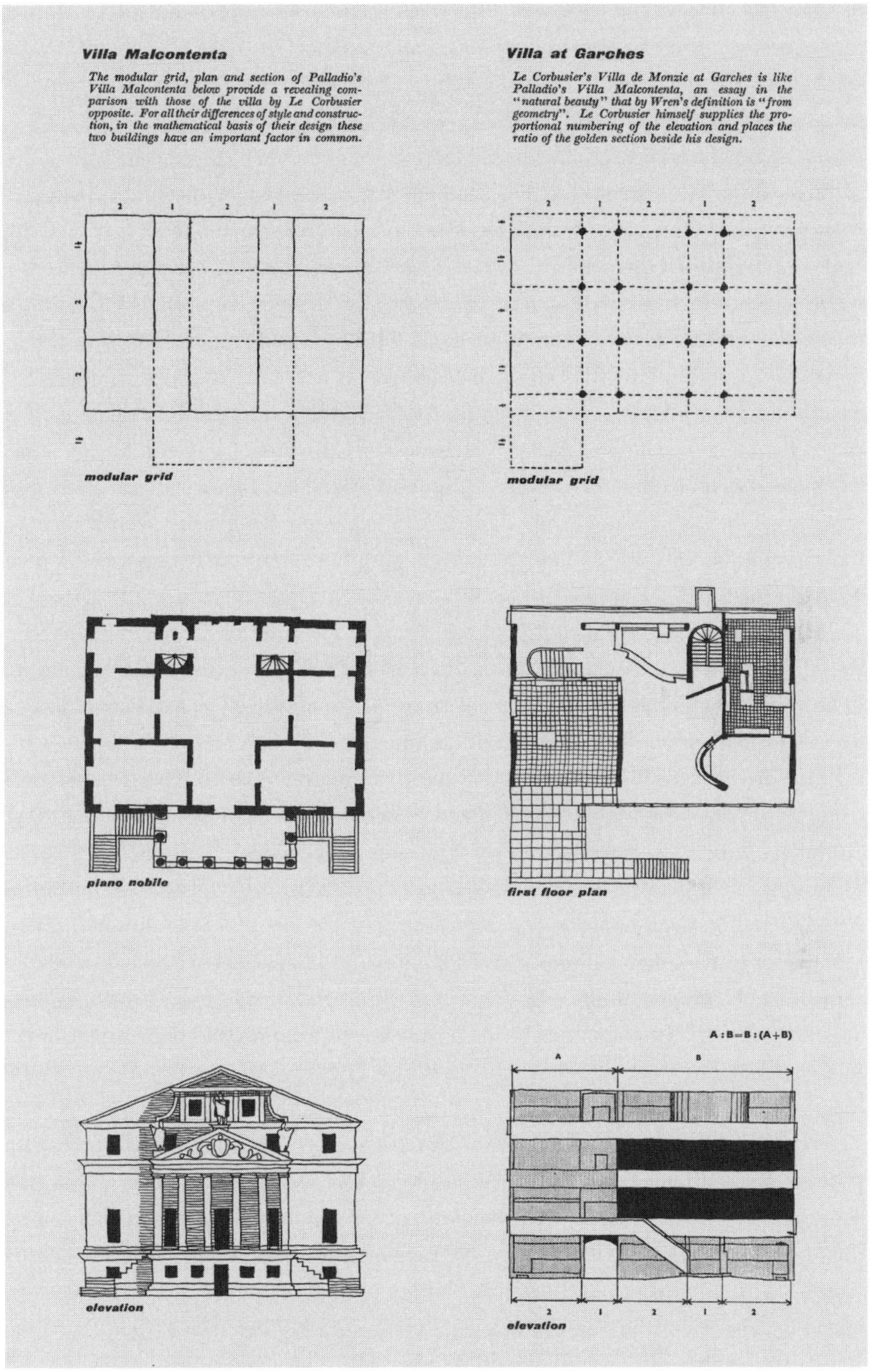

FIGURE 2.7. Colin Rowe, formal comparison of Andrea Palladio's Villa Foscari and Le Corbusier's Villa Stein. From "The Mathematics of the Ideal Villa: Palladio and Le Corbusier Compared," *Architectural Review* (1947). Reproduced by permission of EMAP Publishing Limited.

of historical context and of "mood," the two houses are in fact organized by similar formal systems and by a shared Platonic conviction that "the laws of proportion were established mathematically and everywhere diffused."[24] In addition, Rowe argues, both architects combined this belief in an idealized, abstract basis for architecture with a reverence for specific historical models that embodied these principles.

The similarity between the "The Mathematics of the Ideal Villa" and Eisenman's early work is obvious. His dissertation is essentially an extension of Rowe's method, both in breadth, as Eisenman provides close formal analyses of examples from a range of modernist architects, and in depth, as Eisenman attempts to discover a theoretical ground for such formal analysis out of first principles. The connection is perhaps even more evident in the first houses. House I, for instance, is organized exactly by the "variation of the formula ABABA" that underlies Rowe's pairing of the villas Malcontenta and Stein.[25] More broadly, Eisenman's entire house series can be read as an extension of Rowe's presentation of Villa Stein as a "slipped," and thereby modernist, version of its Palladian source—an observation that Eisenman builds into the elaborate sequences of slips and disruptions that generate his own contributions to this lineage.

Also in the background of this formalism was the work of Rowe's own mentor, Rudolf Wittkower, under whom he wrote a master's thesis at the Warburg Institute in London (though the relationship is perhaps better described as a collaboration).[26] Rowe's formalism was an extension of the diagrammatic method of Wittkower's influential *Architectural Principles in the Age of Humanism* (1949). There, on a single page, Wittkower presented "Schematized Plans of Eleven of Palladio's Villas" (fig. 2.8) along with a twelfth diagram showing the hypothetical "Geometrical Pattern of Palladio's Villas."[27] It is this last generic diagram, showing a lateral rhythm of ABABA and an even tripartite division from front to back, that is the underlying schema for Rowe's own comparison of Palladio and Le Corbusier. Rowe distorts the schema to accommodate the specifics of the villas, the overall form becoming rectangular rather than square and the axial divisions differentiating their proportions. In a characteristic contrast, Eisenman in House I deploys the more generic, square, diagram of Wittkower.

Wittkower's historical work on the Renaissance contributed significantly to a postwar fascination with proportional systems and with Palladio, one which was especially strong in Britain.[28] An extension of the Cambridge architecture building (fig. 2.9), completed in 1958 just before Eisenman's arrival, was itself, in Vidler's words, "a living memory of the neo-Palladian, pre-Brutalist moment that was influenced briefly by Rudolf Wittkower's publication of *Architectural Principles in the Age of Humanism*."[29] (Vidler has also written that this Palladianism had been "cast aside" as early as 1955, suggesting that Eisenman's return to it in the early 1960s was already untimely.[30])

As Alina Payne has argued, Wittkower's interpretation of Renaissance architec-

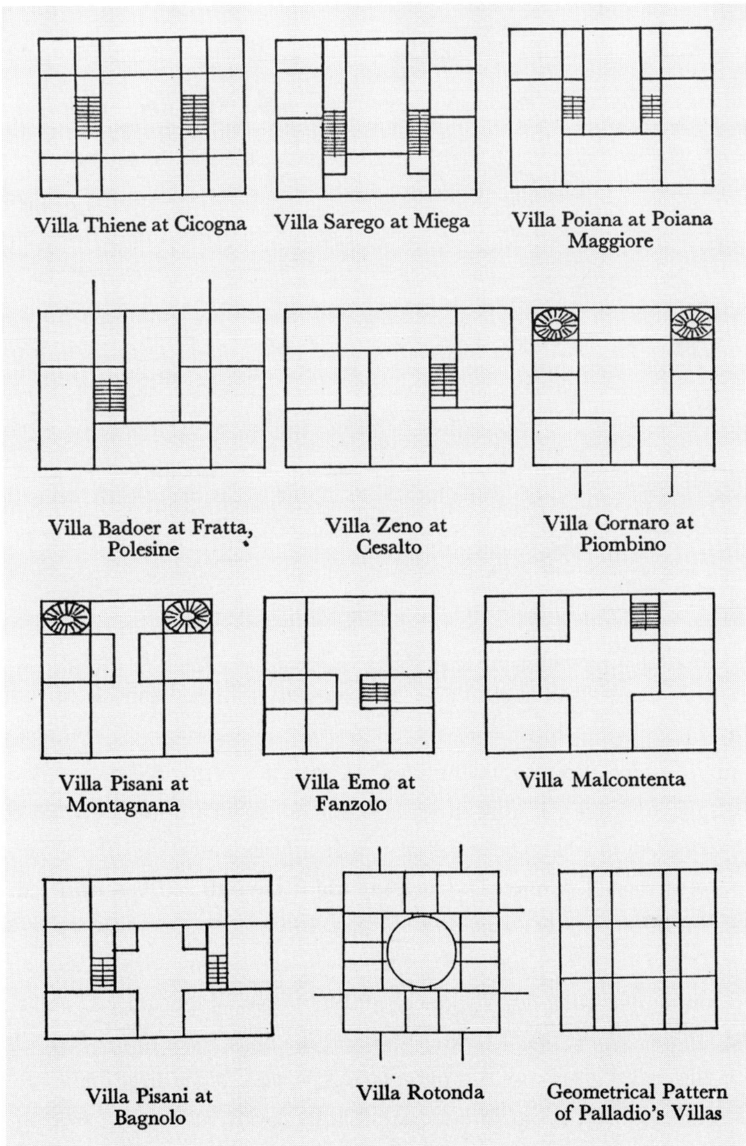

FIGURE 2.8. Rudolf Wittkower, "Schematized Plans of Eleven of Palladio's Villas." From *Architectural Principles in the Age of Humanism* (1949). Copyright © 1949. Reproduced by permission of John Wiley & Sons Ltd.

ture articulated themes that would be central to Eisenman's thinking of the 1960s and early 1970s.

> [P]robably the most significant aspect of Wittkower's thesis about the rudiments of Renaissance architecture is his focus on syntax. . . . In thus approaching form, Wittkower looks beyond its immediate physical presence to a primary structure

FIGURE 2.9. Colin St. John Wilson and Alex Hardy, extension to the School of Architecture, Scroope Terrace, Cambridge, 1958. Photograph by Sam Lambert. By permission of RIBApix.

> and subordinates all other "principles" to that of an essential and willed, rather than intuitive, order that rests upon a scientific matrix. Ultimately, this explicit link between syntax and science via mathematics allows Wittkower to situate Renaissance formal practices within the objective and rational rather than subjective realm.[31]

This focus on syntax allowed Wittkower and Rowe and eventually Eisenman to return select historical examples to architectural discourse at a time when they were largely excluded by mainstream modernism, thereby providing one of the openings for the historicism of postmodernism. However, it bears emphasizing that for Eisenman, a return to architecture's historical lineage was not in the interest of any eclecticism but in order to reveal universal properties of form and formal operations that could resist what he saw as the zeitgeist-driven eclecticism of modernism itself. Here we find another resemblance to mathematics: for Eisenman, architectural history, although contingent in its unfolding, reveals truths about architectural form that are themselves universal and transhistorical, just as the theorems of mathematics are discovered within history.

A sense of a double revelation in Eisenman's houses—of architectural logic and of architectural history—is intensified by following this intellectual genealogy one generation further back. Wittkower's own analysis of Palladio's villas can be seen as an extension of the comparative art historical method of his own *Doktorvater*, Heinrich Wölfflin, with his famous side-by-side formal comparisons. By sighting along this chain of mentor-student relationships, Eisenman's diagrams are revealed as condensations of the comparative methodology, collapsing the historical transformations *between* buildings presented by Wölfflin, Wittkower, and Rowe and replacing them with a set of transformations *within* a single project. The multiple articulations of the nine-square grid superimposed in House II, for example, are analogous to the multiple articulations of the nine-square grid Wittkower identified in a series of individual Palladian villas. In this way Eisenman's diagrams represent not just quasi-logical explanations for his first houses but also fictional genealogies that stand as allegories of architectural history itself.

Reading Eisenman through Wittkower raises another difficult issue in Eisenman's work. As Payne points out, Wittkower's main intellectual foil was Geoffrey Scott. In order to explain our "enthusiasm for architectural form," Scott relied on a theory of empathy based in the humanist subject's body. Wittkower and Eisenman both reject this bodily empathy in favor of a purely intellectual response with mathematics, represented by systems of proportion, providing the content of architecture. By approaching architecture through this extreme formalism, Eisenman's early work intensified the dilemma of communication that had been raised in his dissertation: the indefinitely postponed question of *what* would or could be communicated by an architecture that was deliberately reduced to syntax alone. It is here that the Wittkower/Rowe/Eisenman formulation is, in a disciplinary sense, potentially *less* autonomous than that of Scott. While one answer (described above) to the question of meaning is that architecture expresses nothing other than the syntax of its own history, another possibility, hinted at by the persistent presence of mathematics, is that architecture is ultimately the expression of another, underlying conceptual system. This second response helps to explain why the drive to formulate a thoroughly conceptual architecture has led Eisenman to repeatedly take up, and repeatedly discard, a series of "external" motivators: linguistics, topology, genetics. It also clarifies the obscure meaning of his claim that "beginning with my doctoral dissertation in 1963, this discourse has been an attempt to analogize architecture's previously unarticulated interiority through a variety of seemingly external cultural models."[32]

Finally, the Wittkower/Rowe lineage helps us clarify one of the primary difficulties of Eisenman's theorization of the late 1960s and early 1970s: his attempt to combine the idealized, formalist, "deep inside of architecture" (Eisenman's description) postulated by Wittkower and Rowe with the "deep structure" of language theorized by Chomsky. As part of a Neoplatonic theory, the former is conceived as objective and transhistorical, existing somewhere outside of the individual subject. In contrast, as a neo-Cartesian theory, Chomsky's linguistic model, though still rational, is subject centered. This means that for Eisenman, Rowe, and Wittkower, it is possible that the ideals of architecture are reflected only in certain works by certain architects—notably Alberti, Palladio, Friedrich Schinkel, Le Corbusier, Terragni, and Eisenman himself—while Chomskian linguistics seeks the deep structure beneath any competent expression by any subject. Eisenman's uneasy attempt to merge these models led to an unstated contradiction between his universal claims and his quite selective case studies. Confronted with criticism on this point, most effectively from Gandelsonas, he both abandoned Chomsky and shifted more generally, if always incompletely, away from a search for architectural universals.[33] Counterexamples to Eisenman's approach are provided by the more narrowly scientific architectural research on the topic of "shape grammars" that does map closely onto Chomsky's linguistics. George Hersey and Richard Freedman, in their analysis of Palladian villas, for example, offer clear architectural equivalents of key Chomskian concepts such as deep structure, surface structure, transformation operations, and definable grammaticality.[34]

CONCEPTUAL ARCHITECTURE

In the decade after 1963, Eisenman also began to contrast his work, and architecture generally, with other practices, especially recent "conceptual" sculpture and painting. In doing so he quickly found himself confronted by the complications and paradoxes of medium specificity that vexed the art world after 1945. If the preceding discussion emphasized Eisenman's explorations of what a concept could be in architecture, we will now see him engaged with the question of what constituted architecture itself as differentiated from other formal and material practices.

The fullest version of this aspect of Eisenman's thought appeared in the journal *Casabella* in 1971 as the essay "Notes on Conceptual Architecture: Towards a Definition." In some sense, the essay had been published about a year earlier in *Design Quarterly* in a special issue on "conceptual architecture." However, in the spirit of that project, the main body of the text did not appear, leaving only the footnotes with their reference numbers scattered over four otherwise blank pages. Accompanying information indicated that the full text could be requested by mail from Eisenman.[35] Eisenman begins there by noting that "[although] the influence of painting and sculpture would have been commonly accepted in a treatise on architecture of the 1920's and '30's, this relationship to post-1950 architecture . . . has rarely been the subject for discussion."[36] As his title indicates, Eisenman is particularly concerned with developments in "conceptual art" in contrast to the pop art recently engaged by Robert Venturi and Denise Scott Brown. However, he immediately emphasizes that this interest in the conceptual should not be construed as avant-garde but as persistent throughout architectural history. By using contemporary art as a foil, Eisenman hopes to articulate anew a theory of conceptual architecture. Largely this amounts to a refinement and reformulation of ideas presented in his dissertation through concepts and examples provided by the art of the 1960s as well as by Chomsky's linguistics.

Using LeWitt's mid-1960s structures as illustrations—and with the apparent similarity of his own houses clearly in mind—Eisenman, concerned as ever with establishing architecture's disciplinary autonomy, attempts to differentiate architecture from sculpture. To do so, he first focuses on the relationship of material and concept, noting that the physical qualities of LeWitt's works, though supposedly arbitrary, "still present information which would tend to modify the conceptual intention. But, it is precisely this difference between the concept integer and an actual bar of a grid structure which will be seen to be of critical concern to a conceptual architecture."[37] Going further, he surprisingly argues that in contrast to art, habitation is inseparable from the notion of architecture.

> [T]he idea of an architecture as distinguished from a painting will always contain in the idea, ideas of functional and semantically weighted objects such as walls, bathrooms, closets, doors, ceilings. There is no conceptual aspect in architecture which can be thought of without the concept of pragmatic and functional objects, otherwise it is not an architectural conception.[38]

Paradoxically, in an essay explicitly devoted to "conceptual architecture," Eisenman finds himself needing to claim that in contrast to work such as LeWitt's, architecture is defined by materiality, pragmatics, and function—precisely those concerns of the "actual" that his dissertation had rejected. Here Eisenman was reacting to a problem that other logicians of medium specificity had found themselves confronting: having previously argued that the essence of architecture rested solely in formal concepts, Eisenman's efforts to create buildings purely out of such concepts threatened to result in something that might not be architecture at all as they seemed to slide into the category of sculpture or perhaps simply geometry. The solution advanced here, which represents a key to the house series and to all of Eisenman's most convincing work, is that architecture is defined by the contradictions and tensions between the material and the conceptual, between the "actual" and the autonomous:

> To make something conceptual in architecture would require taking the pragmatic and functional aspects and plac[ing] them in a conceptual matrix, where their primary existence is no longer interpreted from the physical fact of being a bathroom or closet, but rather the functional aspect bathroom or closet becomes secondary to some primary reading as a notation in a conceptual context.[39]

Eisenman's conception of his architecture shifts from the purely conceptual, or autonomous, to the semiautonomous. Or, to use a vocabulary that was not yet available to him, Eisenman recognizes here that the conceptual cannot simply organize a tidy hierarchy of architectural elements as proposed in the dissertation, nor can the conceptual simply negate the material realities of building as in Cardboard Architecture. Rather, the conceptual must overwrite material reality, yet in doing so, it inevitably leaves traces of this reality, which themselves constitute the essence of architecture as differentiated from any other practice.

Yet despite moments marking this important shift, "Notes on Conceptual Architecture" continues to echo Eisenman's dissertation by suggesting that the aim of a conceptual architecture would be to intentionally and legibly present "the inner form or universal formal relationships" of a structure.[40] Here a comparison with the work of LeWitt becomes immensely useful to explicate the complexity and ambiguity of Eisenman's "conceptual architecture." As Rosalind Krauss has argued, the work of LeWitt and other minimalists—such as Donald Judd (whose work also appears in "Notes on Conceptual Architecture"), Robert Smithson, and Robert Morris—was not a celebration of Cartesian thought but an undermining of such "false and pious rationality" through an "absurdist Nominalism" (i.e., Judd's famous "just one thing after another").[41] Krauss points out that in works such as *122 Variations of Incomplete Open Cubes* (1974; fig. 2.10), "[t]he babble of a LeWitt serial expansion has nothing of the economy of the mathematician's language."[42]

In contrast, Eisenman during this same period was still framing his practice through Chomsky's revival of "Cartesian Linguistics" and was still committed to the "deep structure" of a presumed architectural logic. This contrast in attitude between Eisenman and LeWitt explains the differences in results that become apparent with even the mildest attention: it is only because of his belief in a transcendental conceptual logic that Eisenman was compelled to create houses that were so complex

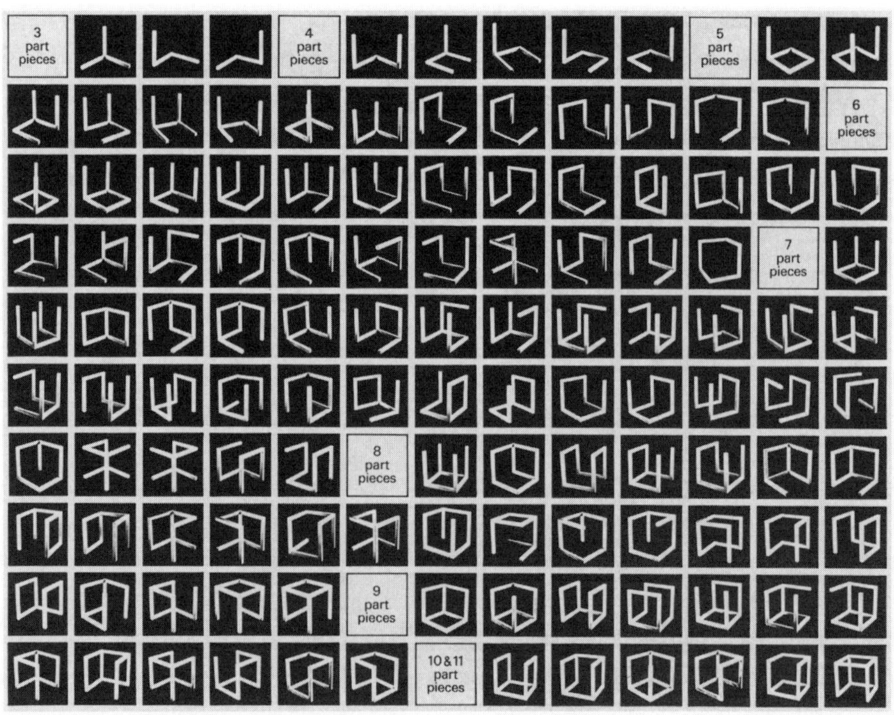

FIGURE 2.10. Sol LeWitt, *122 Variations of Incomplete Open Cubes*, 1974. Copyright © 2016 The LeWitt Estate / Artists Rights Society (ARS), New York.

in their material realization, while LeWitt could use "the idea of error" to spit out arrays of shrewdly mindless forms. Their relationships to historical context thus also diverge: where LeWitt produced deadpan parodies of postwar computation, Eisenman battled the logic of functionalism with an equally earnest logic of form. If Eisenman's work has ever actually resembled LeWitt's, it was only many years after "Notes on Conceptual Architecture." Writing in 1999, Somol—echoing Krauss's description of LeWitt—suggested that "Eisenman's more recent work insists upon a surface reading that questions the possibility of the embodiment of meaning, and seems to operate only as an endless chain of conjunctions—*and, and, and* . . . one thing after the other."[43]

Finally, at the level of technique, Eisenman's continued use, discussed earlier, of "phenomenal transparency"—a device inherited from cubism—demonstrated a willingness to continue or revive prewar approaches that also separated him from contemporaries such as LeWitt or Judd who rejected cubist transparency in favor of demonstrative plainness. Overall, the comparison with work such as LeWitt's invited by Eisenman's essay suggests that extent to which, despite his desire to relate to contemporary art, his work remained a product of an architectural lineage reaching back before the Second World War.

THE INDEX OF THOUGHT

In what sense was Eisenman's early practice automatic? This question takes on wider significance if we recall that it stands as the precursor to an entire lineage of process-based architecture that has firmly established itself within the discipline over the last four decades.

A common answer, one often presumed by critics and by Eisenman himself, is that his design process, at least beginning with House II, is automatic in that it sets up and then lets run a series of transformations that are recorded by his diagrams. This interpretation grows out of a deep conflation of the mental and the physical, one that occurs after Eisenman's initial erasure of materiality via the techniques of Cardboard Architecture. For example, in his 1985 essay "Not to Be Used for Wrapping Purposes," Robin Evans argues that Eisenman's drawings encourage us to believe that static architectural forms are actually dynamic, so his projects appear to be generated by the movement and interaction of animate entities.[44] In some sense this is correct. Because the diagrams are presented like an array of film stills, there is a strong tendency to read them chronologically, and there are subsets of diagrams that clearly imply movement: a single rectangular volume followed by two shifted volumes of the same size that suggest an act of "doubling," or a pair of bars sequentially "rotated" in three successive diagrams. This "movement" conveyed by the diagrams is essential to the sense that the architecture is automatically generated, that is evolves in a pseudophysical environment from simple origins to complex results.

However, while one can read the diagrams as simulations of an unfolding and quasi-physical process, this interpretation is constantly frustrated by ruptures and restarts in the narrative of creation. This nonlinear aspect is succinctly revealed by a short film, *Castelli di Carte: Transformations Series B*, that Eisenman made for the 1973 Milan Triennale. The film, of about one thousand frames, records the diagrams of House IV flipping by, rapidly building up from simple initial forms—a cube of lines, a cube of planes, a solid cube—to a complex palimpsest representing the final state and then decomposing again into the initial cubes. While there are short passages that convey a sense of continuous movement or organic development, the overall effect is determined by the jarring cuts between alternative constructions of the house. Eisenman himself was surprised by the film's disjunctive quality and its demonstration that "What seemed to be a logical set of moves . . . was shown to be flawed."[45]

This notion that the visual evidence of a film could reveal flaws in logic hints at the ambiguous way in which Eisenman conceived of logic. Having set himself the problem of combining a logical method with the creation of architectural form, he needed to connect the discursive, step-by-step, diachronic process of logical justification to the nondiscursive, singular, synchronic objects of architecture. The diagrams collapse the two modes. The effect that Evans interprets as movement is a result of Eisenman's desire to unify logic and form. Logic is represented by diagrams that are superimposed in the final form. Any "movement" then is not the animation of a physical form—though this impression is indispensable to the desired sense that the process is automatic—but the progression of the (pseudo-) logical steps of formal invention. The houses and diagrams represent not the thought of movement but the movement of thought.[46]

As with the postulation of universal formal laws in his dissertation, it may be impossible to defend the transformations documented by the drawings as logical (or even consistent) in any strong sense, but his writings demonstrate that this certainly is what Eisenman set out to achieve in his early houses. This means that the projects are less devious than Evans and others have made them out to be, but they are also less self-aware. If Eisenman's writings and diagrams are not cynical "wrappings" but sincere attempts to describe a logic of form, then the many gaps in that logic have to be taken seriously. What they reveal is that regardless of his rhetoric, Eisenman was an architect, not a logician, and that, as Evans himself notes, "It might only be that topology is the initiator of a train of thought that leads towards architecture, and as such provides the stimulus for the doing of something that would not otherwise be done."[47]

Also emphasizing the pseudophysical nature of Eisenman's process, Stan Allen has suggested that the concept of the index, first proposed by Charles Sanders Peirce and brought to art and architectural theory by Krauss, can help us understand the relationship between process and product in Eisenman's early work.[48] For Peirce the index is a representational mark that records and has an immediate physical relationship with its cause: footprints, shadows, and photographs are classic examples. Krauss had applied this definition to artworks that encode the process of their own making. Allen gives Richard Serra's sculpture *Casting* (1969) as an illustration: the work is made of a series of pieces formed by throwing molten lead into the corner of a wall and floor, the "casting" action being recorded in the frozen forms of the cooled lead. Eisenman's houses, Allen suggests, similarly record the processes of their creation. Yet as Allen himself notes, they entirely lack the physical immediacy of Peirce's examples or of Serra's *Casting*. The elaborately constructed ambiguity of Eisenman's houses is also contrary to the immediacy of the index, which requires a direct material connection between signifier and signified.

Whatever processes the houses record are, as Eisenman repeatedly insists, conceptual, not material, so that the term *index* could only be applied to them metaphorically. Yet what can it mean to speak of a metaphorical use of the index, which, by definition, denotes a literal, nonmetaphorical relationship? Though bordering on self-contradiction, it is precisely this self-canceling quality that Eisenman struggles to achieve in these early projects: the metaphor of the nonmetaphorical; the physical record of purely mental events that are themselves imagined to have the self-determination of material processes; the representation of thought that is as automatic and inexorable (and perhaps meaningless) as a material index. Here, we could recall that Alexander's metaphors for good architecture were also indexical—forms emerging directly from forces that determine them—and relied on the same fiction that the architectural context is full of such "forces" by which form can be shaped.

Speaking of Eisenman, Manfredo Tafuri has described the ultimate motivation of this approach as resolutely negative.

> And, in fact, this invocation [of] Chomsky's transformational linguistics, [of] a geometrical system as well as a topological one, [of] "guided" reconstructions of the compositional process, has as its primary motivation the exorcism of a feared enemy who for this reason is constantly evoked: Eisenman struggles against "meaning" so relentlessly that he compels any observers of his work to ask themselves why he is so tenacious in this pursuit.[49]

In this view, the metaphor of the index, of the nonarbitrary signifier, merely avoids or short-circuits the entwined problems of architectural meaning and architectural authorship that are Eisenman's constant concerns.

HOUSE VI: THE LOGIC OF ALIENATION

While his "conceptual architecture" of the 1970s still pursued the notion of architectural autonomy first put forward by his dissertation, Eisenman began to shift, incompletely but importantly, the means of achieving this autonomy from formal logic to formal ambiguity. Over the course of the house series, the dissertation-like claims for a transcendent, ahistorical architectural logic were increasingly replaced by ambiguity within the formal processes—a trend that in the 1980s would be joined to the antifoundationalism of Jacques Derrida. Yet the desire for an architectural logic has never entirely disappeared: it recurs, for example, in Eisenman's recent summary of his career as an exploration of architecture's "interiority."[50] Given this, we might best characterize the house series, and Eisenman's entire oeuvre, as an anxious use of formal logic, one that constantly suggests and at the same time frustrates the sense that his architecture is generated by some autonomous, rigorous, self-determining process (see the parallel discussion of his "humanism" below).

Similarly, though an interest in formal autonomy runs consistently from his dissertation forward, the purpose of this autonomy shifts from the assuagement of anxiety to its provocation. While Eisenman initially intended his formal logic to be a solution to the anxieties of the postwar condition, he eventually came to understand that this very formalism, especially when deployed to create domestic space, provoked anxieties of its own. The extreme formalism of the houses, their stripping away of semantic references, and their multiplication of competing conceptual readings all work to produce what he has called a Brechtian estrangement, denying the comforting associations conventionally bound up with a house and forcing the occupants to grapple consciously with the architecture.[51] By the early 1970s, Eisenman determined that his anxiety for the autonomy of postwar architecture could only be addressed via anxieties produced by the autonomous architectural object.

This shift grows out of the unavoidable difficulties of materializing a highly abstract, supposedly autonomous formal logic in actual building, emerging at the seam between the conceptual structure and the material structure of the house itself. Though, as noted earlier, Eisenman identified this tension in his "Conceptual Architecture" essay of 1970–71, its full potential was not immediately applied, so that through the publication of *Five Architects* in 1972, he largely continued to maintain the detached, Neoplatonic tone of his dissertation:

> At present most buildings are burdened by their very description as "museums" or "country houses" with a weight of cultural meaning which is here meant to be neutralized . . . .
>
> In House II there is a concern for space as the subject of logical discourse. Such a logical structure of space aims not to comment on the country house as a cultural symbol but to be neutral with respect to its existing social meanings.[52]

In contrast, a truly significant shift came in 1974 with the publication of House III (1971; fig. 2.11). In an accompanying article titled "To Adolph Loos and Bertold Brecht," Eisenman recognized that the "questioning" provoked by his logical structures was in fact a primary and deep attribute of his method, though he still strained

FIGURE 2.11. Peter Eisenman, House III, Lakeville, Connecticut, 1971. Courtesy of Peter Eisenman.

to insist that such provocation arose "quite unintentionally" (a claim that the dedication to Loos and Brecht obviously undercuts):

> It has become clear to me that any attempt to express this concern for the [logical] structure of the form in the actual form itself tends to isolate the individual from the environment of that form. . . .
>
> This expression of the formal system produces an architecture divested of traditional meaning, that admits no adjustment and alteration; it excludes the design of those things which, through design, reinforce traditional meaning, such as interior finishes, the location and style of furniture, or the installation of lighting. Consequently while the architectural system—the formal structure—may be complete, the environment "house" is almost void. And quite unintentionally . . . the owner has been alienated from his environment.
>
> In this sense, when the owner first enters "his house" he is an intruder; he must begin to regain possession—to occupy a foreign container. . . . The interior "void" resulting from a complete architectural structure seems to act as both a background and a foil, almost as a conscious stimulant for the activity of the owner. . . . In such a situation, choosing interior finishes, adding walls, placing furniture, and installing lighting, is no longer concerned with the purpose of fitting some preconceived idea of good taste or completing some "set piece" scheme of either the owner or the architect.[53]

Given the language here, it will be helpful to draw a brief comparison with Viktor Shklovsky's classic description of such "defamiliarization."[54] Importantly, for Shklovsky, it is precisely the amnesia-inducing "automatism"—he even says "algebrization"—of everyday perception that art should work against (his illustration is Tolstoy's inability to say whether, in the midst of some house cleaning, he had or had not dusted a divan). In contrast, by impeding communication through processes of defamiliarization, art should "de-automatize" perception. In these terms, Eisenman's work presents an interesting case in which one automatism, that of domestic mindlessness, is interrupted and "de-automatized" by the presence of another, the automatism of a formal logic that in itself is entirely empty. Either automatism alone would be mindless. It is only the rupture arising from their confrontation that is simulating. When compared with the exemplary methods Shklovsky gives by which poetry impedes language, Eisenman's approach comes closest to the "roughening" achieved through repetition, which makes pronunciation (for architecture, read inhabitation) difficult. Shklovsky adds that this repetition also cannot fall into the regular rhythm of prose or folk song but must itself be disrupted, an observation that applies nicely to Eisenman's troubled repetitions and multiplications.

While the text accompanying House III demonstrates Eisenman's grasp of the potentially estranging effects of his logical structures, the design itself is the most traditionally functional of all of the houses in the series, a point emphasized by one pleasantly surprised reviewer.

> Even though the drawings indicated places such as "kitchen," bedroom," "bath," etc., it was difficult for me to interpret how the volumes so indicated represented . . . spaces that people could actually live in with even a modicum of comfort and privacy. . . .
>
> Not until I was actually inside the house did I gradually come to realize that not only does it function as a house, but it performs well as one, perhaps even better than many that avow a great concern for function. . . .
>
> The arrangement of spaces could hardly be more practical or functional. . . . [Y]ou begin to appreciate . . . that the form and the function of this house are one, that they are inextricably bound to each other, and that neither could exist as it does without the other.[55]

Eisenman must have recoiled from such apparent praise. The next, and last, of his houses to be built, House VI (1975), would prove to be an emphatic rejection of this all too easy reconciliation of conceptual rigor and quotidian existence and the culmination of his exploration of autonomy and domestic anxiety. Taking the Brechtian rhetoric seriously, House VI was a direct, not incidental, attack via "logical structure" on residential norms as evidenced by a catalog of instantly notorious and attentively photographed affronts to sensible living: the column that displaced guests at the dining table; the column on hinges that compensated for a too narrow doorway; the sink packed into an upstairs closet; the inverted "stair" that suggested the entire house might be flipped over; and, most primally, the gap in the "bedroom" floor separating the beds of husband and wife (fig. 2.12).

The effect of these provocations and the extent to which the domestic norms they targeted were shaken was a topic of much discussion, most fully reflected by the book *Peter Eisenman's House VI: The Client's Response* and particularly by Paul Goldberger's article "The House as Sculptural Object" reprinted there.[56] All of the reactions to the project—from the owners Dick and Suzanne Frank, from critics such as Goldberger, and from Eisenman himself—similarly describe the house as a difficult but ultimately domesticated creature. What emerges is a quasi-ritualistic pattern of assimilation in which commentary on the formal abstraction and functional anomalies of the house is immediately balanced by remarks about the phenomenological pleasures of inhabiting it: openings and obstructions appear in all the wrong places, but the play of light is beautiful; the owner bangs his head but learns to bend down and appreciate the architectural lessons he is learning. If the existence of the book is

FIGURE 2.12. Peter Eisenman, House VI, bedroom, Cornwall, Connecticut, 1975. Photograph by Dick Frank. Courtesy Eisenman Architects.

itself evidence of the anxiety the house provoked (and not many dwellings demand a written response), its content also demonstrates the overwhelming strength of the domestic norms Eisenman was supposedly disrupting. In this way, House VI is an important test case for the general question of whether, and how, an architecture of estrangement is possible. Could a building itself ever prevent Tolstoy from slipping into his mindless domestic routine? For how long? Only for as long as he was not in fact "inhabiting" it?

Many of the house's disturbances were also more subtle than such blatant practical affronts. House VI not only disrupted the general concept "house," it was also an inversion of specific tropes of De Stijl houses, by which Eisenman hoped to achieve a "reduction of metaphor."[57] This was approached through a number of strategies: draining the significance of the horizontal datum; the contradiction of horizontal and vertical emphases; the inversion of his own earlier houses in order to place the "facades" at the center; and the opposition of axonometric conception and frontal experience. Through these inversions of established architectural metaphors, which necessarily required acknowledgement of them, House VI moved out of the internalized Platonic world of form that had defined the previous decade of work. Doing so allowed Eisenman to challenge fundamental assumptions that the earlier houses had left intact:

> What was a facade? Why should it be on the outside? Was it a cultural or formal referent? Would it be possible to invert the conception and reality of the facades of the first four houses and place them at the center . . . ?[58]

Lastly, and most radically, House VI attempted to destabilize the very conceptual structure on which it was based.

> House VI . . . represents a change. In House II and IV the architectural notations existed to produce a mental landscape, to suggest an alternative reality and an alternative experience and meaning of architecture. But in House VI, the experience of the physical environment does not lead to any mental structure. . . . [I]n other words a particular juxtaposition of solids and voids produces a situation that is only resolved by the mind's finding the need to change the position of the elements.[59]

Abandoning his desire for the clear communication of formal concepts and radicalizing his use of ambiguity, Eisenman now begins to explore the possibility that not only can the material architecture be ambiguous or multivalent but also that it can suggest a conceptual model that is *itself* ambiguous and irresolvable. This suggests a partial answer to the earlier questions concerning defamiliarization: if a house could produce an irresolvable conceptual ambiguity, perhaps that estrangement would always persist, even after any pragmatic inconveniences had been smoothed over.

HERMENEUTIC PHANTOMS

Collectively, the new strategies of House VI appear to mark an important shift for Eisenman away from his early Platonism and toward another, less idealist, intellectual framework. Krauss has argued as much in an important essay of 1977—the same year that she gave a lecture on the index at the Institute for Architecture and Urban Studies—in which she describes Eisenman's work and her own as parallel developments of, and out of, Clement Greenberg's reflections on modernism in art.[60] Krauss's essay deserves sustained attention for the deep questions it raises about not only Eisenman's work but about the application of key modernist aesthetic concepts to architecture.

As described by Krauss, Greenberg's "formalism" was based on an "ethical necessity" for art to disrupt, or "defamiliarize," representation to make the sign opaque, bringing the viewer (or reader or listener) up short against the material presence of the signifier. Within painting this defamiliarization was to be achieved through medium specificity: "the modernist painting becomes a cognitive object insofar as it is internally coherent, inwardly referential to its own laws or norms, and logically distinct from everything that is not itself painting."[61] Krauss archly notes that "It would seem the easiest thing in the world to apply the same kind of analysis or systemization to architecture."

Of course, as she is about to point out, it is not so easy. Reviewing the efforts of prewar "heroic" modernist architects, Krauss rejects their use of industrial metaphors and their effort to lay bare the materials and structures of buildings. Her rejection of the second strategy remains unconvincing: for example, it is not clear why the brute materiality of Hannes Meyer is unsatisfactory but the rather finessed materiality of Jackson Pollock is exemplary. Krauss then identifies Rowe as the figure who, after World War II, tried to correct these mistakes by focusing attention on "phenomenal transparency" in architecture, an experience of interpretive ambiguity that draws attention to dissociations between the physical presence of a building and its conceptualization. In this way, Krauss offers phenomenal *transparency* as the architectural equivalent of the *opacity* demanded by Greenberg's formalism in painting.

However, Rowe's, and then Eisenman's, strategy is only partially compatible with the formalism of other fields from which Krauss claims it sprang. Where Greenberg champions paintings that deny illusionistic representation by drawing attention to their status as flat, material objects, Rowe is concerned with buildings that are intentionally ambiguous at a material level and that therefore provoke interpretation as representations of concepts. Krauss notes that in constructing this "hermeneutic phantom—a set of readings or interpretations that he substitutes for the real object—[Rowe's] activity veers away" from that of Greenberg and other formalists.[62] Essentially, the two projects work in opposite directions.

What Krauss does not acknowledge is that these "problems of applying formalism to architecture" arise in part because the modernist examples Rowe considers have already largely been stripped of representational elements, so that, in order for modern architecture to have any representational sign to make opaque, concepts must first be reintroduced through the formal ambiguity of phenomenal transparency. Just this two-step strategy of stripping established representational elements—say ornament—and then reintroducing the representation of a limited set of narrowly formal concepts was fundamental to Eisenman's process at this time. It also explains the way in which his work did not follow the linguistic model he claimed to use, which depends on meanings assigned through convention. Devoted to avoiding any conventional meaning, Eisenman had to deny all conventional representational elements, thus "Cardboard Architecture." But then, driven to make architecture "conceptual," he had to reintroduce through his processes and diagrams the smallest quantum of meaning, which is limited to purely formal concepts such as "rotated grid," "shifted volumes," or "the rhythm ABABA." More generally, architecture is rarely representational in a transparent way, at least not in the way that a painting may represent a view or a sentence represent a meaning. So there may always be a shortage of significations with which to work.

Nonetheless, having claimed a parallel between her early formalism and that of Eisenman, Krauss proceeds to argue that in the mid-1970s she and Eisenman, with House VI, shift to a "structuralist" position that "rejects the notion of the perceiver as the privileged subject who confers significance on reality by recourse to a set of ideal meanings of which he is himself the generator."[63] Or, more fully,

> The formalist interest in the work of art as a moment through which experience is thickened and rendered opaque must be viewed in the light of this structuralist critique. For the formalist, opacity is, ultimately, "a kind of secondary transparency through which shines Being." It is a way of using the object as a lever on reality in order to essentialize a certain part of it. It is a moment of essentialization or reduction back to an ontological absolute. If the structuralists think of the work of art as opaque, that is because it is a fragment—the partial articulation of an extended field of signs, one of the terms in a system of differences.[64]

Yet just as Eisenman's thinking was based in Rowe's formalism and not in Greenberg's, so the change in his attitude reflected in House VI is not necessarily to a "structuralist" position neatly equivalent to Krauss's own. In fact, as described above, Eisenman's embrace of estrangement suggests a shift *toward* the existentialist concerns of formalism (following Krauss's use of the term) as does his own contribution to the volume in which Krauss's essay appears.[65] Again the artistic and architectural spheres are out of synch. While Eisenman would later begin to work with such fragments in his larger-scale, site-driven projects such as the Cannaregio Town Square for Venice (1978), he would continue to describe his houses as the results of systems that were hermetic and totalizing—the description of House X eventually fills nearly one hundred pages—and not as fragments of "an extended field of signs."[66]

EVERY MAN OR EVERY MARTIAN

Despite the real changes that are reflected in House VI and in (at least some of) Eisenman's writings at this time, the transition that occurred was more complicated, and less complete, than a wholesale exchange of intellectual frameworks. Take, for example, this scene, filmed in the mid-1980s, of Eisenman and Robert Stern seated at opposite ends of a sofa in House VI:

> **Stern:** You've rather turned five thousand years of culture upside down, it seems to me.
>
> **Eisenman:** Well, I think that architects have traditionally been very slow to understand that culture has been turned upside down all by itself. When we have science fiction movies, the people from Mars come down, and they speak in mathematical terms—in mathematical terms because it's a universal language. This house, in a sense, speaks in mathematical terms the Martians could understand.
>
> What that is saying is that you don't have to be from the elite of society, you don't have to know architectural history, cultural history, social history. You just have to come and experience the house. This is a house that any man can understand and be sensitive to because it speaks in universal terms. . . .
>
> It doesn't speak in the classical conventions that only the learned and the elite understand. It's a house for every man. That's exactly what I'm saying, and it speaks to the America of today, not to the patrician America of two centuries ago.
>
> **Stern:** [*In a voice-over*] Whether for every man or every Martian, House VI is most compelling as a dream monologue of the subconscious.[67]

Here, long after his supposed shift to (post)structuralism, Eisenman is still talking about the importance of his architecture being universally comprehensible, even reassuringly so, precisely the issue that had motivated his dissertation two decades earlier. Of course, the exchange also rather comically emphasizes that it is the very striving for universal comprehension, outside of cultural or even planetary specifics, that turns the house into an alien outpost. This brief interview exposes a conundrum: even with House VI, was Eisenman's conception of the subject—"every man or every Martian"—posthumanist? In one somewhat exaggerated sense, yes: he rejects all "patrician" cultural references in favor of an abstract mathematical language. But, in another sense, no: Eisenman obviously continues to believe that this formal language reaches a "deeper" universal subject that lies beneath the cultural "surface." Here the influence of Chomsky's "Cartesian" linguistics continues.

In a provocative essay on this issue, Sarah Whiting has described a "stark contrast" between Rowe's humanism and Eisenman's posthumanism, which she recognizes as early as Eisenman's dissertation.[68] I think this overlooks the continuity, argued for earlier, of Eisenman's thinking with that of Rowe. While Eisenman did begin developing a formalism of "exteriority," which split from the object-oriented approach of the Rowe/Wittkower lineage, this began only with the Cannaregio project of 1978, meaning that there is a period of nearly two decades during which he worked within Rowe's shadow. Moreover, when it came, this shift in Eisenman's work was paralleled by Rowe's own move to a context-based collage aesthetic, suggesting more similarity than difference between the two. Indeed, in his 1973 addendum to "The Mathematics of the Ideal Villa," Rowe is at pains to point out the "limitations" of his method, including its inability to deal with content and its possible tedium.[69] There is nothing in his tone that suggests a humanist revival, and his only positive claim for formalism closely echoes Eisenman: it may be widely accessible because it relies on few external cultural references.

Further complicating such historiotheoretical parsing is the fact that even in the late 1980s we find Eisenman returning to an explicitly existentialist vocabulary:

> With the scientifically orchestrated horror of Hiroshima and the consciousness of the human brutality of the Holocaust it became impossible for man to sustain a relationship with any of the dominant cosmologies of his past; he could no longer derive his identity from a belief in a heroic purpose and future. Survival became his only "heroic" possibility. . . . For the first time in history, man was faced with no way of assuaging his unmediated confrontation with an existential anxiety.
>
> Man now lives in this *in extremis* condition.[70]

Reflected here is the duration over a long stretch of Eisenman's career of a modernist existential, and ultimately humanist, anxiety, which only incompletely bleeds into a later (post)structuralist view for which, strictly speaking, there would be no humanist subject for which such anxiety could exist.[71] Or, to revise Whiting's description, it is not that there was a rupture *between* Rowe and Eisenman along a humanist/posthumanist fault but a rupture *within* each of their intellectual frames, one that was not so much chronological as conceptual, with both views appearing alternately, or even simultaneously, within either figure's works. This is essentially the description Eisenman himself gave in 1976, just after the completion of House VI:

> [My] new theoretical base changes the humanist balance of form/function to a dialectical relationship within the evolution of form itself. The dialectic can best be described as the potential co-existence within any form of two . . . tendencies. One tendency is to presume architectural form to be a recognizable transformation from some pre-existent geometric or Platonic solid. . . . This tendency is certainly a relic of humanist theory. However, to this is added a second tendency

> that sees architectural form in an atemporal, decompositional mode. . . . Here form is understood as a series of fragments—signs without meaning dependent upon, and without reference to, a more basic condition.[72]

This is not to say that Whiting is wrong to recognize a distinction between Eisenman and Rowe. I want to suggest, however, that this distinction is precisely between the approach that each took to structuring the humanist/posthumanist dilemma rather than each aligning with one side of this dichotomy. A key insight on this point is provided by Vidler's description of an opposition within Rowe's thought between "posthumanist modernism and retrohumanist postmodernism; between an assumption of a humanist subjectivity disseminated and perhaps irrevocably lost, and one precariously surviving, perhaps to be regained."[73] In contrast to which Eisenman's thinking, with its existentialism, foreign to Rowe, and distaste for any hint of nostalgia, can be characterized by the opposition between a humanist modernism and a posthumanist postmodernism. By defining his practice around an anxious logic of form, Eisenman devised an approach that was inherent to architecture—to the "interiority" of its history—which simultaneously reflected and provoked the anxieties of the postwar condition.

3. THE POLITICS OF FORM FINDING: FREI OTTO AND POSTWAR GERMAN ARCHITECTURE

OF THE MORE than thirty national pavilions at the Expo 67 world's fair in Montreal, two stood as signal examples of midcentury architecture: the US Pavilion with its large geodesic hemisphere designed by Buckminster Fuller (fig. 3.1) and the wide-splaying tentlike pavilion of West Germany designed by Rolf Gutbrod and Frei Otto (figs. 3.2, 3.3).[1] In both structures, novel architectural skins protected staggered layers of concrete exhibition platforms below. Yet where the tessellated three-quarter sphere of the US Pavilion monumentalized the crystalline geometries of Fuller's esoteric worldview, the West German Pavilion displayed a contrary sensibility, with relatively low, irregular, draping roofs opening out to the surrounding landscape.

While Otto held Fuller in high regard and often invited him to speak in Germany, he drew a consequential—if casually phrased—distinction between their two Montreal structures:

> Obviously the American pavilion was entirely separate from what we did. . . . [B]y chance we had learned of his project in advance, and then I said to him: "Oh Bucky, you're making a dome [Ach Bucky, Du machst eine Kuppel]."[2]

Underlying Otto's disappointment in Fuller's "dome" were deeply held convictions about the forms and meanings of postwar architecture, about the relationship of buildings to nature, and about the role of semiautomatic form generation in correctly establishing this relationship. Anticipating many topics of contemporary architectural research, such as form finding, biological analogies, minimal structures, complex curvatures, and sustainability, Otto's was perhaps the earliest practice to integrate these concerns into a coherent research and design program.

The West German Pavilion was the fullest expression of Otto's decades-long work on these issues and one of the most important demonstrations of their technical and rhetorical complexities.[3] While echoing the lightweight and lighthearted vocabulary of a festival tent, the pavilion was in fact a work of unprecedented technical complexity built at the limit of existing architectural methods. Rhetorically intended to stand for the

FIGURE 3.1. Buckminster Fuller, Shoji Sadao, Geometrics Inc., and Cambridge Seven Associates, United States Pavilion, Expo 67, Montreal, 1967. By permission of the Estate of R. Buckminster Fuller.

FIGURE 3.2. Rolf Gutbrod and Frei Otto, West German Pavilion, Expo 67, Montreal, 1967. By permission of Ullstein Bild.

FIGURE 3.3. Rolf Gutbrod and Frei Otto, West German Pavilion, Expo 67, Montreal, 1967. By permission of Ullstein Bild.

new easygoing attitude of a reformed West Germany, its tensioned cables and PVC-coated polyester skins actually demanded great precision of planning and fabrication, which the very "naturalness" of its picturesque roof made enormously difficult. Uniting, though not resolving, these contradictions of technique and representation was the research into spontaneous design methods that ran through the course of Otto's long career.

DAS HÄNGENDE DACH

The major themes of Otto's research program appear already in his doctoral dissertation, *Das hängende Dach: Gestalt und Struktur* (The suspended roof: form and structure), written for the civil engineering department at the Technical University of Berlin, completed and first published in 1954, and reprinted several times since (fig. 3.4).[4] This work was prompted by a research trip Otto took to the United States in 1950 and 1951. During this visit Otto sought out many leading architects, including Frank Lloyd Wright, Richard Neutra, Erich Mendelsohn, Ludwig Mies van der Rohe, and Eero Saarinen.[5] Through Saarinen, he met the civil engineer Fred Severud, who was working with the architect Matthew Nowicki on the State Fair Arena in Raleigh, North Carolina. This novel structure, formed by a saddle-shaped suspended cable

FIGURE 3.4. Frei Otto, *Das hängende Dach: Gestalt und Struktur* (The suspended roof: Form and structure [1954]). The cover shows the State Fair Arena in Raleigh, North Carolina, by Matthew Nowicki and Fred Severud, 1952.

roof supported on two parabolic concrete arches, seems to have triggered Otto's particular research focus on suspended roofs. The Arena plays an important role in his dissertation as a rare built example. It also appears on the cover of the published text.

However, older and quite different experiences shaped Otto's research trajectory as well: his interest in building and flying gliders as a teen, his service in World

War II as a Luftwaffe fighter pilot, and his time as "camp architect" while a prisoner of war near Chartres. The nearly mythical story of this early background, retold in both of the major catalogs of his work, highlights the extent to which Otto's concerns for natural forms and processes of formation were, from the start, entangled with the technologies and political valences of the war.[6] Otto himself offers a poetic description of these themes in his dissertation, which, though almost entirely devoted to technical issues, opens with an unusual version of the "primitive hut" trope common to architectural treatises:

> The modern suspended roof is the newest form of building. Completed and widely utilized it claims its place. It is architecture—it is a house.
>
> Now, after the suspended roof has taken on a clear shape, now, after something fundamentally new has been created, we become aware that the suspended roof is very old, for the tent is already a suspended roof.
>
> . . . Today, by our reason and rational way of thinking, through our artistic and spiritual aspirations and creations, amid an overtechnological world—but with the help of modern technology—we have approached again that which is most primordial and simple, that which is as old as man.
>
> As long as man is man, differentiated from animals, differentiated through technology, because he creates tools and transfers experiences from generation to generation . . . the suspended roof is his companion. The tent made of woven twigs or hides—a complete shell or a mere roof over gathered stones.
>
> In contrast to a cave found or dug into the receptive ground, the tent is an artificial work, planned, assembled from parts, and created in a previously barren place.
>
> The instinctive drive that inseparably belongs to life not only directs that dwellings are to be built but also how they are to be built.
>
> The tent is fundamentally of a biological, nontechnical or ur-technical nature. (In contrast, the vaulting of stone buildings is surely a technical act, invented by individuals, grown into a model, and taken up by everyone and used everywhere.) . . .
>
> Two different worlds meet with their aspirations and their desires: In the connection of stone and tent, in the connection of rest and restlessness, transience and duration, an involuntary expression of human existence—as also with the modern suspended roof.
>
> Through the rupture of our time we have become nomads and strive for stability for the sake of peace. The mobile seems to stabilize itself and gives us the support for new urges.[7]

Though limited to this introductory passage and a brief concluding remark, the force of Otto's rhetoric demonstrates that his exploration of the suspended roof was far from a detached technical endeavor. The choice that Otto poses between the

FIGURE 3.5. Frei Otto with Ewald Bubner, Bernd-Friedrich Romberg, and Uwe Röder, retractable roof at the monastery ruins in Bad Hersfeld, Germany, 1969.

world of stone and that of the tent takes on a deep poignancy when one recalls that, as he wrote, he was surrounded by the still-unrepaired rubble of early 1950s Berlin. More than a decade later Otto would help realize a project that embodied this dichotomy: a retractable membrane roof for the open-air theater of the monastery ruins in Bad Hersfeld, Germany (fig. 3.5). In his description of a postwar primitivism, Otto parallels the various forms of brutalism explored by Le Corbusier, Alison and Peter Smithson, and even Louis Kahn, but his choice of the tent as a prototype allows him to combine this perspective with an advocacy of advanced technology and mobility that equals and anticipates that of quite different figures such as Fuller, Cedric Price, and the Archigram group.

Also suggested here is the somewhat strained conflation of biological and technological processes that would color all of Otto's career. The ambiguity in Otto's description of tent making as both instinctive and technological—his unresolved choice between *untechnisch* and *urtechnisch*—anticipates the continual ambiguity in his works between their supposed harmony with nature and their highly sophisticated artificiality, between their rhetorical minimalism and the maximalism of their realization. This pursuit of an architecture that is simultaneously technological and natural will ultimately come to be shepherded, though not resolved, by Otto's quasi-automatic design methods. His notion of "form finding" will assert that, like natural forms, artificial forms can be, in some sense, spontaneous and unauthored. Form finding will allow Otto and his collaborators to deploy spontaneous physical processes to generate architectural form.

In addition to cataloging the small number of existing suspended roofs that he could discover, *Das hängende Dach* also contains Otto's extensive model-based research into the basic forms of membrane and cable-net roofs (fig. 3.6) as well as a profusion of speculative designs based on suspended roofs: various halls, auditoriums, and sheds; gas and train stations; houses (fig. 3.7); churches; an airport; an art gallery; and an Antarctic base (fig. 3.8). One can sense in these schemes Otto's fevered application of the suspended forms he was exploring to almost any architectural problem he could imagine.

He also looked for ways to have these ideas realized and soon began to collaborate with the tentmaker Peter Stromeyer. This led to a series of temporary tensile membrane roofs: three structures for the 1955 Federal Garden Exhibition (Bundesgartenschau) in Kassel (fig. 3.9); four for the 1957 Federal Garden Exhibition in Cologne (figs. 3.10 and 3.11); four, also in 1957, for the Interbau exhibition in Berlin; a large umbrella for the 1958 Garden Exhibition in Saarbrücken; and an ensemble of three roof types for the 1963 International Garden Exhibition in Hamburg. Each of these projects tested a different type projected by *Das hängende Dach*, from the simplest four-point saddle to more complex configurations of peaked, arched, and humped membranes.

While the symmetrical arrays and radial forms of these first built works suggest Otto working toward the demonstration of fundamental principles, the issue of composition and choice quickly arises out of the proliferation of types and the possibilities offered by their combinations. The free compositional possibilities of Otto's tensile roofs became most evident in two projects that were the closest precedents of the Montreal pavilion (both also involved substantial collaboration with other designers). The first of these, an unrealized project of 1963–64 for an auditorium at the University of Stuttgart, was Otto's first collaboration with Gutbrod. The second, strongly echoing the strategy for Expo 67, was an ensemble of large peaked roofs loosely covering a collection of terraces designed with Marc Saugey for the 1964 Swiss Regional Expo in Lausanne (fig. 3.12). Because of the large spans in both of these projects, Otto shifted from a simple membrane covering to the more elaborate

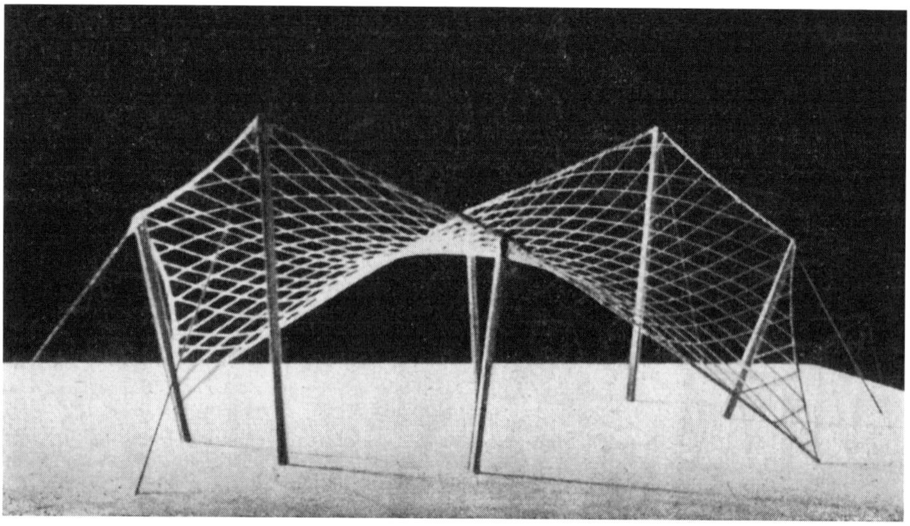

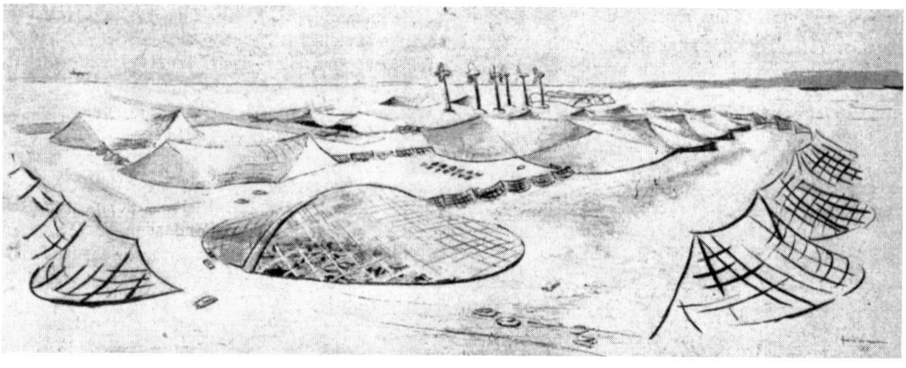

FIGURE 3.6. (*top*) Frei Otto, model of cable net between six high and two low points. From *Das hängende Dach* (1954).

FIGURE 3.7. (*middle*) Frei Otto, design for a house under two suspended roofs. From *Das hängende Dach* (1954).

FIGURE 3.8. (*bottom*) Frei Otto, design for a city in the Antarctic. From *Das hängende Dach* (1954).

FIGURE 3.9. Frei Otto, music pavilion, West German Federal Garden Exhibition, Kassel, 1955.

FIGURE 3.10. Frei Otto, entrance arch, West German Federal Garden Exhibition, Cologne, 1957.

FIGURE 3.11. Frei Otto, dance pavilion, West German Federal Garden Exhibition, Cologne, 1957. By permission of RIBApix.

combination, which would be used in Montreal, of a steel cable net for structural support and a fabric membrane for water, sun, and wind protection (fig. 3.13). Appearing just a decade after Otto's first realized tents, one sees in these projects the productive contradictions between his rhetoric of minimalism, optimization, and naturalism and the competing desire for innovation, expansion, and expression. The result was an architectural vocabulary that went far beyond a mere scientific mapping of structural possibilities.

FINDING FORM FINDING: FROM BUBBLES TO COMPUTATION

As a base for his research Otto established the Development Center for Lightweight Construction (Entwicklungsstätte für den Leichtbau) in 1958. While this institute was only located in a small "glass house" on his in-law's property in Berlin, the scale of Otto's ambitions for it were conveyed by the nine issues of its "Information" journal published between 1958 and 1963. In 1964 this homegrown research organization was superseded by the establishment of the far more substantial Institute for Lightweight Structures (Institut für leichte Flächentragwerke), or IL, at the University of Stuttgart, which Otto would direct until 1991 and which provided the platform for much of his long career. Over the decades the IL would pursue research into a wide range of structures, but much of its early work was devoted to tensile membrane and net structures, particularly for the two major projects of the Expo 67 Pavilion and the

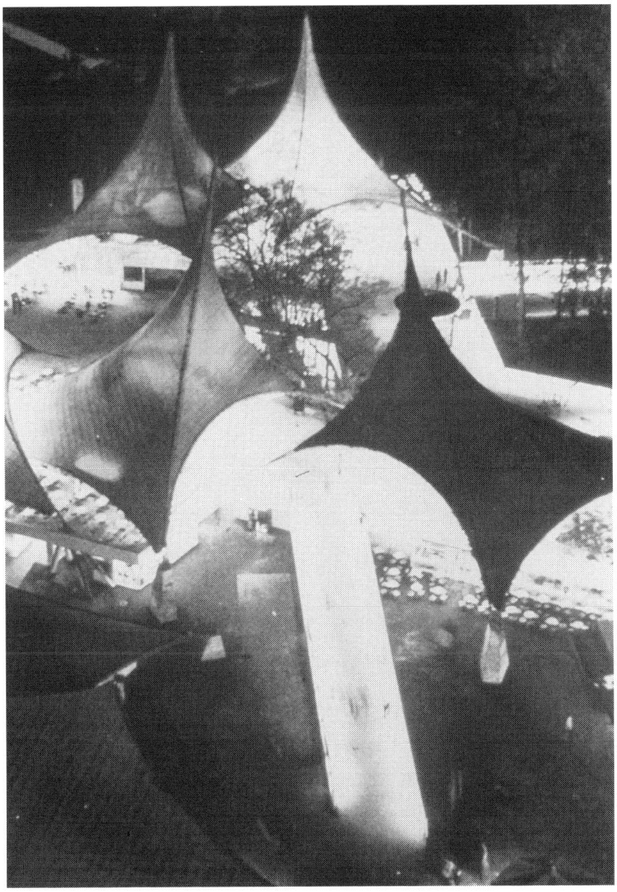

FIGURE 3.12. (*left*) Marc Saugey and Frei Otto, "Neige et Rocs" pavilion, Swiss Regional Expo, Lausanne, 1964.

FIGURE 3.13. (*below*) Hanging the membrane beneath the cable net. Rolf Gutbrod and Frei Otto, West German Pavilion, Expo 67, Montreal, 1967.

FIGURE 3.14. Frei Otto, test structure for the Expo 67 pavilion (later converted to house the Institute for Lightweight Structures), University of Stuttgart, 1966. Courtesy of ILEK, University of Stuttgart.

Munich Olympic roofs. The institute even came to be housed in a structure erected as a test for Montreal (fig. 3.14).

Throughout their work, Otto and his team pursued interdisciplinary research beyond the traditional bounds of architecture or architectural engineering. They also explored a range of novel representational techniques that emphasized semi-autonomy within the design process—that is to say, the active role that models could play in determining form and the comparatively reduced role of the designer. Otto particularly emphasized this aspect of his research in two books: *Gestaltwerdung: Zur Formentstehung in Natur, Technik und Baukunst* (Morphogenesis: On form generation in nature, technology, and building) and *Finding Form: Towards an Architecture of the Minimal.*[8]

The sense that Otto's projects were in some way self-forming was particularly strong in the structures based on tensile surfaces, such as the Expo 67 pavilion. Whether ultimately realized with fabric membranes or cable nets, these forms rely on prestressing in order to become rigid and resistant to the environmental forces of wind, rain, and snow. As Otto discovered, one of the most reliable ways to deploy such prestressing is in the form of a minimal surface: one that minimizes the area spanning a given perimeter. Such forms also minimize the mean curvature at any point on the surface. Membranes or nets in such forms can therefore be placed under great tension and become rigid without experiencing shearing forces that would deform or tear them. Apart from the trivial case of a plane, the simplest example of such a minimal surface is the saddle-like form taken by Otto's Music Pavilion at the 1955 Federal Garden Exhibition in Kassel (fig. 3.9).

It is out of the requirements of minimal surfaces that the sense of semiautomatic form generation arises in this branch of Otto's research, for the definition of a perimeter necessarily defines the corresponding minimal surface that spans it. Therefore, this surface must be discovered, not designed. Any change in the perimeter geometry "spontaneously" results in the redefinition of the minimal surface, implying that the forms of Otto's tents are not designed directly but indirectly through the definition of their edges, which are materially embodied as cables, wires, or threads. Yet while minimal surfaces were crucial for Otto's structural applications, they can only be directly calculated for the simplest perimeter definitions. All other cases require approximation through iterative calculation—a method that only became feasible shortly *after* the construction of the Expo 67 pavilion with the advance of electronic computing. At the time Otto began his research, the minimal surface for an arbitrary perimeter was still inaccessible to calculation.

However, minimal surfaces do occur spontaneously in nature wherever thin films form, as in soap bubbles. This fact had important consequences for Otto. Practically, it allowed him to explore a variety of minimal surfaces before such shapes could be determined computationally. By dipping a small wire model in soap solution and removing it carefully, a spontaneously formed minimal surface was revealed (fig. 3.15). Given their ability to spontaneously determine forms that were otherwise unknowable, these soap film experiments became an important focus for research at the Institute for Lightweight Structures that Otto established in Stuttgart, leading to the construction of a specialized "soap film machine" with a high-humidity climatic chamber to extend the longevity of a film and a parallel light projector to record its geometry on a photographic plate (fig. 3.16).[9] The IL also used the spontaneous optimization of soap films to determine the shortest path connecting points in a two-dimensional constellation. This was the topic of the institute's first publication.[10] This problem is closely related to the path optimization research undertaken by the Cambridge Centre for Land Use and Built Form Studies, which I discussed in chapter 1. Characteristically, Otto's research group explored physically a problem that Cambridge treated computationally.

Of course Otto was not the only figure enamored with bubbles in the 1960s, a period during which pneumatic structures played an important symbolic role in architectural discourse. Hadas Steiner has pointed to an interpretation of this significance that is directly relevant to Otto's work:

> Thomas Herzog explained . . . that "orthogonal forms with hard, cold, machine-produced surfaces" had dominated architecture, and that, "previous attempts to oppose this with a sensuous plastic world have meant a negation of the technical/structural dimension of architecture." Pneumatic structures, Herzog contended,

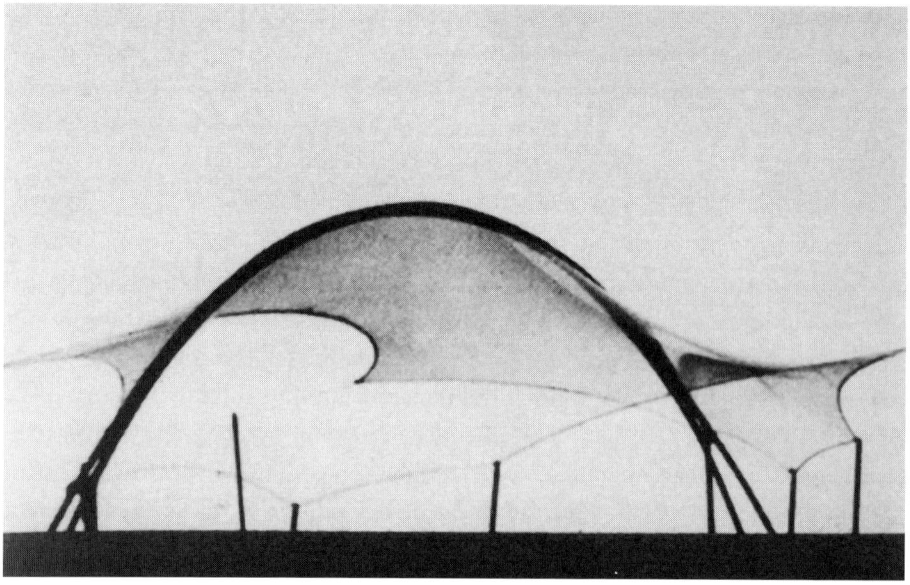

FIGURE 3.15. Frei Otto and the Institute for Lightweight Structures, soap film model of an arch tent. Courtesy of ILEK, University of Stuttgart.

FIGURE 3.16. Frei Otto and the Institute for Lightweight Structures, "soap film machine," climatic chamber and photographic apparatus. Courtesy of ILEK, University of Stuttgart.

offered a synthesis through the use of forms that are "technically highly developed, using soft, flexible, movable, roundly spanned, 'organic' shapes, which can be of great sensuous beauty." In short, pneumatics suggested a blend of the organic world and built form that would not negate the primary role of architecture.[11]

With his tensile surface structures, Otto takes this synthesis further: where others celebrated the antiformal, mutable character of pneumatics, Otto uses soap film as a step toward precise, mathematical forms emphasizing the idealized geometry of the bubbles rather than their flexibility or impermanence. Otto's tensile roofs also provided a solution to a psychological problem presented by pneumatic structures: "Due to their novelty and suggestion of transience, for many, inflatables . . . exhibit[ed] a lack of rigidity that was disturbing even for use at temporary sites."[12] Though in this regard not as radical as inflatable structures, Otto's tensile surfaces nonetheless combined a modernist ethic of lightness and material honesty with the antigravitational aspect of pneumatics.

In preparation for Expo 67, West Germany held a two-stage design competition for its pavilion with Egon Eiermann as chairman of the jury. The first stage, open to all West German architects, received 117 entries, which were judged in February of 1965. Twelve of these proposals were awarded special mention and advanced to the second stage along with five additional architects invited directly by the jury, including the team of Otto and Gutbrod. Their proposal (fig. 3.17) was selected as the winning scheme in June 1965.[13] The schedule for the project was remarkably short—only fourteen months for design, analysis, fabrication, and construction—and there were serious questions as to whether a structure as unusual as that proposed by Otto and Gutbrod could be built so quickly (a pattern repeated a few years later for the Munich Olympic buildings).[14]

FIGURE 3.17. Competition model, 1965. Rolf Gutbrod and Frei Otto, West German Pavilion, Expo 67, Montreal.

While the geometry behind Otto's roof may have been minimal, its realization was entirely maximal. The soap film models gave the IL team important insights into the ideal geometry that the roof should take, particularly in the areas around the teardrop-shaped loops that Otto discovered at a means to avoid excessive stresses, but the use of these models was greatly limited by their size and fragility, which created insurmountable problems of accuracy.[15] Also, while the winning proposal clearly grew out of Otto's early tents, the size and the irregularity of the Montreal scheme produced an entirely new level of difficulty. Given the ubiquity today of complex digital models and of form-generating computer scripts, it may be difficult to appreciate the challenge presented by the geometry of a roof like that proposed for Expo 67: its form needed to be highly precise in order to avoid irregular stresses that could result in failure, yet it was incalculable. Working without three-dimensional computer models and without form-finding algorithms, the coordinates defining the minimal surface had to be located literally "out of thin air."

In order to meet the challenge presented by a form that exceeded drawing and calculation, Otto and the newly established IL relied on a series of novel and complex physical models to drive the design process and to generate construction drawings. In important ways, this working method anticipated current advanced construction practices, often also concerned with complexly curved geometries, for which the computational model has become the document of record, with two-dimensional plots playing a secondary role.[16]

Beginning with the somewhat informal competition model, the design was first refined through a process of trial and error using seven complete models and dozens of partial models at scales of 1:200 and 1:100 with polyester mesh as a stand-in for the roof surface.[17] The elastic fabric offered rough feedback on the distribution of stresses within the surface, allowing the team to approximate a true minimal surface. As an indication of the painstaking level of accuracy required, even the fact that the warp and weft of the fabric had slightly different spacings meant that the surface geometry of the models was distorted away from the ideal form—a problem that then had to be corrected later in the design process.[18] Using a specially constructed drawing device in the form of a large horizontal frame and plumb line suspended over the model, the coordinates of the final fabric model were recorded and became the basis for two new types of models: a solid plywood contour model (fig. 3.18) that was used for wind tunnel testing and an elaborate, multipurpose wire model (fig. 3.19) that was the most complete representation of the project.

To an even greater extent than the earlier models, the large wire model, built at a scale of 1:75, did not passively represent the form of the pavilion but played an active role in *generating* that form and in analyzing its behavior. Made from stainless steel wire of a properly scaled diameter, the large model went through multiple rounds of refinement as the wires were tensioned as they would be in the actual pavilion, measured, and adjusted until the stresses within the net were as even as possible. After

FIGURE 3.18. Wind tunnel model. Frei Otto and the Institute for Lightweight Structures, West German Pavilion, Expo 67, Montreal, 1967. Courtesy of ILEK, University of Stuttgart.

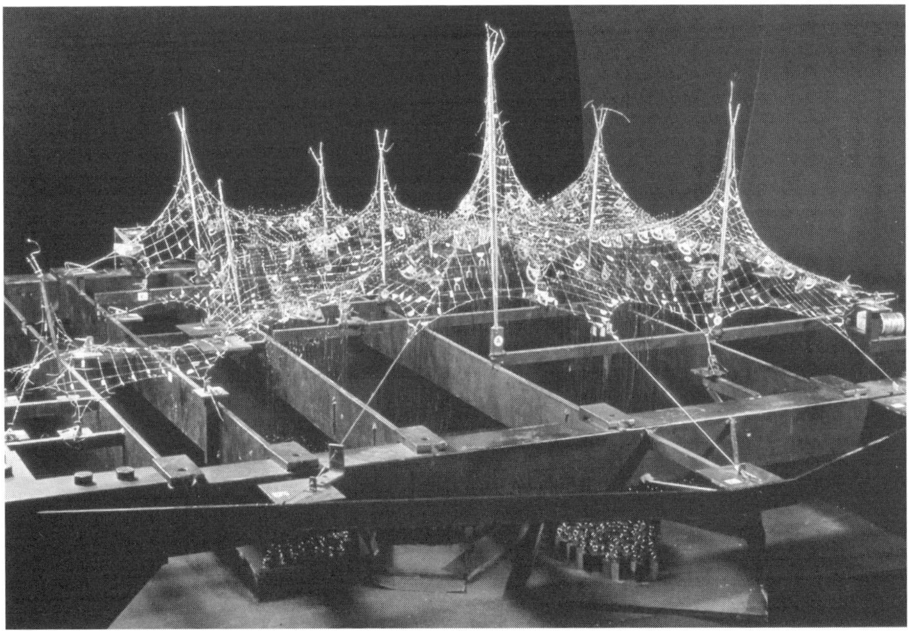

FIGURE 3.19. Wire model. Frei Otto and the Institute for Lightweight Structures, West German Pavilion, Expo 67, Montreal, 1967. Courtesy of ILEK, University of Stuttgart.

this tuning that approximated the ideal minimal surface, the wire model became the source for several further stages of the design process.[19] First, there was a new round of drawings. Echoing the naturalizing descriptions of the pavilion as a landscape, a "contour map" of its roof was created using the drawing machine (fig. 3.20). Working drawings at a scale of 1:10 were also generated by projecting photographs of the wire model and by direct measurement with dividers.

A second wire model was constructed and used as the skeleton for determining the shape and cutting pattern of the membrane skin that would be suspended beneath the cable net. This skin, which in the full scale pavilion would be made of polyester coated with PVC, was approximated in the model by 281 singly curved pieces made first of cardboard and then of tracing vellum (fig. 3.21).Then, because the complex form of the roof made standard structural calculations impossible, the large wire model was used to predict the pavilion's performance under live loads (snow was the main concern). Minute strain gauges were placed within the wire grid and hundreds of scale weights were suspended beneath the net. These could be used to simulate loading. The shape of the net, in both unloaded and loaded conditions, was then recorded in double-exposure photographs taken by multiple cameras simultaneously, allowing the deformation of the surface in three dimensions to be measured.

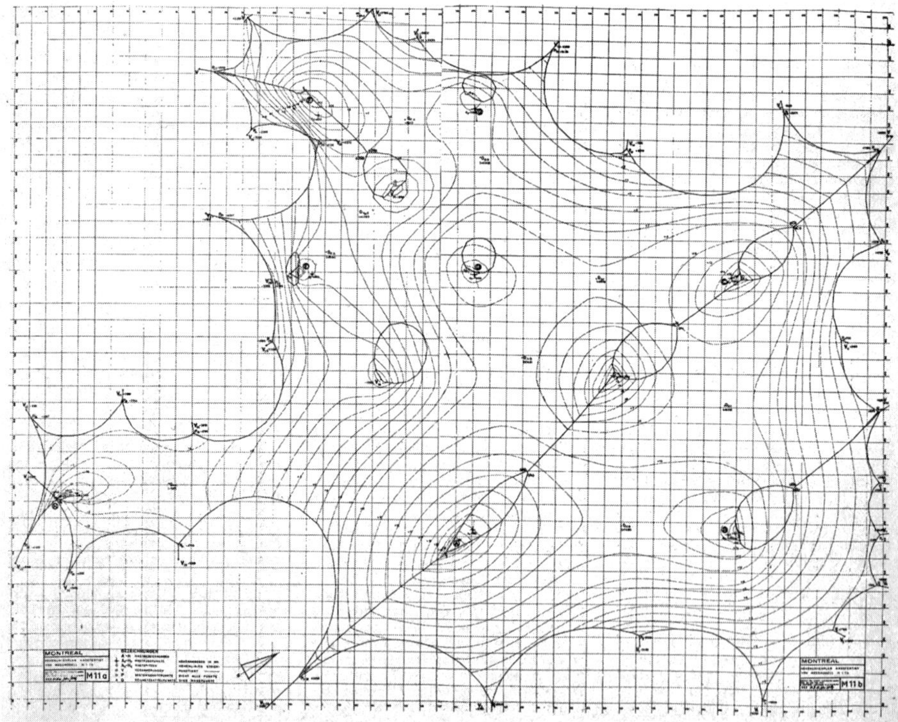

FIGURE 3.20. "Contour map" of the roof surface. Frei Otto and the Institute for Lightweight Structures, West German Pavilion, Expo 67, Montreal, 1967. Courtesy of ILEK, University of Stuttgart.

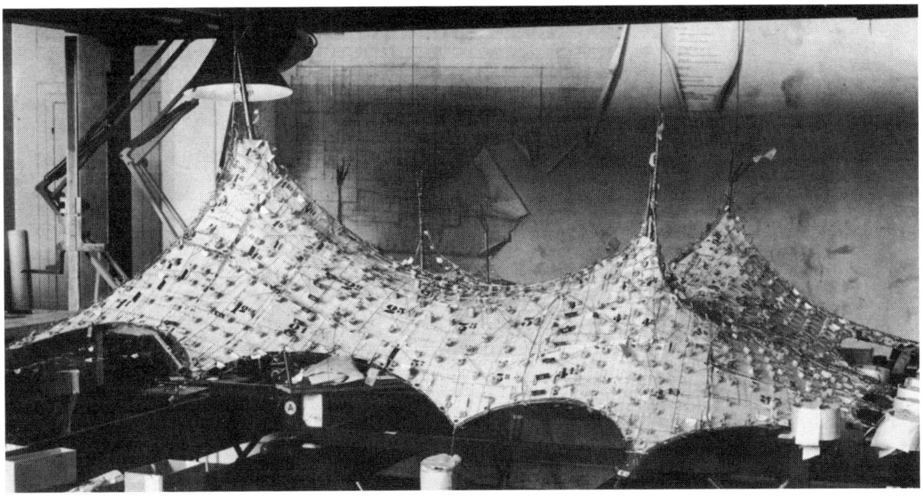

FIGURE 3.21. Model with wire grid and vellum membrane. Frei Otto and the Institute for Lightweight Structures, West German Pavilion, Expo 67, Montreal, 1967. Courtesy of ILEK, University of Stuttgart.

While this ingenious set of physical modeling procedures allowed the Expo 67 pavilion to be realized, they also were conducted at the limit of technical feasibility. Partially in response to these limitations, the physical models of the Expo 67 became the subjects of an even more radical representational experiment: "[a] digital model of the irregular structure was recorded and stored; [so that] any desired cross-section could then be calculated and plotted automatically."[20] While the design team considered this computational work only "supplementary and independent" to the main physical models and tests, it clearly situates the Expo 67 pavilion on the historical cusp of computational methods. The computational approach would be both more advanced and more necessary just a few years later when the size of the Munich Olympic roofs—an order of magnitude greater than Expo 67—exceeded the precision of even the IL's sophisticated modeling methods.

Reinforcing the association of the pavilion with a landscape, the experiment with computational modeling was conducted by a team from the University of Stuttgart's Institute for the Application of Geodesy in Construction (Institut für Anwendungden der Geodäsie im Bauwesen), headed by Klaus Linkwitz. As geodesy is concerned with the measurement and mapping of the earth, Linkwitz's team was accustomed to dealing with the difficulties of representing complex three-dimensional geometries such as those of the Expo 67 pavilion (admittedly at a vastly different scale). Linkwitz's group used the technique of stereophotogrammetry to construct the computational model, photographing the wire model from multiple positions simultaneously and then extrapolating the three-dimensional coordinates of intersections on the wire grid. In a connection that surely pleased him, Otto noted that this technique was also being used by scientists working at microscopic scales.

This early computational modeling led to a significant, if subtle, event in Montreal:

> I [Otto] worked with the geodesic expert Klaus Linkwitz, and we used the stereoscopic method that is used for measuring the surface of the earth. Interestingly, at the same time the biologist Johann-Gerhard Helmcke was testing stereoscopic measurements with electron microscopes.
>
> Helmcke collaborated with Konrad Zuse, who invented the computer and used it in combination with the stereo-comparator for the photogrammetry. We used this method on models for the German Pavilion in Montreal. We also put Konrad Zuse's computer in the World Exposition, together with a computer-controlled drawing machine, plotting the sections of our building.[21]

Konrad Zuse was the leading German computer pioneer. On display in the West German Pavilion was a replica of his Z3, the first programmable electronic computer (fig. 3.22), along with his much more recent Graphomat 64 plotter, which must have been controlled by another, more advanced computer.[22] Built during World War II, the original Z3 was partially funded by the German Aeronautics Research Institute and was used to perform analyses of aircraft wing flutter.[23] The original machine was destroyed in 1943 by allied bombing of Berlin, so what was on display in Montreal in 1967 was a replica built in 1960 (now housed at the Deutsches Museum in Munich).

Appreciated fully, this small scene is an intensive, even poignant, node in the history of architecture, knotting together many strands of the condition of being "postwar." Representing West Germany in 1967 was the replica of a computer that had performed calculations for the Luftwaffe and had itself been destroyed by allied bombing along with Zuse's plotter drawing sections of the complex lightweight doubly curved roof overhead, which itself was an expression of Otto's response to the "rupture" of the war and to his own experience as a fighter pilot. Here also, as physical modeling techniques had been stretched to the limits of their accuracy and despite Otto's own skepticism about computation, was a poetic sign of the transition to a new paradigm in which computation would be the primary driver of advanced architectural form making, especially for the multitude of complexly curved surfaces that were yet to come.

Going forward from Montreal computational methods would play an increasingly important role in the built work with which Otto was involved, especially for the vast structures of the 1972 Olympics in Munich. Researchers at the University of Stuttgart—Linkwitz's geodesy group as well as the Institute for Statics and Dynamics in Aviation and Aerospace Construction (Institut für Statik und Dynamik der Luft- und Raumfahrtkonstruktionen) headed by John Argyris—would make important advances in computing complex minimal surfaces, and developing methods for determining minimal geometries mathematically and for analyzing their structural

FIGURE 3.22. Zuse Z3 computer on display at Expo 67 Montreal, 1967. Courtesy of Horst Zuse.

performance using the Finite Element Method that Argyris had helped formulate. Yet while acknowledging the effect that computation could have, Otto remained highly skeptical of the computational approach:

> Perhaps the Munich structural models, which are basically the same as we used on Montreal, will not be used in the future. The reason is that the mathematicians . . . are able to do exact calculations of the evolution of the surface and to calculate the deformations due to any load conditions. This means we will spend much more time on our design models and deliver them to the mathematicians who will do all calculations including working drawings. . . . Remember that using the computer for advanced work is a very slow and expensive process and, until now, it was not possible to put our know-how for pre-stressed cable nets on the computer. There are other areas of my development work which undoubtedly cannot be put on the computer. . . . The computer is slow and we have had to use models for the preliminary analysis—which is their correct use in the design.[24]

To some extent Otto's attitude was simply pragmatic given the state of technology in the early 1970s ("the computer is slow"), but his skepticism persisted for decades and despite great advances in computation, making it clear that his resistance was also a matter of principle:

> The computer can only calculate what is already conceptually inside of it; you can only find what you look for in computers. . . . If, for example, you do experiments with liquids, the infinite possibilities are restricted to only those forms that can be built with the surface stresses of the liquids, that is, those that tend to form

> minimum surfaces. If this process is done with the computer and this criterion is eliminated . . . you can do an infinite amount of things. . . .
>
> It's a serious problem that the majority of those who work only with computers today are incapable of seeing, because to think of infinite possibilities is tremendously difficult. One can think of everything, one can calculate everything using the computer. It can be said that the computer has created this form, but I think that's a lie because the artist or the mathematician who is behind the computer has created it by using calculation methods to obtain something that he likes, that speaks to his artistic sensibility. I reject the lie that says that the computer has found everything, because new inventions can't arise from it; you only get what you have already placed inside it.[25]

Otto's difficulty with computation grew out of his belief in a design method based on the discovery of forms that are "natural" responses to their environments. Modeled on experimental scientific inquiry, Otto's conception of design was "automatic" in that it involved a search for results, that is, forms, that supposedly lay waiting to be revealed. In contrast to creation through "artistic sensibility," Otto intended his methodology to make design both scientific and harmonious with nature itself.

Yet, despite Otto's continual instance on the spontaneous form-finding aspect of his work, this spontaneity was always conditioned on one side by the highly artificial laboratory conditions that allowed it to occur and on the other by the concrete architectural contexts to which it was applied. The resulting contradictions were recognized by critics and by Otto himself over the course of his career. In his catalog for the 1971 exhibition of Otto's work at the New York Museum of Modern Art, Ludwig Glaeser highlighted the first condition, writing that Otto's "denial of artistic motivations is believable to the extent that he avoids burdening a project from the outset with preconceived ideas. But since he admits to a personal style in problem solving, his forms are not totally automatic results of the design process. However scientific the methods, there is a margin for personal decisions which accounts for the individual style discernible in the work of most engineers."[26] More than three decades later, the catalog of Otto's exhibition in Munich discussed the second condition: "Otto's architecture cannot be understood without knowledge of autonomous formation processes. . . . However, they cannot replace an architectural design. In the preface to *IL* 25 ('Experiment'), Frei Otto wrote: 'It is extremely difficult to apply self-forming processes for architectural design. . . . [D]esign work can only be seen in relation to the complexity of a building task and the integration of the building into its surroundings and into society.'"[27]

Granting the inevitability of these qualifications—that is, the impossibility of an absolutely automatic design process—brings the character of Otto's process into sharper outline. Admitting the "personal style in problem solving" and the "complexity of a building task," Otto's model-based form-finding techniques can be best understood as distancing devices, limiting and shifting his role within the design process. Shaping a minimal surface structure through manipulation of its edge condition or assembling an ensemble of minimal surfaces allows Otto to achieve compositional action at a distance. Otto's sketched fantasias reveal the constant presence of the compositional impulse, as does the general trajectory, for any structural system he engages, from simple, direct, idealized solutions to complex, expressionistic, compositional ones.

A related contradiction is raised by the fact that despite the functionalist overtones of his form-finding rhetoric, Otto's catalog is largely filled with projects that are both very weakly programmed and almost entirely symbolic: exhibition tents for garden festivals, multipurpose halls, and temporary pavilions. In these contexts, such as Expo 67, Otto's experimental use of minimal surfaces does not necessarily conserve resources (certainly not money or time) but is instead symbolic of conservation, of a certain efficiency, and of nature itself. Paradoxically, despite the enormous technical complexity involved in designing and erecting a project like the Expo 67 Pavilion, the unusual characteristics of minimal surfaces and their quasi-spontaneous generation allowed Otto to claim that his schemes were, in fact, merely manifestations of physical laws and, in some sense, not designed by the architects but by nature directly. The official catalog of Expo 67 neatly, though somewhat unknowingly, captured just the conflation of the artificial and the natural that the project presented: "The German Pavilion represents the quintessence of the tent form, posed there like some poetic or philosophical statement on behalf of architectural technology, and expressing the suppleness and freedom of nature itself."[28]

THE POLITICS OF FORM FINDING

The significance and contradictions of Otto's work from this period extend beyond technical and methodological developments. His approach to building, especially for the major national projects of the Expo 67 Pavilion and the Munich Olympic buildings, was enmeshed with the difficulties of postwar West German architecture generally. From his dissertation on, Otto described his interest in form finding as a reaction to the oppressive grandiosity of National Socialism and as an attempt to discover a democratic alternative. His projects illustrate the dilemmas involved in carrying out this vision in structures intended to embody a materially and ideologically reconstructed West Germany.[29]

In an interview, Otto described the qualities that he believed led to the selection of the Expo 67 scheme:

> **F. O.:** The main aspect was, of course, that we offered no firmly tied down [gezurrten] monumental pavilion but instead a landscape; that we also said we are planting the site, the garden runs through, we have this amazing situation

on a lagoon and we are making only a very light roof. A further criterion was that we did not want to put on a German drama but instead an unconventional Germany. Practically a little in the line of Egon Eiermann in Brussels.

P. S. [Paul Sigel]: It worked also as proof of national self-representation.

F. O.: But of course. All world exposition pavilions have not only the function of just exhibiting something, but specifically they are representations of a country.[30]

Here, Otto presents a rapid sketch of the complex, and nearly contradictory, symbolic role that the West German Pavilion needed to perform. First, it must avoid monumentality and any dramatic nationalism, which were forever tainted by associations with Fascism. Second, the way to avoid architectural monumentality was by conceiving of the pavilion as a landscape project, with a garden running through it and only a "very light roof" overhead. This vision is far more evident in the proposal models, constructed with highly transparent fabric nets, than in the realized pavilion, where the open cable net was necessarily supplemented by an opaque membrane of PVC-coated polyester.[31] Sounding a theme that runs throughout his career, Otto's suggestion is that the West German Pavilion essentially succeeded by avoiding architecture entirely—by becoming part of nature.

However, a third aspect of the pavilion's role nearly overturns these first two, for while the project must avoid national dramatics by becoming part of nature, it must, by definition, still perform as an instance of national self-presentation. Given Germany's history, the "unconventional Germany" that the pavilion represented was precisely a nation trying to move beyond nationalist representations of itself. Otto's approach to this projection of self-effacement relied on automatic methods of form generation to fulfill a rhetoric of transparency, lightness, naturalness, and efficiency in projects of great technical novelty and complexity. The results, notably the Expo 67 pavilion, were both symbols of a new Germany and, paradoxically, of an architecture that attempted to slip away from symbolic representation entirely.

The inescapable need for the Expo 67 project to serve as a representation of West Germany and its success in avoiding the direct fulfillment of this need were somewhat comically demonstrated by a minor scandal that erupted when a reporter, after viewing the pavilion from a helicopter, claimed that, in fact, its irregular form depicted a map of the "großdeutsche Reich," that is to say, of a united Germany.[32] Seized on by East Germany, this supposed revelation nearly prevented Otto and Gutbrod from receiving the 1967 Prix August Perret, the highest honor awarded by the Union Internationale des Architects.[33] Decades later, while laughing off this claim, Otto indicated precisely the representational shift he was attempting to achieve in his work:

> It's true, my buildings often look like landscapes. Clearly this is due to the structure. But one must have a very large imagination and above all really not know the greater German empire to detect a similarity in our pavilion.[34]

The Expo 67 pavilion was meant to be analogous to landscapes *generally*, not to a specific land, and yet just this shift made the project a winning representation of a reformed postwar West Germany.

Another aspect of this complex relation of national and natural representations is hinted at by Otto's suggestion that the Expo 67 pavilion was "a little in the line of Egon Eiermann in Brussels." The reference here is to the West German pavilion of the 1958 Brussels World's Fair designed by Eiermann and Sep Ruf, a project that extended the vocabulary of highly refined orthogonal modernism developed by Ludwig Mies van der Rohe. Though differing in form, structure, and methodology from the complexly curving surfaces of the Expo 67 pavilion, Otto nevertheless recognized an important continuity between the Brussels pavilion and his own:

> **P. S. [Paul Sigel]:** The reason for this can perhaps be seen in an ultimately consistent lineage of understatement [Tiefstapeln] as characteristic of West German self-expression.
>
> **F. O.:** That's right. In Montreal we understated [tiefgestapelt] in so far as we followed the minimal principle and actually measured in grams what we would ship to Canada.
>
> **P. S.:** Still, the attempt in Montreal was to show something completely innovative and at the same time elegant.
>
> **F. O.:** You have to make beautiful symbols. In Brussels Eiermann had also in some ways understated. You have to search for the pavilion in contrast to the buildings of other nations. . . . The Eiermann construction was quite restrained, yet distinguished itself through outstanding details. Very elegant and absolutely nothing too much, it was just right. . . . We understated in so far as we have just hung a little something in the air, but we were beautiful to see.[35]

Here then the "minimal principle," which was the guiding idea of Otto's career and which he invariably described as a principle of nature, is instead discussed as a historically specific national tendency to use restraint as the motif of national symbols—an approach crystallized first perhaps by Mies van der Rohe's pavilion in Barcelona, which had made a similar virtue of restraint, in the context of Germany's interwar economic crisis.[36]

While minimal by a geometric measure, the formal complexity and exuberance of Otto and Gutbrod's roofs obviously departed from the "understatement" of Eiermann's modestly scaled pavilion blocks. This exuberance was nonetheless linked to strict technical characteristics: one characteristic of minimal surfaces is that they are also "anticlastic." The simplest example of an anticlastic surface is the saddle-like form of Otto's four-point Music Pavilion at the 1955 Federal Garden Exhibition in Kassel (fig. 3.9). Such a shape displays *opposed* double curvature, which is to say that, at each point on its surface, two curves of equal but opposite curvature intersect at right angles. In contrast, a dome is a surface with *allied* double curvature and can be termed "synclastic" (fig. 3.23). In tensile roof structures, the use of anticlastic surfaces becomes crucial because at every point on these surfaces the opposed curvatures cancel each other, resulting in a net local curvature of zero, which, in turn, means that the surfaces can be placed under tension and become rigid without deforming or tearing.

Although it was central to the success of this vocabulary of anticlastic curves that it could be, and frequently was, described by Otto and by critics as historically unencumbered and related only to forms of nature or to some prehistoric fantasy of primitive tents, it did in fact have many ties to recent German architecture. Formally, the most direct precedent for the Expo 67 pavilion was Hans Scharoun's Philharmonie (1960–63; fig. 3.24), which had used a similar "antidome" roofscape as a solution to the problem of representing West Germany on the highly charged site of Berlin's Kulturforum, overlooking the scar of the recently constructed wall. Yet, where Scharoun's roof remained traditionally supported and composed, the tensile structures in Montreal, and later Munich, represented a rejection of the dome that was technically and geometrically precise.

This echo of Scharoun, and thereby of German expressionism, was not accidental. Otto has described how his father, a sculptor, had "a very active role in the Deutsche Werkbund and personally knew Erich Mendelsohn," and how after World War II, Otto took part in Werkbund and CIAM discussions, where he learned

> in detail about the fights and arguments arising in Germany about two opposing trends—one of them linked to the imaginary and to the current green movement. The roots of Wassili and Hans Luckhardt, Hans Poelzig, and Erich Mendelsohn went beyond the limits of the classical modern movement; this has interested me a lot: why and how at the end of the 1920s one of the two trends continued to exist while this fantasy architecture, which I have called "proto-green," suffered a set-back.[37]

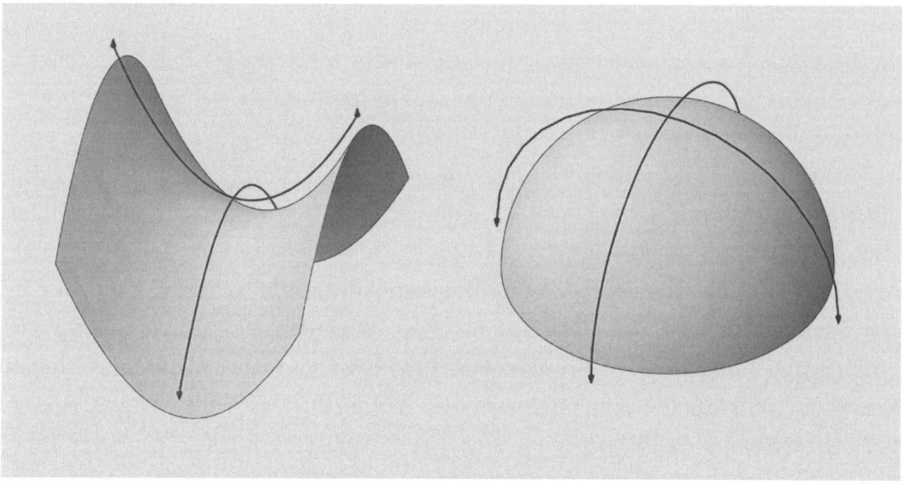

FIGURE 3.23. Anticlastic (*left*) and synclastic (*right*) double-curved surfaces. Image by author.

FIGURE 3.24. Hans Scharoun, Philharmonie, Berlin, 1963. By Permission of Geoffrey Taunton / Alamy Stock Photo.

Otto's turn to nature as a reaction to World War II was, then, also a conscious historical revival of the reaction that expressionists, such as Scharoun, Mendelsohn, Poelzig, and the Luckhardts, had to World War I. Formally, Otto's work can be described as a combination of two strains of earlier expressionism: the technologically enabled "light" architecture of Bruno Taut and the spatially complex compositions of Mendelsohn. Correspondingly, the success of Otto's vocabulary for high-profile national commissions was part of a general revival of interest in expressionism in West Germany, where architects such as Scharoun were seen to have had a "good war," and where the movement stood for a rejection of both fascist historicism and the posthumanism of *neue Sachlichkeit* (as well as its postwar bureaucratic counterparts). Indeed, taking the Philharmonie as a close precursor and Munich 72 as a successor, one begins to realize that the tented roofs of the Expo 67 pavilion were instances in an emerging West German typology of antinationalist, antimonumental national monuments.

Looking further, however, this was not an exclusively German development. Anticlastic geometries appeared as a frequent solution to the dilemma posed by postwar monumentality. A cluster of projects, some tensile, others not, suggest the widespread use of the doubly curved roof from the mid-1950s to the mid-1960s: Le Corbusier's chapel at Ronchamp (1954; fig. 3.25); Le Corbusier and Iannis Xenakis's Philips Pavilion (1958; fig. 3.26); Félix Candela's chapel Lomas de Cuernavaca (1958; fig. 3.27); Eero Saarinen's Ingalls Rink (1958; fig. 3.28); and Kenzo Tange's sports complex for the 1964 Olympics in Tokyo (fig. 3.29). Indeed, even at Expo 67, the West

German Pavilion was only one of several "antidome" structures, as the Italian and Soviet pavilions were also structured around "hanging" geometries (figs. 3.30, 3.31).

The cultural significance of these works had already been projected at the outset of this period by Sigfried Giedion in 1954—the same year that Otto's dissertation was completed—in an essay titled "The Need for Imagination," the second part of his reflections on "The State of Contemporary Architecture," written for *Architectural Forum* (fig. 3.32). There Giedion describes what he sees as the two principal difficulties facing postwar architects: the speed of purely technical advances, which mean that "science and industry constantly pile up a perturbing mound of new materials," and the challenge of creating a vibrant community in a population numbed by the passive habits of watching "a ball game or a television screen."[38] Arguing that meeting these difficulties will require both "social" and "spatial" imagination, Giedion shifts his discussion in a somewhat unexpected direction:

> The area where the spatial imagination has always had the greatest freedom—where it could unfold with the least interference—has been the area that lies above normal utilitarian requirements. This is the space that floats over our heads, lying beyond the reach of our hands. It is here that the fullest freedom is granted to the imagination of the architect.
>
> In two words, we are talking of the *vaulting problem*.

FIGURE 3.25. Le Corbusier, chapel Notre Dame du Haut, Ronchamp, 1954. Photograph by author.

FIGURE 3.26. Le Corbusier and Iannis Xenakis, Philips Pavilion, Expo 58, Brussels, 1958. © Wouter Hagens. CC BY SA 3.0: https://creativecommons.org/licenses/by-sa/3.0/legalcode.

FIGURE 3.27. Félix Candela, Guillermo Rosell, and Manuel Larrosa, Chapel Lomas de Cuernavaca, Cuernavaca, Mexico; 1958. Under construction. Photograph by Dorothy Candela.

FIGURE 3.28. Eero Saarinen, Ingalls Rink, Yale University, New Haven, CT, 1958. Courtesy of Carol M. Highsmith's America, Library of Congress, Prints and Photographs Division.

FIGURE 3.29. Kenzo Tange, Yoyogi National Gymnasium, Tokyo, 1964. By Permission of Arcaid Images / Alamy Stock Photo.

FIGURE 3.30. Leonardo Ricci and Leonardo Savioli, Italian Pavilion, Expo 67, Montreal, 1967. Courtesy of William Dutfield.

FIGURE 3.31. M. V. Posokhin, A. A. Mdnoyants, and A. N. Kondretlev, Soviet Union Pavilion, Expo 67, Montreal, 1967. Courtesy of William Dutfield.

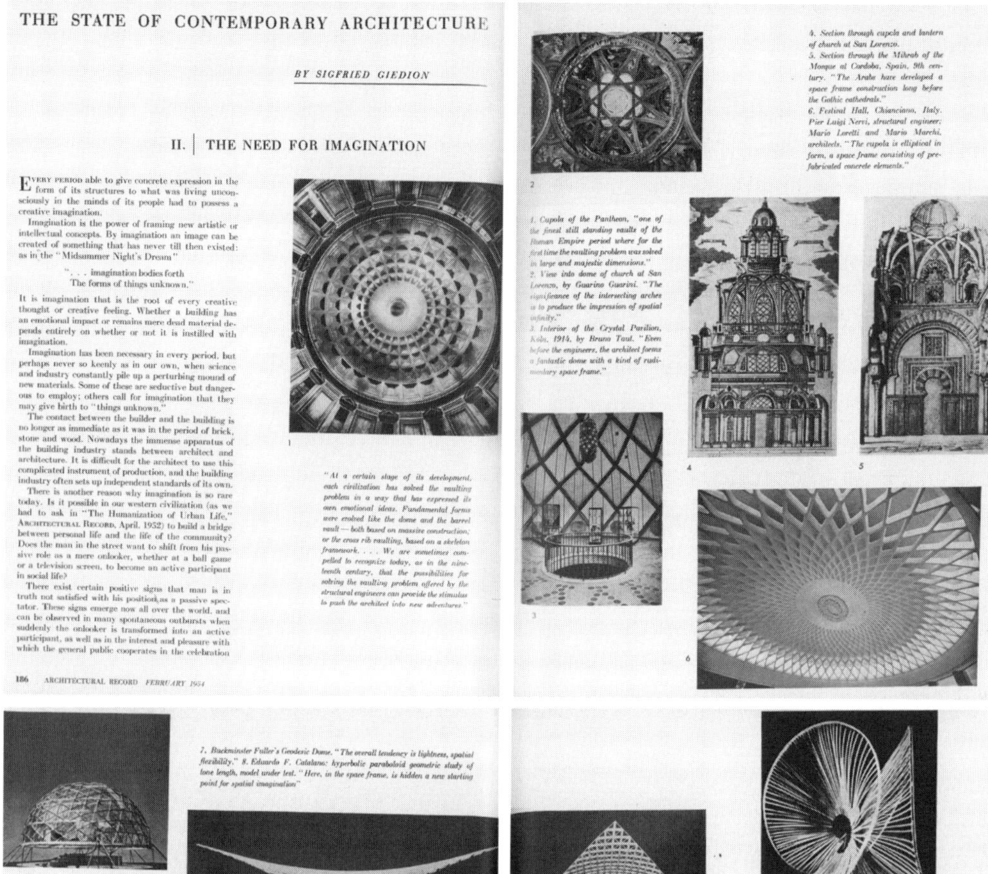

THE STATE OF CONTEMPORARY ARCHITECTURE

BY SIGFRIED GIEDION

II. | THE NEED FOR IMAGINATION

Every period able to give concrete expression in the form of its structures to what was living unconsciously in the minds of its people had to possess a creative imagination.

Imagination is the power of framing new artistic or intellectual concepts. By imagination an image can be created of something that has never till then existed: as in the "Midsummer Night's Dream"

> ". . . imagination bodies forth
> The forms of things unknown."

It is imagination that is the root of every creative thought or creative feeling. Whether a building has an emotional impact or remains mere dead material depends entirely on whether or not it is instilled with imagination.

Imagination has been necessary in every period, but perhaps never so keenly as in our own, when science and industry constantly pile up a perturbing mound of new materials. Some of these are seductive but dangerous to employ; others call for imagination that they may give birth to "things unknown."

The contact between the builder and the building is no longer as immediate as it was in the period of brick, stone and wood. Nowadays the immense apparatus of the building industry stands between architect and architecture. It is difficult for the architect to use this complicated instrument of production, and the building industry often sets up independent standards of its own.

There is another reason why imagination is so rare today. Is it possible in our western civilization (as we had to ask in "The Humanization of Urban Life," Architectural Record, April, 1952) to build a bridge between personal life and the life of the community? Does the man in the street want to shift from his passive role as a mere onlooker, whether at a ball game or a television screen, to become an active participant in social life?

There exist certain positive signs that man is in truth not satisfied with his position as a passive spectator. These signs emerge now all over the world, and can be observed in many spontaneous outbursts when suddenly the onlooker is transformed into an active participant, as well as in the interest and pleasure with which the general public cooperates in the celebration

1

"At a certain stage of its development, each civilization has solved the vaulting problem in a way that has expressed its own emotional ideas. Fundamental forms were evolved like the dome and the barrel vault — both based on massive construction; or the cross rib vaulting, based on a skeleton framework. . . . We are sometimes compelled to recognize today, as in the nineteenth century, that the possibilities for solving the vaulting problem offered by the structural engineers can provide the stimulus to push the architect into new adventures."

186 ARCHITECTURAL RECORD *FEBRUARY 1954*

2

1. Cupola of the Pantheon, "one of the finest still standing vaults of the Roman Empire period where for the first time the vaulting problem was solved in large and majestic dimensions."
2. View into dome of church at San Lorenzo, by Guarino Guarini. "The significance of the intersecting arches is to produce the impression of spatial infinity."
3. Interior of the Crystal Pavilion, Köln, 1914, by Bruno Taut. "Even before the engineers, the architect forms a fantastic dome with a kind of rudimentary space frame."

4. Section through cupola and lantern of church at San Lorenzo.
5. Section through the Mihrab of the Mosque at Cordoba, Spain, 9th century. "The Arabs have developed a space frame construction long before the Gothic cathedrals."
6. Festival Hall, Chianciano, Italy. Pier Luigi Nervi, structural engineer; Mario Loretti and Mario Marchi, architects. "The cupola is elliptical in form, a space frame consisting of prefabricated concrete elements."

3 4 5 6

7. Buckminster Fuller's Geodesic Dome. "The overall tendency is lightness, spatial flexibility." 8. Eduardo F. Catalano: hyperbolic paraboloid geometric study of lone length, model under test. "Here, in the space frame, is hidden a new starting point for spatial imagination"

7 8 9 10

9. Model of experimental space frame structure, being designed by graduate students of Institute of Design, under Konrad Wachsmann, in collaboration with Mies van der Rohe. Structure spans 200 feet, using identical length members allowing various means of support. 10. Space truss hangars, by Wachsmann.

of age-old customs. This was very evident in the recent coronation festivities in Britain, when many half-forgotten ceremonies were introduced anew.

This latent demand for a more developed social life is breaking through in many countries and is made manifest in new plans and projects which, once again after a long lapse of time, provide points of crystallization for the social life of the people. This self-healing process starts from different sides. In USA, recent plans for a new center in Philadelphia, the redevelopment of large blighted areas in Chicago, where four independent schemes are being carried out, the planned Boston Back Bay Center, or the enormous shopping center at Roosevelt Field, Long Island. Nearly all these schemes are showing traces of a new social imagination.

SOCIAL IMAGINATION

The fulfillment of this worldwide trend to create centers of social activity can no longer depend solely upon the technical capacities of the architect. His task today is far more complicated than, for instance, that of his Baroque predecessor, who was required to give form to the programs of a clearly structured society.

Most schemes of this sort that have been prepared are still in early stages of execution or remain mere paper plans, but one of the few examples where this social imagination has been given three dimensional expression is the much discussed and much decried "*Unite d'Habitation*," 1947-52.

The boldness of this venture does not consist in housing 1600 people under one roof. This has often been done in America. Its boldness consists in the elaborate way in which the architect has given form to the half-conscious tendencies of the crowd: its boldness lies in its *social imagination*. The individual inhabitant may prefer to remain a lost number in a huge building, or he may help to develop a social life that can draw him out of the melancholic isolation that is the common form of existence in every large city. The architect can do no more than provide the physical points of crystallization, and this Le Corbusier has done.

SPATIAL IMAGINATION

The need for imagination implies that there exists a need for something more than the bare interpretation of functional requirements.

Nothing is so difficult to find today as an imaginative handling of space — a *spatial* imagination. An

188 ARCHITECTURAL RECORD *FEBRUARY 1954*

8 11

11. Naum Gabo: spheric construction, Fountain, 1937, of plastic 16 inches high. "The development of space frame structures demands that sculptor and architect work together from the start, as well as the engineer." 12. Eduardo F. Catalano: Stadium La Pinta for 8,000 spectators, with aluminum space frame

12 12

imagination that can dispose volumes in space in such a way that new relations develop between differing structures, different edifices, so that they can merge into a new synthesis, a symbolic oneness.

Even greater hesitations arise when the building program demands that the architect create an interior space which transcends its purely technical and organizational requirements, as in great halls destined to reflect general aspirations — whether they be the nave of a Cathedral or the meeting place for a world organization.

The need for a monumental expression in art and architecture is one that has existed, and has been solved, in all civilizations. Our own cannot be an exception.

The area where the spatial imagination has always had the greatest freedom — where it could unfold with the least interference — has been the area that lies above normal utilitarian requirements. This is the space that floats over our heads, lying beyond the reach of our hands. It is here that the fullest freedom is granted to the imagination of the architect.

In two words, we are talking of the *vaulting problem*.

At a certain stage of its development, each civilization has solved the vaulting problem in a way that has expressed its own emotional ideas. Fundamental forms were evolved like the dome and the barrel vault — both based on massive construction; or the cross rib vaulting, based on a skeleton framework. The same form could be very differently handled (the Pantheon, the Byzantine Santa Sophia, or Michelangelo's Saint Peters), *but each civilization was able to find a solution which expressed its emotional convictions.*

What will be our answer to the vaulting problem? There is no certain answer. It is not possible to foretell, but a few signs do exist which point the direction in which we are moving.

We are sometimes compelled to recognize today, as in the nineteenth century, that the possibilities for solving the vaulting problem offered by the structural engineers can provide the stimulus to push the architect into new spatial adventures. But it seems that these possibilities are moving faster than the imaginative power of the architect to give them a symbolic human significance.

The space frame, as it has been developed in recent years by the engineers, uses the principle of equilibrating all forces within the vault itself, so that it can be

ARCHITECTURAL RECORD *FEBRUARY 1954* 189

FIGURE 3.32. Sigfried Giedion, lineage of the "vaulting problem." From "The State of Contemporary Architecture, II. The Need for Imagination," *Architectural Record* (February 1954). By permission of *Architectural Record*.

> At a certain stage of its development, each civilization has solved the vaulting problem in a way that has expressed its own emotional ideas. . . .
>
> What will be our answer to the vaulting problem?[39]

Giedion's suggestion is that the answer will emerge from new approaches to long-span structures, specifically space frames and doubly curved shells. Crucially, though, it is precisely because they rise "above normal utilitarian requirements" that these forms offer hope:

> The vaulting problem is certainly not the main factor in creating a community life. But the moulded sphere above the head always gives a decisive stimulus to the places where the community gathers for religious or political reasons, for a music festival or for theatrical performances. It is not the creation of an all-embracing sphere which changes immediately a chaotic crowd into an integrated community, but it is its foremost symbol.[40]

Giedion's illustrations offer a condensed historical lineage of "the vaulting problem": the Pantheon, Guarino Guarini's San Lorenzo, Taut's Crystal Pavilion, Pier Luigi Nervi's Festival Hall in Chianciano, Fuller's geodesic dome, Eduardo Catalano's study of a hyperbolic paraboloid structure, Konrad Wachsman and Mies van der Rohe's space frame structures. While, according to Giedion, this trajectory heads toward lightness and formal freedom, which were precisely the qualities that Otto would exploit, his images emphasize the historical continuity of "the vaulting problem" in the creation of symmetrical centralized spaces. This contrasts both with Otto's view of two distinct building lineages—one of compression and one of tension—and with his development away from centralized solutions toward naturalistic compositions.

One other image from Giedion's miniature gallery suggests another line of historical comparison with Otto's tensile roofs: the example of a "spheric construction" titled *Fountain* (1937) by the sculptor Naum Gabo. Ludwig Glaeser would make just this connection, as well as to the similar work of Gabo's brother Antoine Pevsner, in his catalog for Otto's exhibition at the Museum of Modern Art while also noting that these works had "no direct influence" on Otto.[41] The formal comparison is understandable given that both Otto's minimal surfaces and the constructions of Gabo and Pevsner feature complexly curving surfaces determined by their edge conditions. However, the similarity quickly breaks down, because the surfaces of Gabo and Pevsner are comparatively simple "ruled surfaces," that is, surfaces constructed by straight lines regularly spaced along the edge curves (a technique also used by Le Corbusier and Xenakis in their Philips Pavilion). While more challenging to represent than rectilinear forms, these "ruled surfaces" are nonetheless amenable to straightforward geometric and mathematical techniques. For instance, Robin Evans has shown how Le Corbusier's office was forced to convert large portions of the Ronchamp roof to ruled surfaces in order to simplify the representation and construction of the project.[42] In contrast, the great challenge of Otto's minimal surfaces, and the reason for the development of his elaborate design methods, was precisely that apart from the simplest cases, they had no mathematical definitions. Further, while the constructions of Gabo and Pevsner may use elements of string or wire in tension, the surfaces formed by these elements are typically not themselves tensile surfaces, meaning that they are unable to be made rigid in the way that Otto's surfaces can be and are therefore unsuitable as large-scale structural forms.

A better and deeper comparison of Otto's work to constructivism—and to better and deeper constructivism—can be made not at the formal level of curves in space but through a similar attitude toward materials and representation. Characterizing the work of the constructivist sculptor Karl Ioganson, Maria Gough argues that his work "constitutes an unrelenting investigation of tensility in the name of formulating a constructive practice with the greatest possible economy of both materials and energy. (In this regard, Russia's material shortage in the post–Civil War period has productive poignancy insofar as it could be said to have stimulated, rather than circumscribed, this investigation.)"[43] The parallel to Otto's attitude emerging from World War II is quite precise: the material constraints during and immediately after the war were, at least theoretically, a productive spur to his investigations. We should also note that Ioganson's use of tensility, like Otto's, was intrinsic, not compositional, creating works that were rigid or, in Gough's fine term, "locked in," just as Otto's roofs were.

However, we cannot simply transfer Gough's reading of Ioganson's tensile "cold structures" to Otto's pavilions. Paralleling the circumstances of postwar West Germany, Otto's works, though stimulated by a condition of material limitation, actually came to represent the opposite, as they tacitly but forcefully embodied the technical and economic power of the West German *Wirtschaftswunder* (economic miracle). In its form and materiality, the Expo 67 pavilion may not have been traditionally monumental, but it was surely not humble in its display of technological prowess. Furthermore, where Ioganson's structures pushed beyond the context of existing references, Otto's structures work within a postwar context of existing anticlastic forms and consciously rely on references to natural forms and processes. In this regard, one broad implication of Otto's pavilions for postwar architecture is that structure and processes of structuring will themselves become representational in newly important ways.

Here at last we come to see all that was implied in Otto's sighing disappointment with Fuller's grand geodesic dome. For just as important as any positive associations Otto's tensile surfaces may have had with landscapes or tents or bubbles was their negative significance: their ability to avoid the most traditional method of spanning a monumental space—the dome—any echo of which was foreclosed by its associations with the pomposity of National Socialism. Otto's roofs were important not just technically but because they advanced a new and acceptable formal vocabulary for

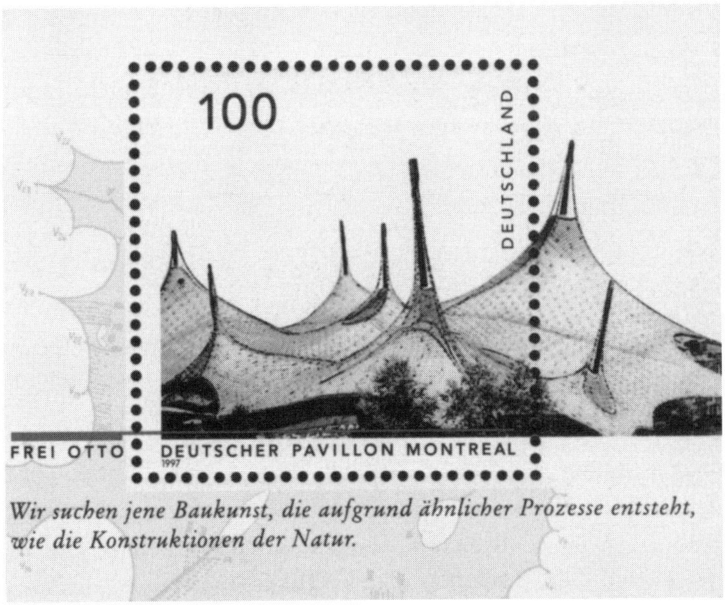

FIGURE 3.33. German postage stamp issued in 1997 depicting the West German pavilion at Expo 67, Montreal. From a four-stamp series titled "Deutsche Architektur nach 1945." The quotation from Otto translates as "We seek those building arts that arise due to similar processes as the constructions of nature."

large-scale national structures, a vocabulary reached through form-finding processes that did not escape design or representation but that were themselves representative of a new attitude toward design and its relationship to power. The conflation of the organic and the technological, the flexible and the rigid, the minimal and the elaborate, the automatic and the composed, and the natural and the political endowed Otto's projects with symbolic stresses that redoubled their structural tensions and were the key to their success as representations of postwar West Germany (fig. 3.33). Around the issues of monumentality, national expression, and technology, this architecture offers a series of incomplete negations, of concepts under erasure. The result was a symbol of a new Germany and, paradoxically, of an attitude toward design and building that struggled to move beyond symbolic representation, beyond nationalism, and in some sense beyond architecture itself.

The anticlastic vocabulary developed by Otto and others after 1945 reflects a fundamental distinction between prewar and postwar architecture, one specifically shaped by the issue of monumentality. The horrific abuses of power leading up to and during World War II produced a fundamental shift in architecture such that straightforward monumentality became a near impossibility. If Nietzsche famously claimed that "Architecture is a kind of eloquence of power in forms," the war, with its Nietzsche-dazzled ideologues, forced that age-old equation to be rethought.[44] Prewar architecture—what we might call the long synclastic age of architecture—could create monumentality by aligning technical achievement with monovocal assertions of power. Postwar architecture, apart from obviously regressive exceptions, had to find new ways to express power, whether national or institutional. We continue to live in this anticlastic era in which technical, economic, or political power cannot be celebrated directly but must be put under erasure so that it both is and is not expressed.[45]

THE MANNHEIM MULTIHALLE

The remarkable "landscape" of the West German Pavilion's tensile roof became immediately famous and served as the model for a grander project of national self-representation at the 1972 Munich Olympics. Much less attention was paid to another novel construction, now nearly forgotten, nestled beneath the pavilion's tented roof: the sprung wooden grid of a complex double-arched vault enclosing the pavilion's auditorium (fig. 3.34). Several years later, this small structure, too, would serve as the prototype for a larger project in which Otto played a leading role: the Multihalle in Mannheim, which was built as a large exhibition space for the 1975 West German Federal Garden Exhibition (figs. 3.35, 3.36). Using a contrasting structural approach and deployed within a national rather than international context, the Multihalle offers a second paradigmatic example of Otto's quasi-automatic design methodology and its resonances.

FIGURE 3.34. Rolf Gutbrod and Frei Otto, auditorium with wooden grid shell roof, West German Pavilion, Expo 67, Montreal, 1967. Courtesy of ILEK, University of Stuttgart.

FIGURE 3.35. Carlfried Mutschler + Partner with Frei Otto, Multihalle, Mannheim, Germany, 1975. By permission of RIBApix.

FIGURE 3.36. Carlfried Mutschler + Partner with Frei Otto, Multihalle, Mannheim, Germany, 1975. Courtesy of ILEK, University of Stuttgart.

Characterized as a whale, a satisfied snake, or perhaps a sculpture by Niki de Saint Phalle, the humped wooden grid-shell roof of the Multihalle covers a layer of concrete platforms and ramps on and under which activities can occur (the same strategy used at Expo 67). Unlike the Montreal pavilion, which was based on a grid of tensioned steel cables suspended between columns and edge cables, the Multihalle is made of timber lathes, which were assembled on the ground into a flat grid, then arched into place and held at, or near, the ground along the building's perimeter (fig. 3.37). The result is a "sprung" structural shell that was covered with a PVC-coated polyester membrane to provide a weatherproof skin. While the resulting space contains moments that recall the geometry of domes and arches, its highly irregular perimeter and overall horizontality result in a continually varying curvature that is entirely unlike the regularity of even the most baroque cupolas. As in Montreal, Otto's structure both intentionally mirrors and yet remains alien to the sculpted landscape in which it is nestled.

The relationship between this amorphous shell and what happened, or might happen, beneath it was much discussed during and after the Multihalle's completion, as was the question of what the form itself might mean. Although Otto did not take part in the initial project proposal, and although architect Carlfried Mutschler was responsible for the overall scheme, and although a vast team of designers and builders contributed—including a group of engineers led by Ted Happold of Ove Arup + Partners—the Mannheim roof was, in its essence, conceived by Otto and the IL. Apart from the short-lived Montreal pavilion, the Multihalle is the most significant realization of Otto's views on the entanglement of form, design process, and politics to create a democratic architecture in the postwar period. The Multihalle also demonstrates the most literal connection to his wartime experience. Asked about the technique of the Multihalle, Otto remarked that "I arrived at grid shells through building fuselages of gliders and not by constructing buildings."[46]

Extending their experience with the comparatively small Montreal auditorium roof, the IL ran a joint research program focused on grid shells from 1972 to 1974 with a Japanese team directed by Kenzo Tange and Takeshi Hasegawa. The result of this work was an extensive catalog of techniques for the determination and analysis of grid shells, which Otto's group utilized in Mannheim and which was published in 1975 as the tenth volume of the institute's journal. Much of this research was devoted to the exploration of catenary chain models (fig. 3.38), meshes suspended from variable fixed points that simply by hanging under their own weight demonstrate the idealized forms that a grid shell could take when the catenary forms are inverted. Previously, catenary models were used most famously by Antoni Gaudí as part of his design process for the Sagrada Família cathedral in Barcelona.

For Otto, the catenary models offered another method of "form finding" in which forces of nature were used to automate part of the design process, and one based on something far hardier than delicate soap bubbles. Though beginning with simple and

FIGURE 3.37. Carlfried Mutschler + Partner with Frei Otto, Multihalle, Mannheim, Germany, 1975; raising of the wooden grid shell. Courtesy of ILEK, University of Stuttgart.

symmetrical cases, the chain models, recorded in high-contrast photographs, were also used to demonstrate that an endless range of irregular catenary forms could be produced. In order to understand the architectural potential of the spaces that could be created through this method, the IL journal instructs the reader that the sequence of model photographs should be viewed one time in their original orientation with the chain nets hanging down and then a second time turned upside down to show how the nets might exist if constructed as grid shells.

For the Mannheim Multihalle, members of Otto's practice, Atelier Warmbronn,

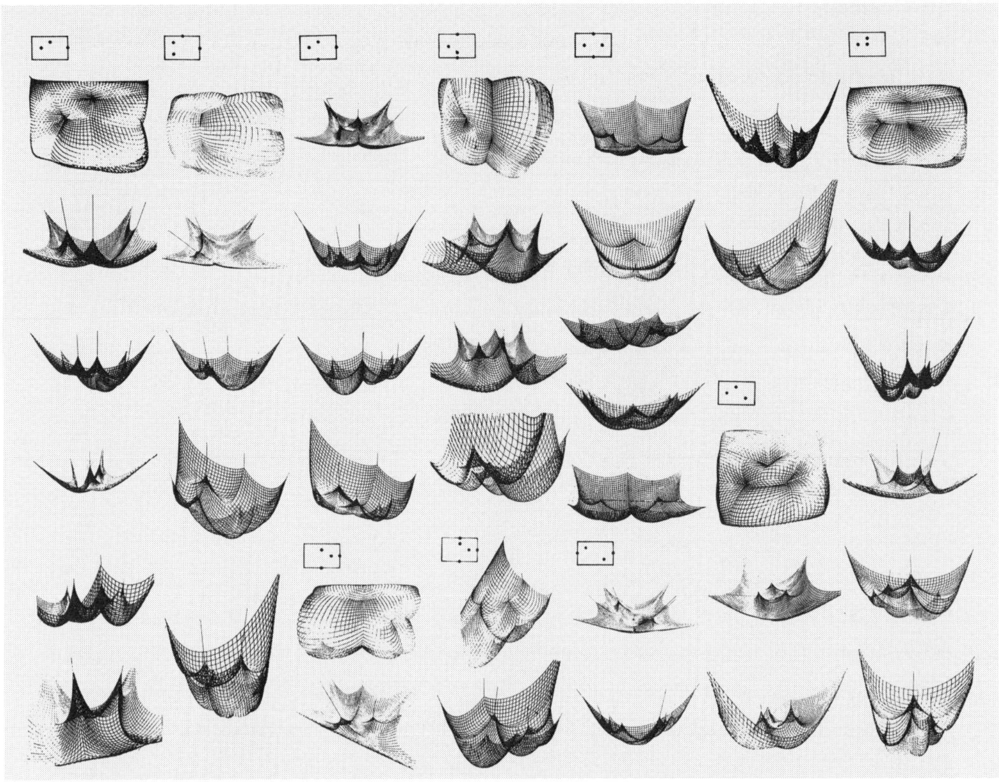

FIGURE 3.38. Jürgen Hennicke, Kazunori Matsushita, Frei Otto, Keizo Sataka, Eda Schaur, and Toshiyuki Shirayanagi, grid-shell forms determined by hanging chain nets with interior suspension points, Japanese-German research project at the Institute for Lightweight Structures, Stuttgart; published in *IL* 10 (1974). Courtesy of ILEK, University of Stuttgart.

and Mutschler and Partners created a catenary model at a scale of 1:100 with a chain grid representing every third wooden lath in the completed building (fig. 3.39). As with the Expo 67 pavilion, this physical model played an important part in the initial phases of the design process. However, because of developments in computational methods that had begun with Expo 67 and then had been greatly advanced during work on the Munich Olympics, the role of the physical model in the Mannheim design process, underway in 1974 and 1975, was greatly changed. In adjacent descriptions given by the physical and computational modeling teams in *IL* 13, one can see the physical model reluctantly giving way to the computational as the debate over their relative merits takes shape. The physical modelers open the issue in a defensive posture: "As manual work is expensive in constructing models, the question has to be asked whether, instead of the model construction, other methods for form finding could not be found, i.e., by means of draughting or calculating."[47]

The argument for the physical model is then made on three grounds: that any calculation process must begin with an initial rough form that can only be obtained from the physical model, that the computational model would not be interactive enough to allow exploration of the form, and that a computational model alone would itself be too expensive to produce. The subsequent summary of the computational modeling by the Institute for the Application of Geodesy in Construction at Stuttgart confronts exactly these points, noting that the initial rough values could have been obtained by pure calculation, demonstrating multiple perspective views of the calculated form, and emphasizing the low cost of the calculations (fig. 3.40). However, beyond all of this stood one undeniable reason for the computational approach, which was simply the physical limitations of a complex model one hundred times smaller than the realized building.

Ironically, given Otto's skeptical attitude toward computational models, it was his very interest in spontaneous form finding and his "minimal principle" that led to their necessity. For it was the integral binding of complex and continually varying geometry with optimized structural performance—the very factors that suggest comparison to organic structures—that pushed Otto's forms beyond the limitations of physical models. A more traditional architectural design process could separate the physical model as a representation of the appearance of a project from structural calculations, that is, the performance of the materials used to make the model need not have a relationship to the performance of the materials used in the building itself. In contrast, Otto's use of the model as a form-finding device meant that the model

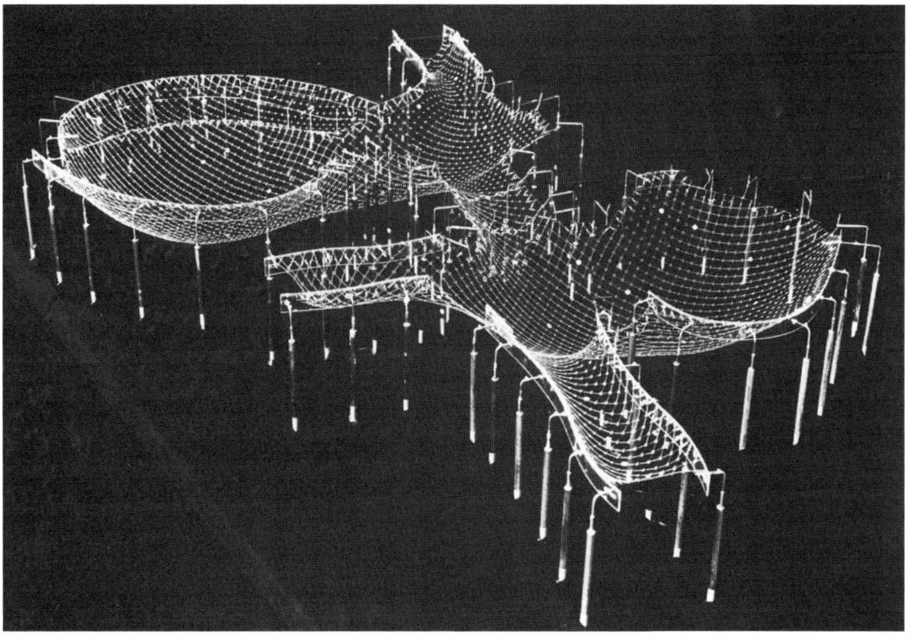

FIGURE 3.39. Carlfried Mutschler + Partners and Atelier Warmbronn (Frei Otto, Ewald Bubner, et al.), hanging chain model of the Multihalle Mannheim, ca. 1973. Courtesy of ILEK, University of Stuttgart.

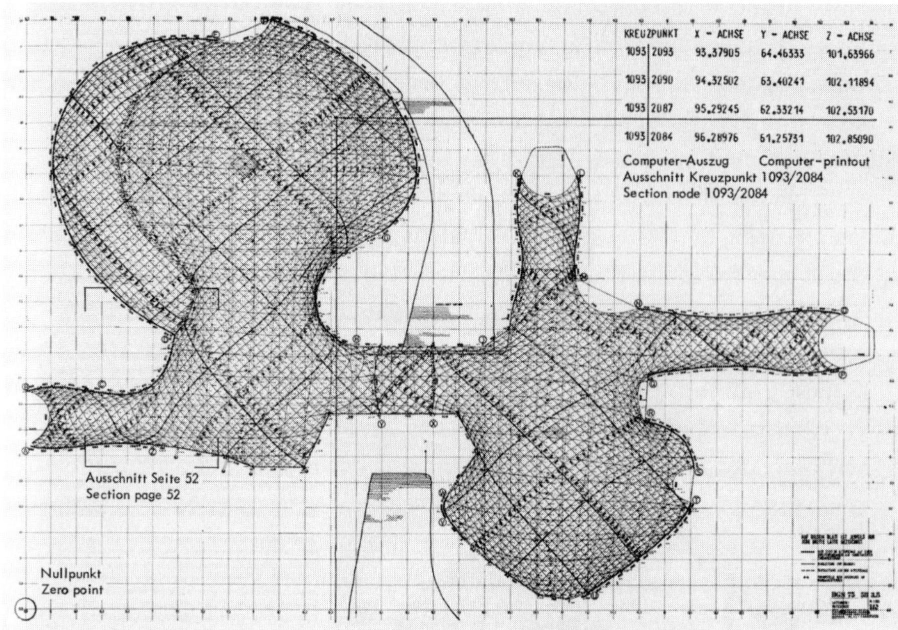

FIGURE 3.40. Institute for the Application of Geodesy in Construction (Lothar Gründig, Ulrich Hangleiter, and Hans Preuss), University of Stuttgart, computer generated plan, with hand notations, of the grid shell for the Multihalle Mannheim ca. 1974. Courtesy of ILEK, University of Stuttgart.

did not just passively represent but actively determined the form of the building. The somewhat perverse implication of this was that for larger buildings, physical models could not determine the form accurately enough, and the "spontaneous" physical form finding that Otto prized needed to be replaced by computational simulations of natural forces. Yet once moved to a simulated environment, there was no need that the forces be limited to "natural" ones—a possibility about which Otto was deeply distressed.[48]

Still, even with more advanced computational methods, Otto's devotion to a "minimal" attitude pushed his work beyond the wide margins of security normally used by structural engineers so that they found themselves in uncertain territory:

> I was really amazed at being able to build this work, a structure that, on the one hand, supported a load test that we carried out well. The building is still standing. . . . It's the work I've been the most afraid of; the most audacious work that really went beyond my knowledge back then and perhaps even my current knowledge. . . .
>
> The structure was correctly calculated, but we knew and had a feeling of the difficulties it could have. I must be thankful that it has never had to support excessive loads, which could have destroyed it. Originally, the pavilion was supposed to remain only during the Federal Garden Exposition. It was allowed to continue

standing there but surely one day it will be taken down. Nevertheless, the older it gets, the more anxious I become. I don't know what I should do: Should I warn the owner that it would be better to tear it down so that I can sleep better?[49]

If one explanation of the unusual Multihalle can be found in Otto's structural and design methods research, another, one offered at the time and hinted at by its very name, is that the building's form is the result of its program. Winfried Langner, one of the project architects, has given a comically deferred description of the way in which ideas about program were reflected in the project's shape:

> [N]ot the roof was the goal of all planning—the roof was only a means to some purpose.
>
> The purpose was space formation. Space formation, what for? . . .
>
> [The] contest [for the Garden Show] required ideas, not concerning the architectural design of [a] functional programme fixed by the institution arranging the contest, as is customary, but first of all proposals and suggestions about the necessary and or potential functions themselves.
>
> . . . In addition to the relatively handy term "restaurant-coffee shop-snacks," [the proposal] shows such flowery terms as "festival garden" [Kerwegarten], "dance hall," "revolving stage with music and show," "climbing mountain," "snail noodles," "[w]ell of light," etc. . . .
>
> . . . let us list the various stations covered when looking for a use:
>
> Youth meeting place
> Sport hall
> Citizens' forum
> Exhibition hall
> Room for entertainment
>
> Owing to the fact that in spite of desperate efforts, [we] could not agree on a final utilization programme as a tangible basis for . . . planning, the designed structure was called "Multihalle" [the German text adds, "und schon schien alles klar zu sein" (and then everything seemed to be alright)].[50]

Yet as Langer admits, this obviously only restated the original problem of what the building was for (other than a temporary exhibition of flowers).

> The expert reader surmises that even with such a clever term the problem and question with which the architect bothers the contractor are far from solved. . . .
>
> What is the purpose of this hall?
>
> "Build an exhibition hall in which other events can be organized."[51]

He continues with a criticism of this very idea.

> Nobody will ask from a small car that it should be simultaneously a racing car, cross-country vehicle, amphibian car, armoured car and luxury car and should cost, if possible, only half the amount paid by the neighbor for his serial car.

> Everybody knows that one function almost excludes the other function and that all the functions can never be accomplished in one vehicle in an optimal fashion.
>
> Therefore, in general language usage there is no general term "multipurpose car" [Mehrzweckauto].
>
> [In architecture however] another word . . . became familiar as the essence of progress; surprisingly it is associated with the commercial slogan: good value, cheap and economical: Multihalle.[52]

In its unlimited desire for multiplicity and flexibility of program, the Multihalle was clearly a somewhat late child of the 1960s. Although according to one prediction, it arrived right on time. In 1968 Peter Cook of the Archigram group produced a projection of architecture's near future, a time line in which the rectilinear buildings of modernism give way to biomorphic forms and where he imagined that soon the use of a great numbers of parts "means that a system can be bent" into curvilinear geometries (fig. 3.41). The Multihalle in Mannheim, the amorphous grid-shell structure of which is literally a system that is bent, was perhaps the only built project to fulfill this formal and political prophesy on schedule. Even its combination of programmatic platforms and shell-like enclosure resembles Cook's vision. Indeed, the desire for flexibility was so overriding that the competition proposal showed several alternatives for covering a cluster of programmatic bubbles, including rather direct copies of the Montreal pavilion, and even a roof suspended beneath a flock of balloons, but not the grid shell that was eventually built.

Created out of Otto's naturalizing techniques, the Multihalle demonstrates the programmatic and political weaknesses of total flexibility. As Langner kept asking, "What is the purpose of this hall?" Still guided by their reactions to World War II, the planners and architects, certainly including Otto, envisioned an architecture that was democratic by virtue of being as open and as undefined as possible. But openness can so easily slip into emptiness, that—absent the sort of collective and ritualized events that Giedion had imagined—the multiplicity of the Multihalle might be simply apolitical (fig. 3.42). While in the larger, fraught context of 1970s Germany such gaps in social space might have their own political use by offering momentary escapes from engagement, these were negative virtues. And here, finally, Otto's construction did perhaps come to resemble nature itself in that it was not so much *Mehrzweck* (multipurpose) as *Zwecklos* (purposeless).

POSTSCRIPT ON A POSTSCRIPT

After standing historically isolated for twenty years as a radically singular building, the Mannheim Multihalle made a revealing reappearance in a short postscript to Greg Lynn's 1996 essay "Blobs (or Why Tectonics Is Square and Topology Is Groovy)."[53]

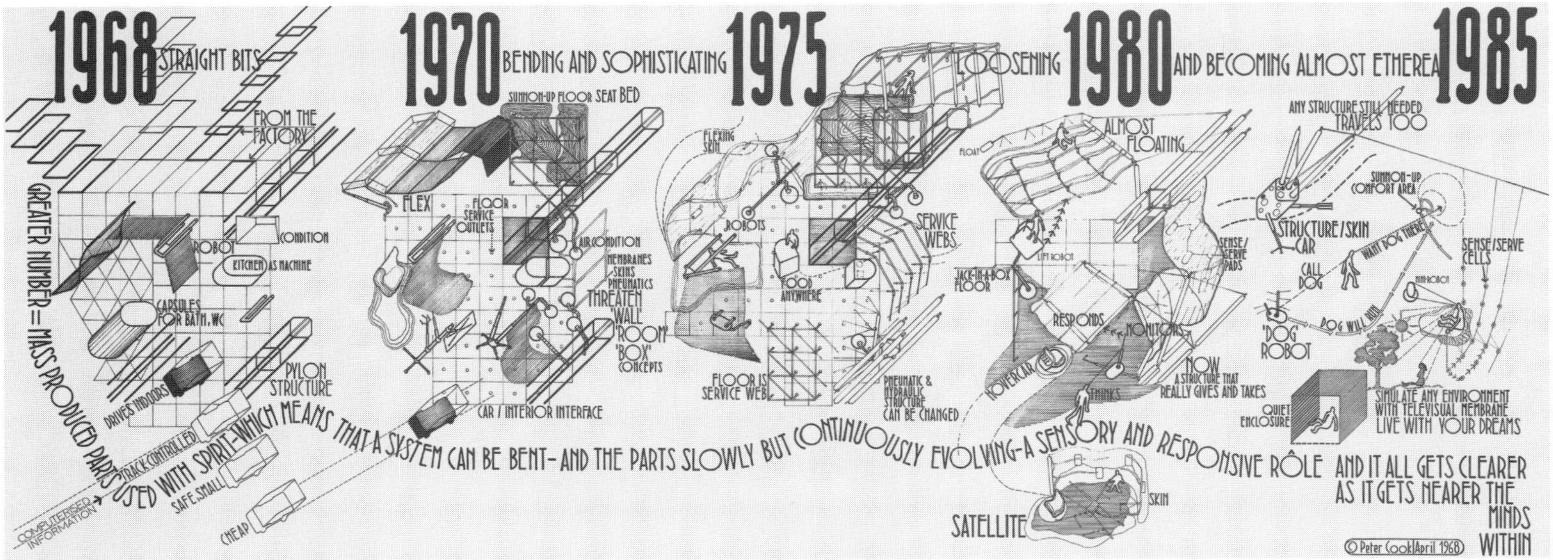

FIGURE 3.41. Archigram, "Control and Choice, Metamorphosis Sequence. Some prognostications on how a Control and Choice situation might evolve," 1968. Copyright © 1968 Peter Cook / Archigram.

FIGURE 3.42. Performance from the Annual Exhibition of the Association of German Artists in the Multihalle, Mannheim, Germany, 1976. Courtesy of ILEK, University of Stuttgart.

Lynn suggests there that the "Mannheim Pavilion" stands as one of the most important precedents for the amorphous forms he identifies as a new direction in contemporary architecture. The Multihalle surely was one of the few built precursors for the new "blob" topology that Lynn was advocating.

Echoing in part, and one assumes unintentionally, Giedion's discussion of the "vaulting problem," Lynn suggests that, although blob construction has so far been limited to complex roof forms, this has often been true of architectural experiments because "it is there that form, structure and tectonics are so intricately entwined."[54] (Giedion would have added "signification," which Lynn characteristically leaves as a tacit assumption.) Two aspects of "blob tectonics" seem particularly relevant to the Multihalle. First, that "Blobs suggest alternative strategies of structural organization and construction that provide intricate and complex new ways of relating the homogeneous or general to the heterogeneous or particular."[55] Though Otto would not have emphasized intricacy or complexity, this description exactly fits the most spectacular projects with which he was involved, particularly the Multihalle, the Expo 67 pavilion, and the Munich Olympic roofs. In each case a semiautomatic form-finding process determined with great precision the complex and varying organization of thousands of elements into a single pseudobiomorphic system. Second, Lynn argues that blobs challenge the fundamental assertion of traditional tectonics, which he calls a fallacy, that architecture must "stand upright."[56] Though again the terminology has shifted, we can see here a parallel reaching back to Otto's dissertation and his interest there in developing an alternative to the traditional architecture of stone, monumentality, and permanence.

However, equally important are two distinctions between Otto's worldview and that of Lynn. First, it is of fundamental importance to Otto that his form finding is driven by natural forces so that its results are, in his view, harmonious with the natural world. As described above, he specifically identified what he saw as the danger of computational modeling becoming detached from these natural forces. In contrast, it is just the freedom of such computational tools that Lynn celebrates as well as the accompanying possibilities of their "plasmaticity," their ability to turn any form into another. If Lynn has elsewhere shown great interest in certain biological processes, such as epigenesis and evolution, it has not been in order to idealistically reunite architecture and nature but to bring the alterity of nature into design. On the other hand, one can see that despite Otto's goals, the Multihalle turned out to be as alien as any of Lynn's projects.

The second difference between Otto's work of the 1960s and 1970s and Lynn's twenty to thirty years later is that of political context. While, as suggested above, one could question the political effect of the Multihalle, its aformal form was nonetheless politically legible against the context of a West Germany that was still very much postwar. Its amorphous shape and lightweight construction still represented a rejection of monumentalized power. In comparison, Lynn's late 1990s vocabulary of blobs, folds, and pliancy is explicitly situated within both the formalist architectural lineage of Peter Eisenman and Colin Rowe and the technical context of the film and aerospace industries of Southern California. It is therefore difficult to read a political valence in these forms that echo the Multihalle. Making a similar point, Michael Hays and Catherine Ingraham suggested that such revivals were neutralized by being embedded in the "diffuse utopia of the computer" and that political assessment would be possible only once they were actually built.[57]

And now they are being built. The last fifteen years have seen the construction of projects that directly take up the forms and strategies developed by Otto for Expo 67 and Mannheim, including projects in which he has been directly involved, such as his collaboration with Shigeru Ban on the Japanese Pavilion for Expo 2000 in Hannover and with Christoph Ingenhoven on the controversial new main train station for Stuttgart, or a project like Ban's Centre Pomidou-Metz, which is clearly the product of a marriage between the Montreal pavilion and the Multihalle. What these and many other major recent built works demonstrate is that the sense of a "diffuse utopia" can be extended beyond computation to a general apolitical naturalism that positions itself beyond the "end of history," which is certainly where Otto has long hoped we could build. Yet it is crucial to recognize that Otto's own work was, nonetheless, always lodged within a very specific and highly charged national political context. Deployed as the vocabulary of a politically indifferent globalized architecture, that specificity is lost, and Otto's form-finding forms are reduced from signs of political aspiration to evidence of political indifference.

CONCLUSION: FROM AUTOMATIC ARCHITECTURE TO ARCHITECTURAL AUTOMATISMS

[T]he task of the modern artist [is] one of creating not a new instance of his art but a new medium in it. One might think of this as the task of establishing a new automatism.

—Stanley Cavell, *The World Viewed*

POSTMEDIUM ARCHITECTURE

No one could say that as a discipline, architecture has ignored the influence of computation and the vast new ecosystem of form generation, representation, analysis, and fabrication that is computationally based. If anything, the flood of books, journals, exhibitions, conferences, studios, and projects has been enough to induce widespread fatigue as evidenced by the list of overexposed terms such as *virtual*, *digital*, *algorithmic*, and *parametric*. Yet these explorations have too often been solipsistic and isolated, both historically and aesthetically, as if the new technologies had generated their own contexts ex nihilo rather than having emerged within a preexisting cultural skein. What is needed is the maturation of architectural practice and criticism beyond these isolated positions so that computational methods can be considered within, rather than simply against, broader historical and aesthetic contexts. So, although we might perhaps like to simply get beyond thinking about computation, we are obliged to continue working through its implications.

One of the consequences of the computational turn is that architecture has belatedly become, like contemporary art generally, a postmedium practice, understanding that "postmedium" does not mean a lack of mediation but a lack of stable and canonical mediums. In some sense, we could say that architecture has always been a post- or transmedium art, deploying an ever-expanding range of representational modes, including many varieties of drawing, physical models, photography, film, video, texts, legal contracts, and ultimately buildings and landscapes themselves. Still, while recognizing the complexity of architectural practice and the range of representational modes that deserve consideration, there has been for many centuries a "special relationship" to drawing. The stability of drawing conventions has provided cover for the actual variety of architecture's mediums. The disruption of those conventions by computational representation both exposes and entirely reconfigures this complexity, with computation now demanding special attention.

As Rosalind Krauss has argued, even after the implosion of essentializing medium specificity, what could inelegantly be called "Greenbergianism," critically minded art practices must still grapple with the dilemmas of mediums. However, these mediums must be understood to refer to what Krauss calls the "layered, complex relationship that we would call a *recursive structure*," that is, the historically constructed conditions that shape practices rather than mediums differentiated simply by materiality, such as painting, sculpture, film, or video.[1] I want to suggest that if, through the displacement of drawing, architecture has belatedly also reached a "postmedium condition," then critical thinking about contemporary architecture would need to follow a similar path. In this postmedium condition, centered around computation, the automatic becomes a theme of new importance, and the cases I have discussed in the preceding chapters function as important transitions between the previous state of modernism and that of our present.

While the dissolution of modernism in the 1960s left architecture without an ideological consensus, the development of computational design media since that time has overturned the long-established convention by which the discipline, despite many revolutions, has identified itself since the Renaissance: that is, architecture as drawing toward building. For fifty years now, research in architecture and related disciplines has pursued, and increasingly realized, a vision of a design process fully integrated through computation, in which a highly flexible model carrying all geometric, material, and performance data could be seamlessly translated into a material result. Though often rhetorically burdened by architecture's own versions of medium specificity, by fundamentalisms holding that architecture can be reduced to function or structure or form or energy use, the main result of advances in computation-based architecture has been only a proliferation of possibilities, an explosion in the range of what is buildable.

On their arrival in firms during the 1970s, computer-aided drafting systems were typically understood simply as digital drawing boards, offering a more efficient way to produce the same types of drawings (primarily construction documents) that had previously been made by hand. Yet even in its primitive states, the representation of architecture by computer held greater implications, implications inherent to the system of representation. Whereas in physical drawing a static material ground receives marks of nearly equal stability, in a digital representation the "ground," if there is one, is a continuously looping and reactive cycle of algorithms invisibly humming behind (or beneath or beside) a graphic display that offers a fleeting and partial glimpse of this activity. Thus, the shift from material to digital representation has entailed the inherent activation of the representation so that any stable state becomes not the default condition but a highly artificial construction, a form of suspended animation. Material outputs, such as prints or models, are now momentary impressions—life masks—of the ever-variable computational model (in the most advanced building practices computational models have even displaced paper documents as the legal object of record). Even a completed building may appear to be little more than the record of the computation-based process of its creation.

A series of consequences flow from the dynamism—one could nearly say vitalism—of computer-based representation. To an unprecedented extent it becomes natural (or, better, "second nature") to conceive of design as the process of designing a process and to think of architectural form as the product of a sequence of semiautomatic transformations. The capacity to embed ever-more complex automated processes within architecture's representational system is unprecedented and lies behind the range of complex forms that have become the face of advanced architecture. Under a variety of labels—*algorithmic, parametric, genetic, nonlinear, nonstandard, intricate, animate, blob*—the most significant examples of this work disrupt the core presumptions of architecture, altering both the architect's authorial role and the conventional understanding of a "design" as a singular and static referent. Distinct from the now universal employment of computers to represent and realize a project first designed by traditional means, fully computational architecture explores the possibilities of *generating* architecture, wholly or in part, by algorithmic methods.

As we advance onto a computational ground for architecture, we should be interested in theoretical and historical parallels that might help us understand this transition more deeply. It is in this spirit, and as a means of advancing our understanding of the automatic, that I want to turn to the work of Stanley Cavell, particularly his 1971 book *The World Viewed* and the essays "Music Discomposed" and "A Matter of Meaning It" from a few years earlier. By extension I will also be touching on the work of his conversational partner Michael Fried and that of Krauss, whose thought has been fundamentally shaped by Cavell. Apart from a handful of asides, Cavell does not speak about architecture directly and, perhaps because of this, he has been almost entirely absent from architectural discussions.[2]

It is necessary to my argument that we recognize that developments within the arts need not be synchronized and that at least since industrialization, architecture has always been a special case, often moving in its own direction, at its own speed, and reacting to cultural conditions in ways that can be quite distinct from other disciplines.[3] We must also understand, as Cavell does, modernism not as a strictly delineated historical period but as a worldview available over an extended, and still extending, stretch of time. It is in this spirit that writing in the late 1960s he noted that "within the last decade film has been moving into the modernist environment inhabited for generations by other major arts, within which each art has had to fight for its survival, to justify its existence in its own way."[4] By parallel, and though it may sound odd, my argument is that it is only within the last two decades that architecture has also, at last, moved into the modernist environment or at least has done so more fully than ever before.

To make better sense of this claim, it will help to follow Cavell's distinction between *modernist* and *modernizing*. According to these terms, architectural modernism was typically *modernizing* not *modernist*.[5] What does this mean? Modern architecture, from Otto Wagner to Ludwig Mies van der Rohe's last works and beyond, was not modernist in the sense that it rarely understood self-critique as its fundamental and unsurpassable task. Instead, with rare exceptions, since the beginning of architectural modernism, architects have repeatedly attempted singular rejections of inherited systems (the classical orders, academic styles, modernism, postmodernism) only in order to assert the establishment of an equally singular new paradigm once and for all. Not incidentally, this recurring desire to "solve" the modernist condition allowed these modernizing architectures to be easily co-opted by mere expediency, whether commercial or political.

In my introduction I described the examples treated here—the design methods theories of Christopher Alexander and Lionel March, the dissertation and early houses of Peter Eisenman, and the form-finding research of Frei Otto—as varied attempts to relaunch the *modernizing* project of modern architecture, to stabilize the methods and values of architecture by an appeal to fields beyond architecture (mathematics, logic, form, nature). Initially at least, they all attempted an escape from the dilemmas of the *modernist* critical position as it has been understood from Kant onward. Yet these cases are also not simple continuations of earlier modernisms. Given the disruptions of World War II, they could not be. Instead, they revive certain modernizing aspirations within a new context in which computation made automation conceptually pressing and technically plausible. Each, in its way, summons a desire of modern architecture across the cataclysm of the war and remakes that desire within what is still largely our own context today. This distinguishes these cases from figures such as Mies van der Rohe and Walter Gropius, who carried *themselves* across this upheaval and often across an ocean, in order to continuing working in a world that had changed around them. For these postwar figures, the notion of a de-authored, automatic design method took on a new importance and a new zreality.

However, while each of these practices attempted to purify itself, to become fully automatic, each in the course of its explorations also came to acknowledge, if intermittently, the limitations of the automatic and to understand itself more accurately as a practice that included and responded to automatic aspects without in fact being entirely automatic. Each follows a trajectory from the automatic to the semiautomatic. This condition of practicing semiautomatically, which emerges in these practices of the postwar period, has extended and developed to become a constitutive mode of contemporary architecture. It is also this shift, from the automatic as a supposed absolute end to the automatic as a historically characteristic means, that makes Cavell's reflections on artistic production so relevant to architecture today.

ARCHITECTURAL AUTOMATISMS

With historical distance, it has become clear that the modernizing and unifying efforts of architecture in the first half of the twentieth century were in fact an exception within a much longer stretch, since the Enlightenment, of more fundamental instability. Or, to paraphrase a remark by Jacques Herzog, modernism has left us with technologies but no codes.[6] Just this is what Cavell insists is *the* modernist problem for the arts: that there are no longer viable conventions or forms of practice available to the artist within which works can be created. Absent these given forms, each art is left to discover what it is as art. As Cavell describes the situation,

> [w]hat modernist painting proves is that we do not know a priori what painting has to do or be faithful to in order to remain painting. . . . [W]hat a painter or poet or composer has to achieve in his painting or poetry or music is not a landscape or sonnet or fugue, but the idea of his art as such.[7]

This is the consequence for art of Kantian modernism, for which critique must be both individually internalized and ever ongoing.

For Cavell, the importance of the genres, forms, and techniques of traditional arts is that they provided structures and limits within which meaningful expression could occur, what he calls "the taking and seizing of chances." As these traditional modes dissolved, he argues, each artist was left to formulate a practice, a way of working, and a set of concerns that has the potential to generate meaningful works. "Modernism," he writes,

> signifies not that the powers of the arts are exhausted, but on the contrary that it has become the immediate task of the artist to achieve in his art the muse of art itself—to declare, from itself, the art as a whole for which it speaks, to become a present of that art. One might say that the task is no longer to produce another instance of an art but a new medium within it.[8]

In order to emphasize the externality of these formulations—their status as more than personalistic styles—Cavell names these ways of working, these new mediums, *automatisms*, a term he borrows from surrealism and deploys in new senses. The concept of automatism is at the center of Cavell's reflections on problems shared by the arts around the middle of the twentieth century and, in turn, has had a great influence on Krauss's analysis of the "postmedium condition" of the arts since the 1960s. Cavell's use of this term is complicated, perhaps irredeemably so, encompassing within it the mechanical automation of the motion-picture camera, the material techniques of painting and music, and the working methods of artists generally. Clearly the choice of the term *automatism* rather than one of the more established possibilities that suggest themselves, such as *medium*, *form*, or *genre*, expresses the importance he attaches to the idea that at all of these levels, it is necessary that there be something literally, or effectively, automatic in the process of artistic production. For although an automatism is emphatically not simply automatic, some variety or sense of the automatic plays an indispensable role in this concept. It is crucial that with an automatism the artist establishes a form of practice that, to some extent, proceeds on its own, independently of the artist, that the artist creates a process in which he or she is then caught up.

Similarly, while one could identify a number of other efforts to reformulate architecture during the period of modernism's dissolution—for example, around the concepts of typology or pop culture or tectonics—the cases I have described here function as automatisms, in Cavell's sense, by placing a special emphasis on the design process itself and on its automation. Or, more precisely, automatism is what each of these practices moved into as it passed beyond a desire for the fully automatic. For while some sense of the automatic is central to his concept of automatism, as is reflected in the term itself, it is equally important that an automatism is not merely automatic. Instead, an automatism is shaped by a dialectic of what is automatic, or systematic and the spontaneous artistic moves that are possible within or against this system. Thus, productive automatisms are always semiautomatic, impure systems disrupted by external influences.

With the dissolution of traditional forms, Cavell sees modern artists confronting two unacceptable varieties of the completely automatic: the meaninglessness of either absolute organization or absolute chance. On one side is the risk of "total organization," demonstrated by the compositions of Karlheinz Stockhausen, where artistic responsibility is displaced by an empty formal system. On the other side is the "radical ceding" of artistic control, and even the dissolution of art itself, proposed by John Cage's chance operations.

The objection to either of these extremes is only that they leave us—with our unsystematic bodies, histories, and politics—out. It is only we who prevent the completion of a system; only we who require artistic automatisms that are not entirely automatic. Cavell's argument is that art, in order to remain art, must not collapse into the fully automatic, but must offer both recognizable coherence and the possibility of improvisation, of discovery, of "taking and seizing chances." Such tendencies toward total automation are surely present in each of the cases I have considered here, but each also offers a historical example of that tendency being tempered, resisted, and complicated by other concerns. The concept of automatism becomes significant to an architectural world in which computation, with its many automations, has become the pervasive means of production. Paraphrasing Cavell, one could say that what architects today must propose are automatisms of automation. That is, architects must attempt to wrest substantial ways of practicing out of the various, and variable, constellation of automated technologies available.

The concept of automatism anticipates the stance of reflective users of computation in architecture. Greg Lynn, for instance, has said that his Embryological House was motivated by the desire to use computers in a way that was unpredictable, but not completely arbitrary; and has described the computer as a "pet" which is partially domesticated and partially wild.[9] Or consider Michael Meredith's anthology *From Control to Design*, the title of which indicates the importance of bending computational methods toward problems of meaning and affect that are beyond mere calculation. The book expresses the desire for a generational shift, so that the use of computational methods is no longer an end in itself, as it has often seemed to be, but becomes integrated into broader practices exploring new expressive terrain. For example, the project "Afterparty" (2009), designed by Meredith's firm MOS for P.S. 1 in New York, used computational form finding to map a cluster of hyperbolic paraboloids, but these were then materialized as the vision of a future ruin resonant with themes of environmental and economic collapse. The presumption here is that technical automation should lead to meaningful aesthetic discoveries, discoveries that must be, in Cavell's word, "seized" and developed alertly through an active effort to "mean it." This self-aware effort distinguishes Cavell's automatism from the more automatic "automatisms" of surrealism.

A principal challenge for contemporary practice is that the freedom offered by computation seems to be of the "nothing left to lose" variety, prompting a motivational crisis to which self-imposed restraint—the discovery of an automatism—is the only productive response. The question is, when anything goes, what matters? In this respect architecture today reenacts the dilemmas of composition and expression that were central to postwar art. As in postwar abstraction, contemporary architecture has come to be constituted by a great variety of approaches, each of which strives to be autonomous and internally systematic. Because projects can now be designed, at least in part, by code, by computational algorithm, the architect stands farther removed from the realized building, no longer composing representations of reality but manipulating computer scripts that generate representations of reality. The potential for systematic variation offered by computation along with the sheer speed of computational representation allows the exploration of vast series of possible solutions for any one project. In this way March's vision of computers enabling the "artificial evolution" of architectural possibilities now plays out within individual practices and for individual projects rather than publicly and collectively as he had hoped. This difference separates the current neoliberal environment from the neosocialist one March hoped to summon. One result is that taste enters in a new way as architects adjust limits and select versions, pruning and nurturing quasi-animate representations of projects, and become, in some sense, clients of their own semiautomatic design processes.

The emphasis on process means that the aesthetic project of contemporary architecture has come to resemble that of minimalism in painting and sculpture, with a similar interest in creation through series and by selection rather than through the intuitive gesture. In this sense we can say that contemporary architecture is for the first time confronting the issues of postwar abstraction rather than those of cubism or constructivism. For Cavell, working in series becomes indispensable as a way of developing and expressing significance, of discovering and displaying what matters for an automatism. He repeatedly stresses that while there are undeniable technical bases to artistic practice, especially in a case such as film, technical innovations do not automatically lead to meaningful artistic discoveries: "To make them 'possibilities of the medium' is to realize what will give them *significance*. . . . What it means is that the aesthetic possibilities of a medium are not givens."[10] Series become essential because they play out and test the relationship between technical automation and the historical and existential conditions of art. Similarly, serial work tests the relationship of forming and form, of process and result. If contemporary architecture now emerges from these same dualities, then working in series takes on a new importance, though the possibilities for working in series may be different, and more limited in realization, than those available to painting or music. Nonetheless, the use of serial techniques is of equal importance for gaining conviction in what is being done.

Looking back, March and Eisenman were both unusual in pointing to the importance of serial practices in music (already well established) and in the visual arts (the contemporaneous work of minimalism and conceptualism). By the time March established the Centre for Land Use and Built Form Study at Cambridge, he was already, and would remain, a practicing serial artist. In 1962 he described his work as an attempt to translate into the visual arts the "almost half century of musical tradition" of serialism. At nearly the same time, it was just this musical serialism that provided a major impetus for Cavell's thinking on the aesthetic problems of postwar art generally and his development of the notion of automatism.

Over the course of five decades Eisenman has interrogated architecture through means that are central to Cavell's notion of automatism: systems, series, authorial distance, and quasi-spontaneous technical generation. Initially foreclosed, it was only with the recognition of the alienating effects of his formal logic—of the conflicted interface between his abstract forms and the existing world of materials, bodies, and norms—that Eisenman's work became a full realization of automatism. Within this conflict it is always autonomous formalism that is emphasized in order to ward off the collapse of the disciplinary autonomy for which he has struggled. By formulating a quasi-autonomous method out of the history of the discipline, Eisenman had produced an architectural version of postmedium practice.

Further, I would argue that it is precisely the humanist/posthumanist dilemma, so important to Eisenman's career, that is also central to Cavell's formulation of automatism, turning as it does around the desire to generate meaningful choices, however precariously, within a postwar world in which "the dominant cosmologies of the past," as well as artistic forms, have been lost. With House VI, Eisenman produced the architectural result of such an automatism: a building formed in a quasi-systematic way out of an intensely elaborated artistic exploration; derived from the discipline's own history; deployed as a confrontation of the subject, the discipline, and society at large; and thereby offered as a context for choices about forms of inhabitation and forms of meaning.

PLASMATICITY AND WORLDLY AUTOMATISMS

With computation as the new ground of architecture, processes of form generation can now take a leading role. Architectural form becomes the product of dynamic, often quasi-automatic forming processes. When combined with a proliferation of possibilities, with an explosion in the range of what is buildable, new aesthetic difficulties arise. One of these, prefigured by March's distortion of the Seagram Building, is identified by Cavell's remarks on animation and his argument for distinguishing animation from film (or what he means by film). His thinking about animation is informed by, though opposed to, Sergei Eisenstein's interest in the metamorphic ability within animation for anything to become anything else. Mickey Mouse's gloved hands, for example, can become two dancing figures with arms and legs of their own, and then just as easily return to being Mickey's hands, a quality Eisenstein described as animation's "plasmaticity." (Though for Eisenstein this was not a problem but a source of fascination.[11])

In animation the laws of our reality—of gravity, of the conservation of mass, of mortality—do not hold. Because of similarities in the technical support of computational representation—the fact that the geometric model underlying the display is inherently transformable—computational architecture presents a similar situation with similar risks. After all, among the first polemically computational architectural projects in the 1990s were the "blobs" of Lynn and others, the "plasmaticity" of which was embraced and theorized by Lynn through the term *animate*. Like their cell-based predecessors, these forms seemed to have the capability of becoming anything, although the static condition of architecture meant that capability remained only potential. Designed within the void of virtual space, these speculative projects often contained no sense of gravity or of materiality.

In contrast, the importance that Cavell attaches to film, or any art, is its ability to present the world to us and to make us present in the world. From this view, the risk of computational representation lies in its ever-tempting capacity to present a world without us—a cartoon world, or a world of cartoon qualities, in which we do not have a place. And if these worlds are not just projected but are built, then our world becomes punctuated by unworldly buildings. True, architecture, not being solely reproductive, has always been defined by projections. Architecture constantly remakes the world, especially in modernism. Still, these projections should include our worldly conditions: the conditions of bodies, materials, sensations, families, places, languages, and histories. What Cavell's remarks on animation suggest is that for mature art, there is, and should be, no escape from these conditions. The artistic challenge, then, perhaps the central challenge for architecture today, is to discover ways of reintroducing these worldly conditions into practices built around computational means.

Here it must be said that despite their parallels, strategies that were polemical and provocative in postwar art have so far often seemed diminished in computation-based architecture, smoothed into a professional working method drained of intensity. If LeWitt famously claimed that for conceptual practices "the idea becomes a machine that makes the art," then too often today it looks as if the (computational) machine becomes the idea that makes the building. Or perhaps it would be more fair to say that systems, series, and fields—those vaunted artistic methods of the postwar avant-gardes—have always posed risks of mindlessness. This is where the example of postwar abstract painting is most valuable to contemporary architecture: as an intense, critical articulation of exactly this problematic.

If in the age of computation, architecture faces a dilemma of possibilities that resembles that confronted by postwar painting and music, where can parallel constraints be found? Given the multiplicity of architecture's postmedium condition, the answer can only be that there are many potential sources and many configurations that such self-imposed restraints could take, all concerned with themes that computation itself does not easily accommodate: the body, scale, materiality, and history, among others.

One key issue, as Krauss outlined in her 1971 article "Stella's New Work and the Problem of Series," is the inimical relationship between the material, phenomenal presence of a specific work and its simultaneous determination as the result of an abstract, conceptual process, what could be called the mind/body problem of serial work. In Krauss's view, "the lesson that Stella seems to have drawn from his own work with serialization is that as the painting tends toward diagram, it enters the condition of the mathematical formula . . . in which both its presence and the viewer's physical presence to it are no longer part of its meaning."[12] The reaction of Stella and his peers was to search for strategies that would resist or at least complicate this emptying out of the work's presence. As a generation of critics have taken pains to point out, the works of artists such as Jackson Pollock, Barnett Newman, Stella, and LeWitt center on the mind/body problem presented by systems and series, and not as attempted solutions but as engaged and engaging "worryings" of the problem. Take the example of LeWitt's wall drawings and paintings. As sets of instructions for the generation of form, these are the most literal precursors of today's computational methods. However, it should be obvious that though the works are algorithmic in conception, to automate the execution of one would be a travesty, because it is only the friction of abstract thought and concrete act, rule and freedom, that gives LeWitt's wall drawings and paintings their artistic heat.

A tangle of issues surround this fundamental relationship of abstract conception and material realization, all of which should offer contemporary architecture possibilities for interrupting the overly smooth translation from the former to the latter. If anything, what I am offering here is an argument against a smoothness of form and ideology that has been all too tempting in recent years. As computation is more thoughtfully integrated into architecture, we might imagine, and perhaps now begin to see, practices that work on the antinomies of the scaleless and the bodily, the abstract and the material. As I tried to show in chapter 2, it is just such engagement that has defined Eisenman's most compelling projects and that distinguishes these from his projects that simply ignore the material world.

A related and more pressing provocation, conspicuously dodged by much automatic architecture, is us: the presence of people and our stubbornly corporeal bodies in confrontation with an abstract architectural system. One of the well-recognized problems of computational models is that there is effectively no marker of, and no limit to, scale, especially when the model is generated directly by code and not "by hand" (i.e., with a mouse). When this limitless depth of scale is combined with parametric modeling and with fabrication processes of mass customization, a new relationship of part and whole becomes possible, a highly intricate and totalizing organization. Born in the scaleless world of pure geometry, computation-based projects are then faced with the troublesome problem of reintroducing the body and all of its architectural indexes: stairs, doors, ceiling heights, bathrooms, etc. To a great extent this explains the tendency for computational generation to remain on the surface of buildings, where the constraints of human occupation can be minimized.

Again Eisenman's early houses stand as precedents in their handling (or denial) of this theme. We might, though, also recall the struggles and compromises needed to convert Otto's polemically "natural" surfaces into occupiable buildings. Described as landscapes, these roofs had no intrinsic relationship to human bodies, to enclosure from weather, or to the use of space. This work was left to the concrete trays, glass partitions, and awkward pneumatic gaskets that converted Otto's natural forms into spaces for people. The disjunction between these two spheres, between the biomimicry of Otto's formal vocabulary and the actual bodies of building occupants, stands as a cautionary example: rather than articulating the difference Otto largely chose to simply pass over it.

A third worldly ground for automatism can be located in building type, which connects architecture both to use and to its disciplinary history. If, as Krauss has it, critical postmedium practice must be both "differential and self-differing," this requires reflection on the historical conventions out of which the practice emerges.

For architecture these conventions are perhaps best represented by the notion of type, which offers the possibility of conventions that are historically grounded but also adaptable within new technical and social contexts. As in Krauss's assessment, I would argue that engagement with typology enables the differentiation of architecture from the homogenized field of a digitally saturated culture.

The possibilities for the engagement of the automatic with typology are illustrated by Eisenman's houses, which despite their superficial detachment from historical context are, in fact, entirely based on a type—call it the idealist villa—that through Rowe and Wittkower stretches back four hundred years to Palladio. What Eisenman discovers is a way of extending and exaggerating this type within a new historical context. Without recreating Palladian villas (an approach that was being followed in the same years of postmodernism), he generates an automatism out of the historical type, thereby lending disciplinary specificity and resonance to these houses. They are thus not exchangeable with apparently similar sculptures such as LeWitt's.

Continuing this lineage, Lynn's unbuilt Slavin House marks an important shift in recent architecture. The complex curvilinearity of its support continues a drive toward computation-based form making, recalling his long-standing fascination with the continuously variable geometry of spline curves. Yet what is most surprising and significant about this house is the extent to which it looks something like a house, the extent to which it engages and distorts a recognizable historical type: specifically, Le Corbusier's Maison Domino. This is all the more notable because Lynn's first publication, "Multiplicitous and Inorganic Bodies," was an argument for thinking outside of the typological lineage represented by Le Corbusier's villas.[13] When contrasted with the alien and hermetical detachment of his earlier Embryological House project, the incorporation of a known type, arguably the quintessential domestic type for modernism, represents a significant shift in his approach.

In a different mode, type was also central to March's mature theory of design process. As the very name of his Cambridge research center suggests, "built form"—the underlying organizational possibilities of occupied space—provided the basis for the quantitative analysis and then possible "evolution" of architecture. Importantly, for March, this was always understood as bound up with "land use," especially urban land use, with building type mediating the scalar relationships from the city through the particular building and down to the individual occupant. March's PDI theory provides an early but sophisticated vision of how type might be deployed within a computational regime.

It is useful to emphasize the difference between the possible role for typology suggested here and Mario Carpo's notion of the architect designing what he calls "generic objects" or "objectiles."[14] Where Carpo's generic objects are individually authored, a type is historically and collectively received—and therefore meets Krauss's concept of medium as a "layered, complex relationship that we would call a recursive structure." Thus, I would argue, it is in fact type and not the generic object that corresponds to the idea of "normative genus" that Carpo takes up from Erwin Panofsky and Richard Krautheimer. As such, type offers an indispensable way for contemporary practices to gain productive artistic friction.

AUTOMATISMS OF THE AUTOMATIC

In conclusion, I propose that Cavell's concept of automatism suggests what a "critical" contemporary architecture could be—critical in a Kantian sense of questioning its own ground—one that encompasses but also moves beyond the mere automations of computation. It is perhaps only now, with the collapse of the long regime of drawing, that architecture confronts the dilemmas of modernism as dilemmas, as conditions that cannot simply be overcome but have to be endured. These dilemmas center on the problem of producing an architecture that places us in the world. It is an existential problem, the problem of us as individual beings with bodies, us as collective cultures with histories, and of architecture as a discipline of both, a discipline of cultured bodies. Our historical position means that our particular relationship to these conditions must run through, but not be run by, computation. In architecture as elsewhere, we must today be constantly learning to deploy the automatic, not be deployed by it.

A reading of Cavell also suggests that it is only through such an approach that meaning is produced, meaning as an unfolding, as an ongoing questioning. Such meaning occurs not for a singular, universal public but within multiple, limited, though perhaps interrelated groups: "while the community of serious art is small it is not exclusive—not the way an elite is exclusive. It is esoteric, but the secret is open to anyone."[15] For such communities, the practices of automatism are central. When combined with critical reception, they establish a discourse. Even more than other arts, architecture has been uncomfortable with such limitations of its discourses, understandably because of its necessary entanglements with so many "publics." But within late modernism the alternative, pretending to have a truly general *sensus communus*, is intolerable, leading only to shallow populism or essentialism.

The activity of seeking and expanding an artistic automatism is in essence romantic, or, thinking of Cavell, it might be better to say transcendental. For while it attempts to disclose truths about its world, it achieves this disclosure through testing, struggle, daring, and reflection. It cannot be anticipated or mapped in advance, and it cannot be imitated except by being reduced to a formula that destroys it. Each automatism must be positioned in knowledge of all others, but there is no possibility of establishing complete consensus around any one automatism, though some may expose more terrain than others.

Finally, there is, in this turn to Cavell's thinking, something untimely in that it resists positivist narratives of technical and formal advancement that have surrounded computation in all its forms. In as much as this implies an interruption of the too smooth running of the too many automatic processes surrounding us, I think it is to be supported. As Cavell observed already in 1971,

> To speak now of modernism as the activity of an avant-garde is . . . empty. . . . [I]t implies a conflict between a coherent culture and a declared and massed enemy; when in fact the case is more like an effort, along blocked paths and hysterical turnings, to hang on to a thread.[16]

What is suggested by the contexts I have explored here as well as by the notion of automatisms of the automatic is that, ever more so, this thread must run from our computing devices out to the material world that we inhabit still.

NOTES

INTRODUCTION

1. Immanuel Kant, *Critik der Urtheilskraft* (Berlin: Lagarde und Friederich, 1790), §16.

2. Reinhold Martin has made a similar point about some of the same figures. See Reinhold Martin, "Naturalization, in Circles: Architecture, Science, Architecture," in *On Growth and Form: Organic Architecture and Beyond*, ed. Philip Beesley and Sarah Bonnemaison (Halifax: Tuns, 2008), 100–111.

3. Reyner Banham, ed., "Stocktaking: 1960," pt. 1–5, *Architectural Review* 127 (1960): 93–100; 183–90; 253–60; 325–32; 381–88.

4. See Peter Galison and Bruce William Hevly, eds., *Big Science: The Growth of Large-Scale Research* (Stanford, CA: Stanford University Press, 1992).

5. See Arindam Dutta, ed., *A Second Modernism: Architecture, MIT, and the "Techno-Social" Moment* (Cambridge, MA: MIT Press, 2013).

6. Eduard F. Sekler, "The Function of Architectural Theory and Criticism," *Architectural Design* 38 (1968): 347. First presented at a conference on architectural theory and criticism at the Technische Universität Berlin in December 1967.

7. See Peter Galison, "Aufbau/Bauhaus: Logical Positivism and Architectural Modernism," *Critical Inquiry* 16 (1990): 709–52.

8. Alan Colquhoun, "Frames to Frameworks," *Encounter* 48 (April 1977): 41.

9. Colin Rowe, introduction to *Five Architects: Eisenman, Graves, Gwathmey, Hejduk, Meier* (New York: Wittenborn and Company, 1972; New York: Oxford University Press, 1975). Citations refer to the 1975 edition.

10. Ibid., 7.

11. Alan Colquhoun, "Typology and Design Method," *Arena* 83 (June 1967); reprinted in Alan Colquoun, *Essays in Architectural Criticism: Modern Architecture and Historical Change* (Cambridge, MA: MIT Press, 1981), 50. Citations are to the 1981 reprint.

12. Royston Landau, *New Directions in British Architecture* (New York: G. Braziller, 1968), 114–15.

13. The earliest use given by the Oxford English Dictionary of the word *computer* in this sense is in 1646. Peter Galison has noted that the term was still used during World War II to refer to teams of women employed to calculate differential and integrodifferential equations, especially for nuclear weapons work. The term eventually shifted from the women to machines. See Peter Galison, *Image and Logic: A Material Culture of Microphysics* (Chicago: University of Chicago Press, 1997), 375.

14. Mark Wigley, "Network Fever," *Grey Room* 4 (2001): 84.

15. Among the most important of these works are Beatrice Colomina, *Domesticity at War* (Cambridge, MA: MIT Press, 2007); Sarah Williams Goldhagen and Réjean Legault, eds., *Anxious Modernisms: Experimentation in Postwar Architectural Culture* (Cambridge, MA: MIT Press, 2001); Reinhold Martin, *The Organizational Complex: Architecture, Media, and Corporate Space* (Cambridge, MA: MIT Press, 2005) and *Utopia's Ghost: Architecture and Postmodernism, Again* (Minneapolis: University of Minnesota Press, 2010); and Felicity Scott, *Architecture or Techno-utopia: Politics after Modernism* (Cambridge, MA: MIT Press, 2007).

16. Robert Venturi, *Complexity and Contradiction in Architecture* (New York: Museum of Modern Art, 1966).

17. Colquhoun, "Typology and Design Method."

CHAPTER 1

1. "Statement on the Department of Architecture, from a Spokesperson for the General Board of the University of Cambridge, in Response to News Reports Speculating about Its Future," University of Cambridge press release, November 1, 2004.

2. Luke Layfield, "Architecture under Threat at Cambridge," *Guardian* (UK), October 29, 2004.

3. *Research Assessment Exercise 2001: Assessment Panels' Criteria and Working Methods* (Bristol: RAE, 1999).

4. Robert Maxwell, "Education for the Creative Act," *Architectural Research Quarterly* 4 (2000): 59.

5. Edward Prior, "Art Study at Cambridge," *Journal of the Royal Institute of British Architects* (1912): 593–98.

6. Richard Rogers, "The Doyen: Influential, Generous and European," *Architectural Research Quarterly* 4 (2000): 304.

7. Peter Carolin and Trevor Dannatt, eds., *Architecture, Education and Research: The Work of Leslie Martin: Papers and Selected Articles* (London: Academy Editions, 1996), 115.

8. Leslie Martin, Ben Nicholson, and Naum Gabo, eds., *Circle: International Survey of Constructive Art* (London: Faber and Faber, 1937).

9. Jeremy Lewison, "*Circle*: a Determining Effect on the Practice of Architecture," *Architectural Research Quarterly* 4 (2000): 306.

10. Naum Gabo, "The Constructive Idea in Art," in Martin, Nicholson, and Gabo, *Circle*, 7.

11. Leslie Martin, "The State of Transition," in Martin, Nicholson, and Gabo, *Circle*, 218.

12. Ibid.

13. Maxwell, "Education for the Creative Act," 63.

14. Leslie Martin, "Conference on Architectural Education Held at Magdalen College, Oxford," *Royal Institute of British Architects Journal* 65 (1958): 279.

15. Clinton Rossiter in 1961 as quoted in Colin Rowe and Alexander Caragonne, *As I Was Saying: Recollections and Miscellaneous Essays* (Cambridge. MA: MIT Press, 1996), 1:131.

16. Lionel March, ed., *The Architecture of Form*, Cambridge Urban and Architectural Studies 4 (Cambridge: Cambridge University Press, 1976), ix.

17. Dean Hawkes, "'Only Connect . . . ,'" *Architectural Research Quarterly* 4 (2000): 303. Robert Maxwell makes a similar point in "Education for the Creative Act."

18. Anthony Jackson, *The Politics of Architecture: A History of Modern Architecture in Britain* (London: Architectural Press, 1970), 79.

19. Ibid.

20. Royston Landau, *New Directions in British Architecture* (New York: G. Braziller, 1968), 15.

21. Ibid.

22. M. Batty, "From *Environment and Planning B* to *Planning and Design*: Traditions, Transitions, Transformations," *Environment and Planning B* (anniversary issue, 1998): 1–2.

23. John Paterson, "Autobiographical Manuscript," John Paterson Papers, Royal Institute of British Architects Library, London.

24. Stephen Grabow, *Christopher Alexander: The Search for a New Paradigm in Architecture* (Stocksfield, UK: Oriel Press, 1983), 29.

25. Ibid., 30.

26. Ibid., 31.

27. Christopher Alexander, "Perception and Modular Co-ordination," *Royal Institute of British Architects Journal* 66 (1959): 425–29.

28. Christopher Alexander, "The Revolution Finished Twenty Years Ago," *Architect's Yearbook* 9 (1960): 181–85.

29. Colin Rowe, introduction to *Five Architects: Eisenman, Graves, Gwathmey, Hejduk, Meier* (New York: Wittenborn and Company, 1972; New York: Oxford University Press, 1975), 3–7. Citations refer to the 1975 edition.

30. Serge Chermayeff and Christopher Alexander, *Community and Privacy*, 2nd ed. (New York: Anchor Books, 1964); Christopher Alexander and Marvin Manheim, *The Design of Highway Interchanges: An Example of a General Method for Analysing Engineering Design Problems*, MIT Department of Civil Engineering Systems Laboratory Publication 159 (Cambridge, MA: MIT School of Engineering, 1962); Christopher Alexander and Marvin Manheim, *The Use of Diagrams in Highway Route Location: An Experiment*, MIT Department of Civil Engineering Systems Laboratory Publication 161 (Cambridge, MA: MIT School of Engineering, 1962).

31. Christopher Alexander, "The Synthesis of Form: Some Notes on a Theory" (PhD diss., Harvard University, 1962); and Christopher Alexander, *Notes on the Synthesis of Form* (Cambridge, MA: Harvard University Press, 1964; repr. 1971). Citations refer to the 1971 edition.

32. See Alexander's "worked example" in Alexander, *Notes on the Synthesis of Form*, 136–73.

33. Alexander, *Notes on the Synthesis of Form*, 131.

34. Ibid., 7–8.

35. Alexander performed his analysis on an IBM 7090 at the MIT Computation Center. See Christopher Alexander and Marvin Manheim, *HIDECS 2: A Computer Program for the Hierarchical Decomposition of a Set with an Associated Graph*, MIT Department of Civil Engineering Systems Laboratory Publication 160 (Cambridge, MA: MIT School of Engineering, 1962), and Christopher Alexander, *HIDECS 3: Four Computer Programs for the Hierarchical Decomposition of Systems Which Have an Associated Linear Graph*, MIT Department of Civil and Sanitary Engineering Research Report (Cambridge: MIT School of Engineering, 1963).

36. Alexander, *Notes on the Synthesis of Form*, 137–42.

37. Christopher Alexander and Barry Poyner, *The Atoms of Environmental Structure* (London: Ministry of Public Building and Works, 1967), 4.

38. Ibid., 14.

39. Ibid., 16.

40. Alexander, *Notes on the Synthesis of Form*, preface to the 1971 edition.

41. Ibid.

42. Ibid., 134.

43. D'Arcy Wentworth Thompson, prefatory note to *On Growth and Form: A New Edition* (Cambridge: Cambridge University Press, 1942).

44. Ibid., 16.

45. Ibid., 13.

46. Alexander, *Notes on the Synthesis of Form*, 134.

47. Anne Massey, *The Independent Group: Modernism and Mass Culture in Britain 1945–59* (Manchester: Manchester University Press, 1995), 42. See also Isabelle Moffat, "The Independent Group's Encounters with Logical Positivism and Searches for Unity in the 1951 Growth and Form Exhibition" (PhD diss., MIT, 2002), and "'A Horror of Abstract Thought': Postwar Britain and Hamilton's 1951 Growth and Form Exhibition," *October*, no. 94 (Fall 2000): 89–112.

48. Lancelot Law Whyte, *Aspects of Form: A Symposium on Form in Nature and Art* (London: Lund Humphries, 1951).

49. Ibid., 1–2.

50. Herbert Read, preface to Whyte, *Aspects of Form*, v–vi.

51. Lionel March, "Modern Movement to Vitruvius: Themes of Education and Research," *Royal Institute of British Architects Journal* 81 (1972): 101.

52. Lionel March, "Research and Environmental Studies," *Cambridge Review* (February 2, 1973): 85.

53. March, "Modern Movement to Vitruvius," 101.

54. See Lionel March, "The Logic of Design and the Question of Value," in March, *Architecture of Form*, and Alexander's introduction to the paperback edition of Alexander, *Notes on the Synthesis of Form*.

55. In 1974 LUBFS merged with the smaller Technical Research Division of the Department of Architecture to create the Martin Centre for Architectural and Urban Studies—it continues to operate under this new name.

56. Lionel March, "'Setting Out the Possibilities': Leslie Martin and the Advancement of Architectural Knowledge," *Architectural Research Quarterly* 4 (2000): 298.

57. Ibid., 298–99.

58. March, "'Setting Out the Possibilities,'" 299; and Batty, "From *Environment and Planning B*," 2. March refers to the "Centre for Urban Studies" but he must mean the "Centre for Environmental Studies" as in his "Research and Environmental Studies," 87.

59. March, "'Setting Out the Possibilities,'" 298–99.

60. March, "Research and Environmental Studies," 90.

61. Ibid., 92.

62. Lionel March, "Geometry and Arithmetic," *Royal Institute of British Architects Journal* 86 (1979): 171.

63. Ibid.

64. Ibid.

65. Nigel Lloyd, "Description of the Centre for Land Use and Built Form Studies," 1971, Library of the Martin Centre, University of Cambridge.

66. March, *Architecture of Form*, xii.

67. March, "Modern Movement to Vitruvius," 109.

68. March, *Architecture of Form*, vii.

69. Ibid. (brackets in original).

70. Andrew Saint, "Catherine Cooke: Passionate Authority on the Architecture of Russian Constructivism," *Guardian* (UK), March 11, 2004.

71. See especially Catherine Cooke, "'Form is a Function X': The Development of the Constructivist Architect's Design Method," in *Russian Avant-Garde Art and Architecture*, Architectural Design Profile 47 (London: Academy Editions and *Architectural Design*, 1983), 34–49.

72. Lionel March, Marcial Echeñique, and Peter Dickens, eds., "Models of Environment," special issue, *Architectural Design* 41 (1971).

73. Ibid., 275.

74. March, *Architecture of Form*, xiii.

75. Ibid., xiv.

76. Philip Steadman, "Graph-Theoretic Representation of Architectural Arrangement," *Architectural Research and Teaching* 2/3 (1973): 161–72; reprinted in March, *Architecture of Form.*

77. March, *Architecture of Form*, vii.

78. Philip Tabor, "Analysing Communication Patterns" and "Analysing Route Patterns," in March, *Architecture of Form*, and T. M. Willoughby, "Computer Aided Building Planning for Minimal Circulation" (PhD diss., University of Cambridge, 1972).

79. Tabor, "Analysing Communication Patterns," 284.

80. Ibid., 289–309.

81. Ibid., 309.

82. Ibid., 347.

83. Alan Colquhoun, "Typology and Design Method," *Arena* 83 (June 1967); repr. in Alan Colquoun, *Essays in Architectural Criticism: Modern Architecture and Historical Change* (Cambridge, MA: MIT Press, 1981). References are to the 1981 reprint.

84. Karl Popper, *Conjectures and Refutations: The Growth of Scientific Knowledge*, 5th ed. (London: Routledge and K. Paul, 1974), 376.

85. Karl Popper, *The Poverty of Historicism* (London: Routledge, 1957).

86. March, "Logic of Design," 5.

87. Ibid.

88. Ibid., 14.

89. Ibid., 15.

90. Ibid.

91. Ibid., 18.

92. Ibid., 21–22.

93. March, "Modern Movement to Vitruvius," 108–9.

94. Ibid., 101.

95. Ibid.

96. Lionel March, "Serial Art: Notes on the Cover Design 'Rotations around a Square,'" *Architectural Design* 36 (1966): cover, 62–63.

97. Ibid., 62.

98. March, "Modern Movement to Vitruvius," 101.

99. March, "Serial Art," 63.

100. Ibid.

101. Ibid.

102. Lionel March, "A Boolean Description of a Class of Built Forms," in March, *Architecture of Form.*

103. Ibid., 41.

104. Ibid., 42.

105. Robin Forrest, "Transformations and Matrices in Modern Descriptive Geometry," in March, *Architecture of Form.*

106. Manfredo Tafuri, "L'Architecture dans le Boudoir: The Language of Criticism and the Criticism of Language," *Oppositions* 3 (1974): 37–62, and "'European Graffiti.' Five × Five = Twenty-Five," trans. Victor Caliandro, *Oppositions* 5 (1976): 35–74.

CHAPTER 2

1. Stan Allen, talk given for "Five Architects and After," session 4 of the series "The 70's: The Formation of Contemporary Architectural Discourse," Harvard Graduate School of Design, 2000–2001. A video recording is available at the Loeb Library, Harvard University Graduate School of Design.

2. See Peter Eisenman, "Discord over Harmony in Architecture: The Eisenman/Alexander Debate," *Harvard Graduate School of Design News* 2 (1983): 12–17, and "Contrasting Concepts of Harmony in Architecture," *Lotus International* 40 (1983): 60–68, as well as George Teysot, "Marginal Comments on the Debate between Alexander and Eisenman," *Lotus International* 40 (1983): 69–73.

3. Eisenman, "Discord over Harmony," 12. Eisenman noted that he had followed Alexander's work "very closely" and that there was a connection between his interest in structuralism and Alexander's talk on the "deep structures" of architecture: "I was very much in sympathy with the things you were saying in your lecture, in fact, I would like to think that for the past 10 or 15 years of my life I have been engaged in the same kind of work."

4. Peter Eisenman, "The Formal Basis of Modern Architecture" (PhD diss., Trinity College, University of Cambridge, 1963; facs., Baden: Lars Müller, 2006), and "Towards an Understanding of Form in Architecture," *Architectural Design* 33 (1963): 457–58.

5. Eisenman, "Formal Basis," 1.

6. Ibid., 29.

7. Ibid., 4.

8. Ibid., 6.

9. Ibid., 33–35.

10. Ibid., 72–73.

11. Ibid., 13.

12. Eisenman returned to this theme most explicitly in "Post-functionalism," *Oppositions* 6 (1976): i–iv.

13. Peter Eisenman, "Cardboard Architecture: House I," in *Five Architects: Eisenman, Graves, Gwathmey, Hejduk, Meier* (New York: Wittenborn, 1972; New York: Oxford University Press, 1975), 15–17. Citations refer to the Oxford edition.

14. Eisenman, "Cardboard Architecture: House I," 17. Louis Martin suggests that Eisenman was introduced to the work of Chomsky in early 1969 by Richard Falk, the client for House II. See Louis Martin, "The Search for a Theory in Architecture: Anglo-American Debates, 1957–1976" (PhD diss., Princeton University, 2002), 561.

15. Eisenman, "Cardboard Architecture: House I," 15–16.

16. Peter Eisenman, "Cardboard Architecture: House II," in *Five Architects*, 26.

17. Colin Rowe and Robert Slutzky, "Transparency: Literal and Phenomenal," *Perspecta* 8 (1963): 45–54.

18. Kenneth Frampton, preface to *Peter Eisenman's House VI: The Client's Response*, by Suzanne Frank (New York: Whitney Library of Design, 1994), 13.

19. Eisenman, "Cardboard Architecture: House II," 25.

20. Ibid.

21. Jaquelin Robertson, "Machines in the Garden," in "Five on Five," by Romaldo Giurgola, Allan Greenberg, Charles Moore, Jaquelin Robertson, and Robert A. M. Stern, *Architectural Forum* (May 1973): 50.

22. Mario Gandelsonas, "Linguistics in Architecture," *Casabella* 374 (1973): 22.

23. Robert E. Somol, "Oubiler Rowe," *ANY* 7/8 (1994): 9.

24. Colin Rowe, "The Mathematics of the Ideal Villa: Palladio and Le Corbusier Compared," *Architectural Review* 101 (March 1947): 102.

25. Eisenman, "Cardboard Architecture: House I," 17.

26. See Anthony Vidler, "Mannerist Modernism: Colin Rowe," in *Histories of the Immediate Present: Inventing Architectural Modernism* (Cambridge, MA: MIT Press, 2008), 60–104.

27. Rudolf Wittkower, *Architectural Principles in the Age of Humanism* (London: Warburg Institute, University of London, 1949), 65.

28. See Alina A. Payne, "Rudolf Wittkower and Architectural Principles in the Age of Modernism," *Journal of the Society of Architectural Historians* 53, no. 3 (September 1994): 339.

29. Anthony Vidler, "Another Brick in the Wall," *October*, no. 136 (Spring 2011): 105.

30. Vidler, "Mannerist Modernism," 70.

31. Payne, "Rudolf Wittkower," 328.

32. Peter Eisenman, introduction to *Eisenman Inside Out: Selected Writings, 1963–1988* (New Haven, CT: Yale University Press, 2004), vii.

33. On Gandelsonas's critique, see Martin, "Search for a Theory," 645–47.

34. George Hersey and Richard Freeman, *Possible Palladian Villas (Plus a Few Instructively Impossible Ones)* (Cambridge, MA: MIT Press, 1992).

35. Peter Eisenman, "Notes on Conceptual Architecture: Towards a Definition," *Casabella*, no. 359/360 (November/December 1971): 49–57, and *Design Quarterly*, no. 78/79 (1970): 1–5. Citations will (necessarily) be to the *Casabella* publication.

36. Ibid., 49.

37. Ibid.

38. Ibid., 51.

39. Ibid.

40. Ibid.

41. Rosalind Krauss, "LeWitt in Progress," *October*, no. 6 (Fall 1978): 46–60.

42. Ibid., 55.

43. Robert E. Somol, "Dummy Text; or, the Diagrammatic Basis of Contemporary Architecture," introduction to *Diagram Diaries*, by Peter Eisenman (New York: Universe, 1999), 18.

44. Robin Evans, "Not to Be Used for Wrapping Purposes," *AA Files*, no. 10 (1985): 68–78.

45. Peter Eisenman, "Diagrams of Interiority," in *Diagram Diaries* (New York: Universe, 1999), 75. My description is based on a videotape of the film shown in the exhibition "Eisenman/Krier: Two Ideologies" at the Yale School of Architecture, fall 2002. Louis Martin curated the Eisenman portion of the show.

46. Pamela Lee has proposed a similar reading of the temporal aspect of LeWitt's sculptures through the concept of "phasing"; see "Phase Piece," in *Sol LeWitt: Incomplete Open Cubes*, ed. Nicholas Baume (Cambridge, MA: MIT Press, 2001), 49–58.

47. Evans, "Not to Be Used for Wrapping Purposes," 71.

48. Allen, "Five Architects and After"; Rosalind Krauss, "Notes on the Index," pt. 1, *October*, no. 3 (Spring 1977): 68–81, pt. 2, *October*, no. 4 (Fall 1977), 58–67. According to Allen, Krauss gave a version of the index article as a lecture at the Institute for Architecture and Urban Studies in 1977.

49. Manfredo Tafuri, "Peter Eisenman: The Meditations of Icarus" (1980), in *Houses of Cards*, by Peter Eisenman, Rosalind E. Krauss, and Manfredo Tafuri (New York: Oxford University Press, 1987), 167.

50. Eisenman, *Eisenman Inside Out*, vii, and "Diagrams of Interiority," in Eisenman, *Diagram Diaries*.

51. Peter Eisenman, "House III: To Adolf Loos and Bertolt Brecht," in "House III: Miller Residence, Lakeville, Conn.," by Peter Eisenman, David Morton, and Robert Miller *Progressive Architecture* 55, no. 5 (May 1974): 92.

52. Eisenman, "Cardboard Architecture: House II," 27.

53. Eisenman, "House III: To Adolf Loos," in Eisenman, Morton, and Miller, "House III: Miller Residence," 92.

54. Viktor Shklovsky, "Art as Technique" (1917), in *Russian Formalist Criticism: Four Essays*, trans. Lee T. Lemon and Marion J. Reis (Lincoln: University of Nebraska Press, 1965), 3–24.

55. David Morton, "One man's fit . . . ," in Eisenman, Morton, and Miller, "House III: Miller Residence," 92–94.

56. Frank, *Peter Eisenman's House VI*, and Paul Goldberger, "The House as Sculptural Object," *New York Times Magazine*, March 20, 1977.

57. Peter Eisenman, William Gass, and Robert Gutman, "House VI (Frank Residence) in Cornwall, Connecticut," *Progressive Architecture* 58, no. 6 (June 1977): 59.

58. Ibid.

59. Ibid.

60. Rosalind Krauss, "Death of a Hermeneutic Phantom: Materialization of the Sign in the Work of Peter Eisenman" (June 1977), in Eisenman, Krauss, and Tafuri, *Houses of Cards*, 166–84.

61. Ibid., 169.

62. Ibid., 171.

63. Ibid., 179.

64. Ibid., 184.

65. Peter Eisenman, "Misreading Peter Eisenman," in Eisenman, Krauss, and Tafuri, *Houses of Cards*, 167–86.

66. Peter Eisenman, "Transformations, Decompositions and Critiques: House X," and "Sandboxes: House Xia," in "Peter Eisenman," special issue, *A + U*, no. 112 (1980): 15–151, 221–43.

67. Robert A. M. Stern, "Dream Houses," *Pride of Place: Building the American Dream*, episode 3, directed by Murray Grigor (Films for the Humanities, 1986), VHS.

68. Sarah Whiting, "Euphoric Ratio," in *Tracing Eisenman: Peter Eisenman: Complete Works*, ed. Cynthia Davidson (London: Thames and Hudson, 2006), 91–111.

69. Colin Rowe, "The Mathematics of the Ideal Villa," in *The Mathematics of the Ideal Villa and Other Essays* (Cambridge, MA: MIT Press, 1976), 16.

70. Eisenman, "Misreading Peter Eisenman," in Eisenman, Krauss, and Tafuri, *Houses of Cards*, 170, 172.

71. Reinhold Martin has persuasively situated Eisenman's humanism within the political context of the early 1970s; see "Language: Environment, c. 1973," in *Utopia's Ghost: Architecture and Postmodernism, Again* (Minneapolis: University of Minnesota Press, 2010), esp. 62–64.

72. Eisenman, "Post-functionalism," iv.

73. Vidler, "Mannerist Modernism," 79.

CHAPTER 3

1. While Jonathan Massey has drawn attention to the rivalry between the US and Soviet pavilions, it was the contrasting architectural approaches of the US and West German pavilions that received special note in the official album of the exhibition (with preference shown for Otto's strategy). See Jonathan Massey, "Buckminster Fuller's Cybernetic Pastoral: The United States Pavilion at Expo 67," *Journal of Architecture* 11, no. 4 (2006): 463–83, and Claude Beaulieu, "Architecture," in *Expo 67: The Memorial Album of the First Category Universal and International Exhibition Held in Montreal from the Twenty-Seventh of April to the Twenty-Ninth of October Nineteen Hundred and Sixty-Seven*, ed. Jean-Louis de Lorimier (Montreal: Thomas Nelson, 1968), 328.

2. Frei Otto, quoted in Paul Sigel, "Interview mit Frei Otto," in *Exponiert: Deutsche Pavilions auf Weltausstellungen* (Berlin: Verlag Bauwesen, 2000), 303 (my translation).

3. While the main athletic venues of the 1972 Munich Olympics took a similar approach—and in far more complex political and material contexts—Otto was added to the design team only after the proposal by Günter Behnisch and Partners had been accepted, and he has always described the final structure as compromised from his point of view.

4. Frei Otto, *Das hängende Dach: Gestalt und Struktur* (Berlin: Ullstein, 1954).

5. On pages 25–26 of Juan Maria Songel, *A Conversation with Frei Otto* (New York: Princeton Architectural Press, 2010), Otto says that he also met Walter Gropius during this trip, but later, on page 29, he explains in more convincing detail that, although he visited Gropius's studio, he only met Gropius himself later. See also Ludwig Glaeser, *The Work of Frei Otto* (New York: Museum of Modern Art, 1972), 7.

6. Glaeser, *Work of Frei Otto*, and Winfried Nerdinger, ed., *Frei Otto: Complete Works: Lightweight Construction, Natural Design* (Basel: Birkhäuser, 2005). For additional details on Otto's early life, see also Songel, *Conversation with Frei Otto*.

7. Otto, *Das hängende Dach*, 9–10 (my translation).

8. Frei Otto, *Gestaltwerdung: Zur Formentstehung in Natur, Technik und Baukunst* (Cologne: Rudolf Müller, 1988), and Frei Otto and Bodo Rasch, *Finding Form: Towards an Architecture of the Minimal* (Stuttgart: Axel Menges, 1995).

9. Rainer Barthel, "Natural Forms: Architectural Forms," in Nerdinger, *Frei Otto*, 19, and Berthold Burkhardt, "The Institute for Lightweight Structures: University Institute and Spinner's Centre," in Nerdinger, *Frei Otto*, 92. See also Daniela Fabricius, "Calculation and Risk: The Rational Turn in West German Architecture 1965–1985" (PhD diss., Princeton University, 2016).

10. "Form Force Mass 5: Experiments," *IL* 25 (1969).

11. Hadas Steiner, "The Forces of Matter," *Journal of Architecture* 10, no. 1 (2005): 102; the quotation is from Thomas Herzog, *Pneumatic Structures: A Handbook of Inflatable Architecture* (New York: Oxford University Press, 1976).

12. Steiner, "Forces of Matter," 93.

13. Hans Rossig, foreword to *Expo '67 Montreal—German Pavilion: Documentation on the Structure*, ed. F. M. Sitte and G. Eisenberg (Düsseldorf: Werner-Verlag, [1967]), 3.

14. C. Mertz, "The Implementation of Construction," in Sitte and Eisenberg, *Expo '67 Montreal*, 4, and Rolf Gutbrod and Frei Otto, "The Design of the Structure," in Sitte and Eisenberg, *Expo '67 Montreal*, 13.

15. Frei Otto, "Model Testing 2," in "Frei Otto at Work," special issue, *Architectural Design* (March 1971): 148.

16. See Mario Carpo, *The Alphabet and the Algorithm* (Cambridge, MA: MIT Press, 2011).

17. "Frei Otto Designs 1.864 Million Cubic Feet of Air," *Architectural Forum* 126, no. 3 (April 1967): 62.

18. Eberhard Haug, "The Large Scale Model," in Sitte and Eisenberg, *Expo '67 Montreal*, 17.

19. For detailed descriptions of the design process see Sitte and Eisenberg, *Expo '67 Montreal*.

20. Klaus Linkwitz, "Application of Photogrammetry and Electronic Data Processing to the Model of the Pavilion," in Sitte and Eisenberg, *Expo '67 Montreal*, 18. See also Mick Eekhout, "Frei Otto and the Munich Olympic Games: From the Measuring Experimental Models to the Computer Determination of the Pattern," *Zodiac* 21 (1972): 38; and Frei Otto, quoted in Songel, *Conversation with Frei Otto*, 76–77.

21. Frei Otto, quoted in "Frei Otto in Conversation with the Emergence and Design Group," *Architectural Design* 74, no. 3 (May/June 2004): 23. Evidence of the collaboration between the research groups of Otto and Linkwitz on the Montreal pavilion is also given by Eekhout, "Frei Otto and the Munich Olympic Games," 38, and Wolfgang Faig, *Vermessung dünner Seifenlamellen mit Hilfe der Nahbereichsphotogrammetrie* (Munich: Verlag der Bayerischen Akademie der Wissenschaften, 1969).

22. Lorimier, *Expo 67: The Memorial Album*, 86.

23. Konrad Zuse, *The Computer: My Life* (Berlin: Springer-Verlag, 1993), 61–64.

24. Otto, "Model Testing 2," 148.

25. Frei Otto, quoted in Songel, *Conversation with Frei Otto*, 38–40.

26. Glaeser, *Work of Frei Otto*, 9.

27. Barthel, "Natural Forms: Architectural Forms," 18. The embedded quotation is from "Form Force Mass 5."

28. Beaulieu, "Architecture," 328.

29. For an analysis of these dilemmas in another prominent case, see Anthony Vidler, "Losing Face: Notes on the Modern Museum," *Assemblage* 9 (1989): 40–57.

30. Sigel, "Interview mit Frei Otto," 300 (my translation).

31. Otto was able to fully realize the degree of transparency he sought only once, in the aviary for the Munich zoo—suggesting that, despite his claims, men and animals really do have distinct architectural needs.

32. Sigel, "Interview mit Frei Otto," 302.

33. Eberhard Möller, "German Pavilion at the Expo 1967 in Montreal, Canada," in Nerdinger, *Frei Otto*.

34. Frei Otto, quoted in Sigel, "Interview mit Frei Otto," 302 (my translation).

35. Sigel, "Interview mit Frei Otto," 303–4 (my translation).

36. On this theme see Detlef Mertins, *Mies* (New York: Phaidon, 2014), 138–39.

37. Frei Otto, quoted in Songel, *Conversation with Frei Otto*, 25–27.

38. Sigfried Giedion, "The State of Contemporary Architecture. II. The Need for Imagination," *Architectural Record* 115 (February 1954): 186.

39. Ibid., 189.

40. Ibid., 191.

41. Glaeser, *Work of Frei Otto*, 8.

42. Robin Evans, *The Projective Cast: Architecture and Its Three Geometries* (Cambridge, MA: MIT Press, 1995), 295–314.

43. Maria Gough, "In the Laboratory of Constructivism: Karl Ioganson's Cold Structures," *October*, no. 84 (Spring 1998): 113.

44. Friedrich Nietzsche, "Twilight of the Idols" (1889), in *The Portable Nietzsche*, trans. and ed. Walter Kaufman (New York: Penguin, 1954), 521.

45. I have discussed this issue as manifest in the buildings of the 2008 Beijing Olympics; see my "Bidden City," *Artforum* (Summer 2008): 137–42.

46. Frei Otto, quoted in Songel, *Conversation with Frei Otto*, 36.

47. Ewald Bubner, "The Form Finding of the Grid Shell," in "Multihalle Mannheim," special issue, *IL* 13 (1978): 40.

48. Frei Otto, quoted in Songel, *Conversation with Frei Otto*, 38.

49. Ibid., 55–56.

50. Winfried Langner, "Programme and Utilization of the 'Multihalle,'" in "Multihalle Mannheim," 183.

51. Ibid.

52. Ibid.; where the original uses the English neologism *Multihalle*, the German has the common word *Mehrzweckhalle* (multipurpose hall).

53. Greg Lynn, "Blobs (or Why Tectonics Is Square and Topology Is Groovy)," *ANY* 14 (1996): 58–61; revised version in Greg Lynn, *Folds, Bodies and Blobs: Collected Essays* ([Brussels]: La Lettre Volée, 1998). Citations refer to the *ANY* version.

54. Ibid., 60.

55. Ibid., 58.

56. Ibid., 60.

57. Michael Hays and Catherine Ingraham, "Computer Animisms (Two Designs for the Cardiff Bay Opera House)," *Assemblage* 26 (1995): 9.

CONCLUSION

1. Rosalind Krauss, *"A Voyage on the North Sea": Art in the Age of the Post-Medium Condition* (New York: Thames and Hudson, 2000), 6. See also Rosalind Krauss, "Reinventing the Medium," *Critical Inquiry* 25, no. 2 (1999): 289–305.

2. The one major exception is Aron Vinegar's *I AM A MONUMENT: On Learning from Las Vegas* (Cambridge, MA: MIT Press, 2008), but this is focused on aspects of Cavell's thought that are removed from what I consider here.

3. This recalls August Schmarsow's description of the arts as a "planetary system," with "lighter" arts moving on fast inner orbits and "heavier" arts (especially architecture) moving slowly on long outer tracks. August Schmarsow, *Beiträge zur Aesthetik der bildenden Künste*, vol. 1 (Leipzig: Verlag von S. Hirzel, 1896): 13.

4. Stanley Cavell, *The World Viewed: Reflections on the Ontology of Film*, enl. ed. (Cambridge, MA: Harvard University Press, 1979), 60.

5. Ibid., 15.

6. Jacques Herzog in a public conversation at the Mies Crown Hall Americas Prize award ceremony, IIT College of Architecture, October 22, 2014.

7. Cavell, *World Viewed*, 106.

8. Ibid., 104.

9. Greg Lynn, "Families," in *Greg Lynn FORM*, ed. Mark Rappolt (New York: Rizzoli, 2008), 172–74, and Greg Lynn, *Animate Form* (New York: Princeton Architectural Press, 1999), 19–20.

10. Cavell, *World Viewed*, 31.

11. Jay Leda, ed., *Eisenstein on Disney* (Calcutta: Seagull, 1986).

12. Rosalind Krauss, "Stella's New Work and the Problem of Series," *Artforum*, December 1971, 44.

13. Greg Lynn, "Multiplicitous and Inorganic Bodies," *Assemblage* 19 (1992): 32–49.

14. Mario Carpo, *The Alphabet and the Algorithm* (Cambridge, MA: MIT Press, 2011), 46–48.

15. Cavell, *World Viewed*, 14.

16. Ibid., 110.

INDEX